Shakespeare's *Sonnets* Among His Private Friends

Shakespeare's *Sonnets* Among His Private Friends

Complete Sonnets of William Shakespeare

Edited with commentary by Carl D. Atkins

Small Latin Press
East Chatham, NY

*For my son, Christopher, who sums my count
and makes my old excuse.*

Table of Contents

Introduction

"His sugred Sonnets among his private friends." That's how Shakespeare's *Sonnets* were described in the only contemporary reference to them (eleven years before they were first printed).[*] This has always intrigued me, especially since there was a trend in the sixteenth century for small groups to get together to listen to sonnets or lectures on sonnets.[†] It brings up the image of a talented, young poet—with a penchant for irreverent fun—getting together with friends to read his new sonnet cycle. (I am thinking of W. H. Auden's comment that "Shakespeare never takes himself too seriously.")[‡] The sonnet cycle was a form of writing in which the poet was expected to write as if he were telling his own story, almost as if he were writing a diary, except in poetry. There is always a story being told but vaguely, heard only from the poet's point of view.[§] Often, we don't even know who the poet is talking to (if anyone). At times it seems we could be listening to a conversation the poet has *thought about*, but never had. But we can tell events are happening, things are changing, relationships are evolving. We may not be sure exactly what is going on and how much is real or imagined, but it's obvious

---

[*] The author was Frances Meres who wrote this in his *Palladis Tamia* in 1598, cataloging the works of great poets of his time. Rollins, *Variorum*, 2:53. I find this much more interesting than the enigmatic dedication in the first edition of *The Sonnets*, presumably written by the printer, Thomas Thorpe: "To the onlie better of these ensuing sonnets Mr. W.H. all happinesse and that eternitie promised by our ever-living poet wisheth the well-wishing adventurer in setting forth. T.T." As Rollins says, an inordinate amount of ink has been spilled over this (he spills eleven pages worth). Ibid., 2:166-76. If you are interested and want a fun read about the mysterious Mr. W. H., pick up a copy of Oscar Wilde's short story "The Portrait of Mr. W. H." in *The Short Stories of Oscar Wilde*. (1921; reprint, Norwalk: Easton Press, 1976), 3-78.

[†] Richard Simpson, *Philosophy of Shakespeare's Sonnets* (London: N.. Trübner, 1868), 4.

[‡] Auden, Lectures on Shakespeare, 319.

[§] In 1898, George Wyndham suggested taking Sir Philip Sidney's advice in believing, as he states in his *Defense of Poetry* (1585), "that there are many misteries contained in Poetrie, which of purpose were written darkly." Wyndham, *Poems*, cvi.

things are different at the end of the sequence compared to the beginning.

Numerous sonnet cycles were published that typically told the story of thwarted love. The same topics are repeated over and over: a chaste and beautiful lady, a love-sick poet dreaming only of his beloved, sunk into despair by her cruelty (cruel only because she decides to remain chaste). Shakespeare's *Sonnets* are like this, but with a twist—as one commentator puts it, standing convention on its head by "turning the sonnet-lady into a whore and attaching all the idealised emotion to a young man."[*] *The Sonnets* increase the reader's fun in trying to work out the details of the vague story they tell by adding a love triangle and intertwining two story lines into the typical tale. I imagine Shakespeare wrote *The Sonnets* both as a literary exercise to show off his talents *and* as a form of entertainment for his "private friends" to enjoy. Working out all the possibilities of the vague story as the sonnets progress is all part of the fun. I will waste no time discussing the possibility that *The Sonnets* are autobiographical—especially given how little we know of Shakespeare's life.[†] It will be simpler to treat *The Sonnets* as fiction, which will at least allow us to follow their story without the distraction of trying to identify characters.[‡] Instead, we can concentrate on the drama (and the humor) of the story that develops through the course of these poems.

Because *The Sonnets* tells its story through a series of poems, you'll miss something if you ignore the fact that they were written in verse. If you want a prose translation of *The Sonnets,* there are some tolerable versions out there. But they won't give you

---

[*] Maurice Evans, *Elizabethan Sonnets,* xxii.

[†] H. E. Rollins ends the better part of his thirty-three-page section on the question of autobiography with three commentators' statements, thirty to forty years apart, to this effect. Some eighty years of further commentary has added no additional light to the subject. Rollins, *Variorum,* 2:132-65, esp. 156.

[‡] W. H. Auden calls this a waste of time: "It is an idiot's job, pointless and uninteresting. It is just gossip. . . ." Auden, *Lectures,* 86. (No, tell us how you really feel!) Putting aside the scorn, the important point is that it is not helpful to the appreciation of *The Sonnets,* as other commentators have noted.

the same appreciation for their beauty. If you pay attention to the meter of *The Sonnets*, you will see how it interacts with the words and emotions. But since the rhythm of a particular sonnet may not always be immediately obvious, I have done my best to help. It's common in Elizabethan poetry for words to be pronounced with fewer or more syllables than in modern pronunciation. I've tried to reduce confusion by using the usual convention of the accented *e* (*è*) to indicate pronunciation of the final *-ed* of past tense verbs as a syllable where we would not and added an acute accent (´) over vowels that are stressed in a position that is usually unstressed in modern pronunciation. Also, where vowels are obviously not meant to be pronounced, I have replaced them with an apostrophe when possible. I have tried to point out the words that might be troublesome (I wanted to make sure you could read the words easily—too many apostrophes are confusing). I will sometimes mention meter in the discussion of a sonnet, but in order to avoid distractions, I've kept it to a minimum, usually in footnotes. I will only give the brief explanation here that *The Sonnets* are written in iambic pentameter, a verse with five feet, each foot made up of two syllables. In regular iambic pentameter, all the feet contain iambs, which have an unstressed first syllable and a stressed second syllable. A good poet, though, will use variations to keep iambic pentameter from sounding dull. There are four variations of stress used in *The Sonnets*: trochees (reversed stress), spondees (both syllables stressed), pyrrhics (both syllables unstressed), and feminine endings (an eleventh, unstressed syllable at the end of a line). When I cite text with these variations, I will put them in **bold**. Stressed syllables are written in ALL CAPS. I will unapologetically discuss how I read the meter of the sonnets. Not everyone will agree. That's fine—there are many ways to read verse depending on how you read a phrase or how much emphasis you put on a particular syllable.* But I hope my readings

---

* I hold to the idea that Shakespeare could make the same metrical effect convey different emotions depending on the mood of the poem, so

will help you pay attention to the meter and how it affects your experience of a sonnet. If you are very interested in the meter of the sonnets, you will find an analysis of all 154 sonnets on my website, www.amonghisprivatefriends.

As for rhyme, there are differences of opinion about that. There are some rhymes that we can be sure about, but it's hard to know how words were pronounced four hundred years ago. Some rhymes that sound off to our ear may have sounded better in Shakespeare's day, but from a practical standpoint, I find it easier to accept imperfect rhymes with modern pronunciation than to try to read *The Sonnets* by guessing how Shakespeare pronounced his words.*

Of course, there is no single correct way to read each sonnet, or *The Sonnets* as a whole. Different people may read each sonnet differently. I find *I* sometimes read a sonnet differently from one day to the next. Shakespeare was a subtle writer—he deserves subtle interpretation.

I'd like you to imagine that that we are among the friends our poet has allowed to see his new sonnet cycle. You will read the poems and the discussion of each one, trying to figure out the story. I think this is what it might have been like to read Shakespeare's *Sonnets* "among his private friends."

---

consistency is not to be expected in my readings. See Wright, *Shakespeare's Metrical Art*, 81.

* Fausto Cercignani argues that prior analyses have ignored evidence to fit particular ideas about what Shakespeare's pronunciation sounded like. Cercignani, *Shakespeare and Elizabethan Pronunciation*, 1-30. Moreover, Sister Miriam Joseph shows that contemporary rhetoricians considered changing vowel sounds to be an acceptable practice in poetry, something that none of the phonologists seem to have considered. Joseph, *Shakespeare and the Arts of Language*, 294.

Note on the Text

The Sonnets were first printed in 1609 (except for versions of Sonnets 138 and 144, which were printed in 1599 in *The Passionate Pilgrim*, which cannot stand up to scrutiny as an authoritative source).[*] I have used the transcription of the Huntington-Steevens Quarto from the variorum edition by H. E. Rollins, who notes that there are very few, minor variations among the different copies.[†] I've kept much of the original punctuation, often retaining commas that would be omitted in modern usage and leaving out commas other editors would insert. I have done this because it often affects the meter of sonnets and it sometimes affects the meaning. I have not changed Shakespeare's use of italics and capitalization since they were used in his day to indicate subtle differences in emphasis.[‡] I don't want to make a big deal about this. I just don't see any reason to make changes out of fear that a modern reader might be confused. Now that I've explained it, I think I'm safe (as long as you've read this note, that is).

I have presented *The Sonnets* in the order in which they were originally printed. Sonnet sequences have been known to be rearranged by their authors and their publishers, leading some editors to question the authority of the order of the 1609 text. Rollins devotes forty-three pages to a discussion of this and various proposed rearrangements, ending with a caution for any newcomers.[§] Few modern editors have dared to ignore that warning, though occasional notes about misplaced sonnets occur.[**] I was prepared for the possibility that I might have a

---

[*] See Rollins, *Passionate Pilgrim*, ix-xl.

[†] See Rollins, *Variorum*, 2:5 and Atkins, *Sonnets*, 288 for the only error I have found in his list.

[‡] See Moxon, *Mechanick Exercises*, 216. I exclude the convention used by the compositor of capitalizing the second letter of each sonnet.

[§] Rollins, *Variorum*, 2:74-116, esp.112.

[**] A recent publication suggests that *The Sonnets* are not a sequence at all and publishes them along with other sonnets from Shakespeare's plays (and some other questionable poems) in a presumed chronological order. See Paul Edmondson and Stanley Wells, *All the Sonnets of Shakespeare*.

problem with a few sonnets not fitting in with the story, but in the end, reading through the perspective of the story presented no problems in sonnet placement. Of course, that's no guarantee that Shakespeare intended *The Sonnets* to be presented in the order we find them, nor that all of them were intended for the sequence. However, many of the sonnets clearly belong together, others clearly relate to one another, and there is some sense of a beginning, middle and end to the sequence. Although some elements of the story might differ with different assumptions about the order of the sonnets and the inclusion of particular poems, the story itself would change little.

Choosing emendations for a modernized version always involves some amount of arbitrariness. I have been more conservative than most in keeping original punctuation, changing it only when I thought there was an obvious error or when it was necessary to help the reader understand the verse.[*] I have also been conservative about word forms—I thought it better to let the reader see some of the variability of Elizabethan English rather than try to make Shakespeare conform to some modern sense of correct spelling and grammar (as long as I felt it wouldn't be too confusing). I would encourage interested readers to explore other editions to get a sense of how emendations may affect the reading of *The Sonnets*.[†]

Below are listed first the Quarto reading then, in italics after the bracket, my emendation, listed after each sonnet and line number where it occurs (using the standard format of sonnet.line number). I have not included obvious misprints, spelling modernizations, or changes in punctuation.[‡] Controversial

---

[*] For my standards for emendation of punctuation errors, see Atkins, *Application of Bibliographic Principles*.

[†] My variorum edition may be a good place to see a sample of others' ideas (Atkins, *Sonnets*). Among my favorites are G. Blakemore Evans and Katherine Duncan-Jones (see bibliography).

[‡] Rollins lists 84 misprints, some of which I would consider spelling variants, contemporary grammatical usage or minor alterations for the sake of better sound. Rollins, *New Variorum*, II, 11-13. For a discussion of

emendations are pointed out in the footnotes throughout the text.

11.11 the] *thee*; **12.4** or] *all*; **13.7** You] *Your*; **23.9** books] *looks* **24.1** steeld] *stelld*; **24.4** it is] *is it*;* **25.9** worth] *might*; **26.12** their] *thy*; **27.10** their] *thy*; **28.12** th'] *the* **34.12** losse] *crosse*; **43:11** their] *thy*; **44.13** naughts] *naught*; **45.12** their] *thy*; **46.3** their] *thy*; **46.8** their] *thy*; **46.13** their] *thy*; **46.14** their] *thy*; **47.11** nor] *not*; **50.6** duly] *dully*; **51.11** naigh] *waigh*; **55.1** monument] *monuments*; **65.12** or] *of*; **69.3** end] *due*; **69.5** Their] *Thy*; **70.6** their worth] *thy worth's*;† **73.4** rn'wd] *ruin'd*; **77.10** blacks] *blanks*; **102.8** his] *her*; **113.6** lack] *latch*; **115.8** Divert] *Diverts*; **128.11** their] *thy*; **128.14** their] *thy*; **129.11** and] *a*; **132.6** th'] *the*; **132.9** morning] *mourning*; **136.14** lovest] *lov'st*; **138.12** t'have] *to have*; **144.6** sight] *side*; **146.2** that thee] *(omit)*; **153.8** strang] *strong*; **153.14** eye] *eyes*

---

misprints, spelling variants and contemporary variation, see Atkins, *Importance of Compositorial Error.*

 * Original emendation (2007 ed.)

 † Original emendation this ed. (conj. 2007)

The Sonnets

1

From fairest creatures we desire increase,
That thereby beauty's *Rose* might never die,
But as the riper should by time decease,
His tender heir might bear his memory.
But thou contracted to thine own bright eyes,
Feed'st thy light's flame with self substantial fuel,
Making a famine where abundance lies,
Thy self thy foe, to thy sweet self too cruel.
Thou that art now the world's fresh ornament,
And only herald to the gaudy spring,
Within thine own bud buriest thy content,
And, tender churl, mak'st waste in niggarding.
    Pity the world, or else this glutton be,
    To eat the world's due, by the grave and thee.

5 *contracted* betrothed **6** *self substantial* of your own substance **10** *only* principal; *gaudy* resplendent; *only herald to the gaudy spring* main embodiment of all that is young and beautiful **11** *thy content* what you contain (i.e., potentiality for parenthood) **12** *churl* miser; *niggarding* being miserly **14** *to eat the world's due* to rob the world of what it deserves to have; *by the grave and thee* i.e., when you die

Sonnet 1: this is the dramatic equivalent to Act I, Scene 1 of a play. We, the readers, are the audience. We're eavesdropping on the writer (we'll call him W.), our first character in the drama of *The Sonnets*. We read the words he writes and hear only what *he* has to say. We find out in line 5 that he's speaking to someone else, the Young Man we'll call him (or Y.M., for short).* He's

---

* I am not the first to use the term "Young Man." There is nothing in this sonnet to indicate that the writer is male. I did indicate in the Introduction, though, that I am assuming that *The Sonnets* were written by Shakespeare and that sonneteers typically wrote as if they were telling their own stories.

urging him to marry and have a child to perpetuate his beauty. This is a conventional Elizabethan theme. What's not so conventional is the way Shakespeare expresses it. Poets commonly spoke as if in their own voice, with or without actually identifying themselves with the person who is speaking in their sonnets, but the object of a poet's sonnets was often given a name, and she was usually a woman. This procreation theme is not the usual stuff of the beginning of a sonnet sequence.

Sonnet 1 sounds like everyday speech. This is one of the features that makes it seem personal and conversational, rather than just conventional. One editor finds the syntax of the last five words (*by the grave and thee*) strained.[*] Everyday speech is like that. The syntax may be hard to make out, but the sense isn't— it means, "by your dying." That's why a first reading can sometimes make more sense than can be teased out of the grammar. Sonnet 1 also has a clinching couplet, the last two lines summing up the sonnet to make a final point. This is just like the rhyming couplets Shakespeare often uses to end his scenes in the plays. It gives emphasis to what has gone before.

Shakespeare's particular way of using the English language, what I will call his diction, takes some getting used to.[†] Shakespeare shared the Elizabethan love for wordplay, especially for what are called rhetorical devices. One of his favorites has remained a favorite to modern times—the pun.[‡] Sonnet 1 uses another one called antithesis: *increase/decrease, famine/abundance, niggarding/glutton.* Many more devices will show up in *The Sonnets,*

This would make the writer by presumption a male. Other characters in our story will be also given names that are used by most editors. (Others use the term "speaker" for the Writer.)

[*] The editor is Tucker Brooke. Brooke, *Shakespeare's Sonnets,* 244

[†] I borrow the term "Shakespeare's diction" from one of his most famous critics, Dr. Samuel Johnson, who called his language "licentious." Johnson, *Dramatic Works,* 19-20.

[‡] Samuel Johnson thought Shakespeare's love of the pun a serious flaw "the fatal Cleopatra for which he lost the world and was content to lose it." (Boswell, *Plays and Poems,* "Dr. Johnson's Preface," 1:60-108, esp. 76.) I love puns.

sometimes adding depth, sometimes just adding fun. Another feature typical of Shakespeare's diction is the insertion of a parenthetical phrase that interrupts the flow of a sentence. You can tell they're parenthetical because if you remove them the sentence still makes sense. They may be short, as in this sonnet with *contracted to thine own bright eyes* (line 5) and *tender churl* (line 12), or much longer, as we'll see later. The problem with these parenthetical phrases is their tendency to muddle syntax, sometimes making it difficult to follow Shakespeare's meaning. Sometimes they even appear to have gotten Shakespeare confused, leading him to get his grammar mixed up. We do this when we speak. We interrupt ourselves with parenthetical ideas and when we return to our original train of thought we get our grammar confused. In conversation, it may go unnoticed, or even if noticed, it's likely to be understood. The same kind of confusion in *The Sonnets* enhances the sense that we're eavesdropping on a conversation (even though it's a written one and we only hear one side of it). I'm not saying Shakespeare deliberately got his grammar mixed up. I'm suggesting he wrote conversationally— he didn't over-examine grammar when he wrote any more than we do when we speak spontaneously.

Returning to the dramatic context of Sonnet 1, we've been introduced to two characters and a theme. We also know something about the relationship between the characters. Y.M. is a person worthy of being implored by W. who, in this sonnet, does so in a variety of tones of voice. In the first quatrain (the first four lines) we hear a dispassionate saying; the second and third quatrains display some emotion, somewhat chiding—these especially give me the impression of someone older and wiser giving advice to a youth; the final couplet ends with an impersonal appeal to morality on behalf of the world.

The combination of Shakespeare's diction, his manipulation of tone, his ability to mimic the way we speak, even in this simple, conventional first sonnet, lead not only to a sense that we are listening to a personal conversation but also to a sense of drama. As if something more is going to happen.

2

When forty Winters shall besiege thy brow,
And dig deep trenches in thy beauty's field,
Thy youth's proud livery so gaz'd on now,
Will be a totter'd weed of small worth held.
Then being ask'd, where all thy beauty lies,
Where all the treasure of thy lusty days,
To say within thine own deep sunken eyes,
Were an all-eating shame, and thriftless praise.
How much more praise deserv'd thy beauty's use,
If thou couldst answer "this fair child of mine
Shall sum my count, and make my old excuse"
Proving his beauty by succession thine.
    This were to be new made when thou art old,
    And see thy blood warm when thou feel'st it cold.

2 *trenches* furrows, wrinkles **4** *totter'd weed* tattered garment **6** *lusty days* days filled with vigor **8** *thriftless* unprofitable **9** *use* investment **11** *sum … excuse* complete my account and excuse my old age

As we read Sonnet 2, we have no doubt that the same writer is addressing the same young man. The theme is also unchanged. We have a new element of Shakespeare's diction, though: *an all-eating shame* is the first use of the condensed adjective. This phrase means "the shame of eating up all" instead of "the shame *that* eats all up," as we might expect. In prose, one might say, "the eating-all shame" or "the eating-all-up shame." Although intelligible, this is not very good prose (and it's horrible poetry). In line 11, *make my old excuse*, is another condensed adjective, where "old" means "for being old," which, in prose, would be placed *after* "excuse". (These are condensed adjectives because of all the meaning packed into two words.) When you're prepared for this aspect of Shakespeare's diction, phrases like these can be very evocative. They help achieve the distillation of thought that distinguish poetry from prose. I find these condensed adjectives add to the dramatic texture of this sonnet. The power of their concentrated thought adds a force that was absent from Sonnet 1.

The first two quatrains address the youth in harsher tones than we've heard, softened by the appearance of the word *beauty* twice. They remind him that he will someday be besieged by age, his *proud livery* becoming *tattered* weeds, his eyes *deep sunken*, his shame *all-eating*, his praise *thriftless*—with emphasis at the end of the second quatrain on the *shame.*[*] The third quatrain brightens, bringing the future's fair child into the present and adding *beauty* twice more, *proving* the child's worth. The couplet ends with antitheses: new/old; warm/cold—but beauty is absent from these lines. These shifts in tone are stronger than they were in Sonnet 1. They give a sense that W. has moods and give more depth and feeling to his voice. W. sounds sterner to me in Sonnet 2. It leaves me wondering what changes the next sonnet will bring.

---

[*] The meter is mostly regular in this sonnet but there's an abrupt change in line 8, which starts out with only one unstressed syllable out of four: ("**WERE an ALL-EAT**ing SHAME"). Those stressed syllables lead into and emphasize the normal stress on the second syllable of the fourth foot, "shame." Here's the rhythm: "DUM-te-DUM-DUM-te-DUM." I can *feel* the thud landing on the shame.

3

Look in thy glass and tell the face thou viewest,
Now is the time that face should form another,
Whose fresh repair if now thou not renewest,
Thou dost beguile the world, unbless some mother.
For where is she so fair whose un-ear'd womb
Disdains the tillage of thy husbandry?
Or who is he so fond will be the tomb
Of his self love to stop posterity?
Thou art thy mother's glass and she in thee
Calls back the lovely April of her prime,
So thou through windows of thine age shalt see,
Despite of wrinkles, this thy golden time.
    But if thou live rememb'red not to be,
    Die single and thine Image dies with thee.

1, 9 *glass* mirror **3** *fresh repair* youthful state **4** *unbless some mother* leave some woman unblessed with maternity **5** *un-ear'd* untilled **7** *fond* foolish **8** *to stop* which stops

Sonnet 3 continues with the same characters and the same theme. Has anything changed? The structure is the same: the sonnet is divided into units of three four-line quatrains followed by a couplet. The argument ("You look like your mother, whose youthful image you perpetuate. You rob some other potential mother of the same blessing by not marrying her and giving her a child.") is stated leisurely in the first two quatrains, then repeated more tersely in the third. After the lilting beginning,* I get a hectoring sense as the sonnet progresses, heightened by the repeated rhymes that run through the last two quatrains into the couplet: *husbandry/posterity, thee/see, be/thee.* (It was considered bad form to repeat rhymes in a sonnet, but Shakespeare didn't always pay attention to rules if they didn't serve his purposes.)

---

* Lines 1 through 4 have feminine endings—an unstressed eleventh syllable at the end of the line. This gives the lines a sing-song quality. Those feminine endings soften the beginning of the argument, making the first quatrain sound gentler, more like Sonnet 1 than Sonnet 2.

Especially after this hectoring, the tone of the couplet sounds severe—the repeated *die* with its harsh "d" sound, like a double dare. There's a definite contrast to the preceding sonnets. Sonnet 1 appealed to pity and Sonnet 2 appealed to flattery. Sonnet 3 sounds more like a warning. There's also a sharper contrast in tone between the quatrains in Sonnet 3 and its couplet. Subtly, the argument of the couplet changes as well. Instead of "if you die single some potential mother's image will die with her" it says, "if you die single *your* image will die with *you*," reverting back to the argument of Sonnet 2. We'll continue to see interconnections among neighboring sonnets like this as we read on.

We have to untangle the change in word order in the couplet to catch the sense. *If thou live rememb'red not to be* means "if thou live to be not remembered [i.e., forgotten]." This is typical for Shakespeare's diction. He changes the order of words—to fit the rhyme, the meter, or just to improve the sound—while usually managing to keep the meaning within reach.

Have we learned anything new about our characters? Y.M. seems implacable to me. W. sounds interested, but not directly involved in Y.M.'s affairs. Is he a concerned friend or relative? Or are his arguments on behalf of another? Has he been asked to intercede? A go-between? It feels like we're missing something. We need to know more.

4

Unthrifty loveliness why dost thou spend
Upon thy self thy beauty's legacy?
Nature's bequest gives nothing but doth lend,
And being frank she lends to those are free.
Then beauteous niggard why dost thou abuse
The bounteous largesse given thee to give?
Profitless usurer why dost thou use
So great a sum of sums yet canst not live?
For having traffic with thy self alone,
Thou of thy self thy sweet self dost deceive,
Then how when nature calls thee to be gone,
What acceptable *Audit* canst thou leave?
    Thy unus'd beauty must be tomb'd with thee,
    Which usèd lives th'executor to be.

4 *frank* generous; *free* generous 5 *niggard* miser 7 *use* use up 9 *having traffic* being involved 10 *deceive* cheat 14 *lives* i.e., in the person of a child

The tone darkens throughout Sonnet 4, dominated by negative references to Y.M.: he is *unthrifty*, a *niggard*, *profitless*. This, despite the more frequent positives: *loveliness, thy beauty's legacy, beauteous, bounteous largesse, thy sweet self, beauty*. The context demands this: he is unthrifty with his loveliness, spends his beauty's legacy on himself, he is a beauteous niggard, abuses his bounteous largesse, cheats himself, and lets his beauty go unused.

There's a change in grammar in line 12. *What* doesn't really fit with the *how* in the previous line. But Shakespeare is writing colloquially. I don't think he cared about the grammar. With correct grammar we would ask, "how can you leave an acceptable audit?" Or, "what acceptable audit can you leave?" But if we're speaking spontaneously, we might start with *how* and continue with *what* as this sonnet does. The lines sound like the way people speak. They're understandable. They're both more natural and more emotional than the grammatically correct form would be.

W.'s argument is more insistent in this sonnet. It lasts thirteen lines—the admonition to do what is required is saved for the last line. Y.M. now seems conceited, W. more exasperated. Is this just a philosophical argument, a ploy on the part of W. to convince Y.M.? At any rate, we're learning more about these characters in our drama. The relationship is developing.

5

Those hours that with gentle work did frame
The lovely gaze where every eye doth dwell,
Will play the tyrants to the very same,
And that unfair which fairly doth excel.
For never resting time leads Summer on
To hideous winter and confounds him there,
Sap check'd with frost and lusty leaves quite gone,
Beauty o'er-snow'd and bareness everywhere.
Then were not summer's distillation left,
A liquid prisoner pent in walls of glass,
Beauty's effect with beauty were bereft,
Nor it nor no remembrance what it was.
 But flowers distill'd though they with winter meet,
 Leese but their show, their substance still lives sweet.

(Sonnets 5 and 6 are a double sonnet meant to be read together.)

2 *gaze* object to be gazed upon **4** *unfair* rob of beauty; *fairly* in beauty **6** *confounds* destroys **9** *summer's distillation* perfumes made from flowers **10** *walls of glass* i.e., the perfume bottle **11** *beauty's effect...were bereft* beauty's lasting effect along with beauty would be taken away **12** *Nor it...what it was* neither it, nor the remembrance of it, being left **14** *Leese* lose

6

Then let not winter's ragged hand deface,
In thee thy summer ere thou be distill'd:
Make sweet some vial; treasure thou some place,
With beauty's treasure ere it be self kill'd.
That use is not forbidden usury,
Which happies those that pay the willing loan;
That's for thy self to breed another thee,
Or ten times happier be it ten for one.
Ten times thy self were happier than thou art,
If ten of thine ten times refigur'd thee,
Then what could death do if thou should'st depart,
Leaving thee living in posterity?
    Be not self-will'd for thou art much too fair,
    To be death's conquest and make worms thine heir.

1 *ragged* rough **3** *treasure* enrich **5** *use* borrowing (beauty from Nature) *forbidden usury* (lending money at interest—"use"—was illegal) **6** *happies* makes happy; *that pay the willing loan* who willingly pay the loan **10** *refigur'd* duplicated **13** *fair* beautiful

W. is now trying even harder than he did in Sonnet 4, where his argument lasted 13 lines. Now his argument lasts through two poems to line 12 of Sonnet 6. Sonnet 5 is only half a poem, being continued in the next one. Its incompleteness is clear when Sonnet 6 is read. These two sonnets were meant to be read together as one poem. This is not unique—there are eight other sonnet pairs in the sequence and one triple sonnet. The idea of linking sonnets together this way wasn't invented by Shakespeare—examples can be found among his predecessors.[*]

The language of these sonnets is harder to follow than the earlier ones. Sonnet 5 is easier than Sonnet 6, presenting the metaphor of the distillation of a flower's essence into perfume as a

---

[*] If you are interested in examples, pick up a copy of the excellent collection by Maurice Evans, which includes Sonnets 29 and 30 of Samuel Daniel's *Delia* and Sonnets 76 and 77 of Edmund Spenser's *Amoretti*. Evans, M., *Elizabethan Sonnets*, 69-70 and 136.

way of preserving its beauty (the flowers buried under snow by winter). Shakespeare's image: *A liquid prisoner pent in walls of glass* is a superb example of the power of poetry's condensed thought. (Compare it to the same image in prose from Sidney's *Arcadia* (1590): "Have you ever seen a pure Rosewater kept in a crystal glass; how fine it looks, how sweet it smells, while that beautiful glass imprisons it?")* We hardly notice the awkwardness of the next two lines: *Beauty's effect with beauty were bereft, / Nor it nor no remembrance what it was.* The sense is understandable, even if the first line is especially hard to make out. The "nor...nor" construction in the next line is standard Elizabethan English, used where we would say "neither...nor." The omission of words that can be easily inferred ("remembrance [of] what it was [left behind]") is also common, especially for Shakespeare. He is doing the same thing with the previous line, it's just less obvious. *Beauty's effect with beauty were bereft* must mean "Beauty's [lasting] effect [along] with beauty were bereft." Of course, *were bereft* must be understood to mean "were taken away,' a common usage by Shakespeare. We now see that the second line simply explains the first, in reverse order: neither beauty nor the lasting effect of beauty, that is, our remembrance of it, would be left to us.

The metaphor in Sonnet 6 is more difficult. The argument seems to be that since all beauty is borrowed from Nature, Nature is lending it out for *use* (that is, at interest). But if you pay Nature back by having children (generating more beauty) you will be willingly paying off the loan since it will benefit you, making you happier (and if you have ten children, you will be ten times happier). There's some verbal awkwardness, as there was in Sonnet 5, but here it extends for five lines, all to expound on the *willing loan*. The loan is *for thyself to breed another thee*—for having a child—or ten times happier *be it ten for one*. All clear, but wordy. The next two lines then say, "ten of you are happier than you, if ten of you duplicates you ten times." The tens can get

---

* The comparison was first noted by Gerald Massey. Massey, *Sonnets*, 36-7. I have modernized the spelling.

27

overwhelming, unless you let the meter be your guide and avoid emphasizing them.[*]

A lot of breath is going into this argument on the same theme as before. Is there anything new here to justify it? Let's review the previous arguments. Sonnet 1: "We expect the fair to have children to keep beauty alive when they die; don't keep to yourself." Sonnet 2: "By the time you are forty your beauty will have faded: have a child to show how beautiful you were." Sonnet 3: "You are the evidence of your mother's lovely youth, don't rob some potential mother of a child who could do the same for her (and for you)." Sonnet 4: "You are so selfish—how can you account for yourself if you let your beauty die with you (without passing it on to a child)?" In Sonnets 5 and 6, W. returns to the same argument as Sonnet 2—it's just laid on thicker. We also see the same alternation of negative and positive that we did in Sonnet 4, but I find in these two sonnets, the sweetness of the English summer dominates. In Sonnet 5 we have the *gentle work* of passing hours, the *lovely gaze*, summer's *lusty leaves*, the flowers' sweet substance. Even though these images are restrained by *tyrants, never-resting time, hideous winter*, frost-checked sap, and the bittersweet, imprisoned rosewater, the word that comes to mind when I read this sonnet is the last one, *sweet*. The sweetness continues in Sonnet 6 with the sweet *vial*, the *treasure* (repeated twice), and *happy* (repeated and multiplied). The only opposition to this pleasantness in Sonnet 6 is weakly offered by the *winter's ragged hand*, and the final conquest of *death* and *worms*, which the youth is cautioned to avoid. In making the argument of Sonnet 2 more leisurely, while using the same kinds of negative images as in Sonnet 4, ending as it does with another image of death, I

---

[*] The meter of lines 7 to 10 are perfectly regular so that the stress lands on the word "ten" only about half the time, making them sound not so insistent to me. Here's how I read the lines:

That's FOR thy SELF to BREED anOTHer THEE,
Or TEN times HAPpier BE it TEN for ONE.
Ten TIMES thy SELF were HAPpier THAN thou ART,
If TEN of THINE ten TIMES reFIGur'd THEE,

hear an entirely new tone especially in the couplet of Sonnet 6:

> Be not self-will'd for thou art much too fair,
> To be death's conquest and make worms thine heir.

Note the alliteration in line 12 (*leaving/ living*). It immediately precedes that image of death. The emphasis in that line falls on *living.*[*]

There's something plaintive about this. Previous couplets have sounded imperative, or scolding. They recommended, recommended strongly, demanded action. This couplet sounds more like a request. A plea. For the first time, it sounds to me like W. *cares* about Y.M.

---

[*] I read the line: "**LEAVing** thee LIVing IN posTERiTY."

7

Lo in the Orient when the gracious light
Lifts up his burning head, each under eye
Doth homage to his new appearing sight,
Serving with looks his sacred majesty;
And having climb'd the steep up heav'nly hill,
Resembling strong youth in his middle age,
Yet mortal looks adore his beauty still,
Attending on his golden pilgrimage.
But when from high-most pitch with weary car,
Like feeble age he reeleth from the day,
The eyes ('fore duteous) now converted are
From his low tract and look another way.
    So thou, thy self out-going in thy noon,
    Unlook'd on diest unless thou get a son.

1 *Orient* east; *the gracious light* the sun **2** *each under eye* each subject's eye on Earth below **3** *new appearing sight* i.e., sunrise **5** *steep up* precipitous; *And having...hill* i.e, having risen in the sky to noon **7** *mortal looks* looks of mortals **9** *high-most pitch* the apex; *car* the sun god's chariot (which carries it across the sky) **10** *reeleth from the day* i.e., toward sunset **11** *converted* turned away **12** *tract* course **13** *outgoing in thy noon* passing your highest point

This sonnet takes a new approach. There's allegory in the quatrains followed by a moral in the couplet. We can *feel* the first twelve lines following the sun, rising from dawn in the east in line 1, toward noon in lines 7 and 8, falling toward sunset in line 10 and its lowly tract at the end. Beauty is not even mentioned. There's a mixed metaphor in this sonnet. On one hand we are shown a picture of the sun personified, his head burning in the east, shining brightly at noon and fading as he sets in the west. On the other hand, we see the sun god pulling him across the sky, grandly raising him up to his full height at midday, then tiring, feebly reeling away as he disappears with him in his chariot at sunset.

I imagine W. trying to catch Y.M. off guard in Sonnet 7.

Y.M. is sitting, just relaxing. "Let me tell you a story," W. seems to say, in the beginning of the sonnet. It appears to be just a beautiful story, at first. And then, as the sun *reeleth from the day* and the eyes *look another way*, Y.M. gets suspicious—maybe he raises an eyebrow. Then comes the couplet.

I hear an even gentler plea than in Sonnet 6. "You don't want to be forgotten like the setting sun, do you? I wouldn't want that for you. Won't you consider marrying and having an heir? I really do care about you." How does Y.M. react? Is he charmed? Is he disarmed? Does he feel cheated? Does he say to W., "I thought this was just going to be a lovely sonnet, at last. And there you went, badgering me about getting married and having a child—again. Do you really care about me or do you have other motives for your incessant pestering? Is someone putting you up to this?" At this point, it's hard for us to judge.

8

> Music to hear, why hear'st thou music sadly,
> Sweets with sweets war not, joy delights in joy:
> Why lov'st thou that which thou receiv'st not gladly,
> Or else receiv'st with pleasure thine annoy?
> If the true concord of well tunèd sounds,
> By unions married do offend thine ear,
> They do but sweetly chide thee, who confounds
> In singleness the parts that thou should'st bear.
> Mark how one string sweet husband to another,
> Strikes each in each by mutual ordering;
> Resembling sire, and child, and happy mother,
> Who all in one, one pleasing note do sing;
> > Whose speechless song being many, seeming one,
> > Sings this to thee "thou single wilt prove none."

1 *Music to hear* you whom it is music to hear; *sadly* without joy **3-4** *Why ... annoy* Why do you love what gives you no pleasure, or take pleasure in what annoys you? **7-8** *confounds...bear* i.e., spoils the harmony (of family life) by performing singly instead of in concert with others **14** *none* no one, nothing

SHAKESPEARE'S SONNETS

This is new. We have the impression that this sonnet is a direct response to something that has just happened or has been said. This is similar to the effect Shakespeare will use in the plays when he opens a scene in the middle of a conversation between two characters. We get that sense here—we're not starting at the beginning of this discussion. We can imagine Y.M. remarking that although he enjoys music, he always feels sad when he listens to it. "You are music to hear," W. begins, "why should you hear music sadly?" He uses the occasion to return to the procreation theme. "Why should something beautiful annoy someone who is beautiful himself?" W. doesn't ask why Y.M. doesn't love music or find it beautiful—that's taken for granted. Instead, he suggests it's the harmony of sounds (implicitly more beautiful than single notes) that reminds Y.M. that a family is more pleasing than single life. The logic of the couplet may go something like this: "The harmony of music, blending many sounds into one, reminds you that everything gets reduced and, as only one, you will therefore become nothing." Even if the logic may appear strained, the progression of the sonnet feels strong enough to hold it up: "The union of strings in harmony, like a happy couple, producing an orderly progression, like a family, chide you for being single and holding yourself apart from the role you should be playing in the harmony of life." The couplet is felt to be correct, if not strictly provable. (For that matter, shouldn't line 7 read "the part that thou should'st bear" instead of "the parts"? But do we notice? Would we notice if someone were saying this to us?)

What is most important, though, is not the argument of Sonnet 8, nor its logic—not whether it will finally convince Y.M. to marry and have a child (by now, this is seeming less and less likely). What is important is that something has happened between Sonnets 7 and 8. Until now there have just been a bunch of written speeches. Now an event has happened. This gives us a strong sense that there is a story going on. Time is passing. Things are changing. But as is typical for sonnet sequences, the story is vague. There is no attempt to make us fully aware of the story; its incompleteness becomes a sort of mystique. We are

32

meant to feel like voyeurs, listening in on this one-sided conversation we're not supposed to hear. It gives the sequence a feeling of privateness, a personal intimacy critical to evoking an emotional response.

We've now had a glimpse of an interaction between W. and Y.M. They have had a conversation. Perhaps they have listened to music together. It has become an opportunity to revisit The Theme—get married, have a child. How does Y.M. react? How does W. feel about Y.M.'s reaction? How is their relationship developing? Whatever is going on, we sense that we are going to learn more as we read on.

9

Is it for fear to wet a widow's eye,
That thou consum'st thy self in single life?
Ah; if thou issueless shalt hap to die,
The world will wail thee like a makeless wife.
The world will be thy widow and still weep,
That thou no form of thee hast left behind,
When every private widow well may keep,
By children's eyes, her husband's shape in mind.
Look what an unthrift in the world doth spend
Shifts but his place, for still the world enjoys it,
But beauty's waste hath in the world an end,
And kept unus'd the user so destroys it.
   No love toward others in that bosom sits
   That on himself such murd'rous shame commits.

3 *issueless* childless **4** *makeless* mateless **5** *still* continually **7** *private* particular **9** *Look what* whatever; *unthrift* prodigal **10** *Shifts but his place* only changes its place (i.e., money) **14** *murd'rous shame* shameful murder

There's a subtle change in approach in Sonnet 9. W. asks Y.M. a question. It sounds like a rhetorical question, meant to set up a false premise that W. can brush aside with a display of brilliance. But it's still a question, asking for the reason behind Y.M.'s decision to remain single. Not just, "don't remain single, have a child," but "why do you insist on remaining single?" It says something about the relationship between the two men. W. can ask the question. He might even expect a reply.

There's also a change in structure. We no longer have three quatrains and a concluding couplet. The phony argument is set up in the first two lines, then answered in the next six, making the first eight lines a complete thought. There's no couplet concluding this simple argument/counterargument ("If you are worried about causing a widow grief, you will cause the world more grief by leaving no child behind, whereas your widow would at least have that consolation.") The next four lines set up an entirely new argument, which is concluded, as usual, in the couplet ("You are worse than a spendthrift who, although he wastes money, at least when he does so the money goes to other people, 'the world,' whereas you waste your beauty—by not having a child—using it up all by yourself, leaving nothing for the world.") Shakespeare connects the two parts of the sonnet with alliteration. Many of the important words in this sonnet begin with the letter "w" and the alliteration extends from the first eight lines through to the next six: *wet, widow, world, weep, wife, wail,* and *waste,* with *world* appearing in both sections. There are also words that refer back to prior sonnets: *user, waste,* and *shame,* reminding us of Sonnets 1, 2, 4, and 6, picking up their themes without repeating them.

As in Sonnets 3 and 4, this sonnet starts out with a mild tone and ends with a stern one. This change in tone is deflected by changing from the direct address of the first eight lines (*thee, thine, thy, thou*) to the indirect address of the remainder of the sonnet (*an unthrift, the user*). Everything is fairly innocent until we come upon *destroys* in line 12 leading up to the stinging rebuke of the *murd'rous shame* in the last line. Was that a slap on the face? "I'm tired of repeating myself. You don't love anybody—not if you are capable of such shameful murder!" (This is another example of the condensed adjective—*murderous shame* means "the shame that comes from being murderous.") This is strong. Where did the murder come from? How did *beauty's waste* get translated into murder? The argument may be: "You are putting an end to Nature's gift of beauty to you. If you had a child, your beauty would live on. Instead, your beauty comes to an end—it dies. You are willfully causing the death of your beauty—you are murdering it." But the most significant word in this line may be *love*. Why does W. mention that Y.M. can have no love toward others? Has Y.M. said he loves someone? Could he have said he loves a woman but does not want to marry her for fear of making her a grieving widow, to which this sonnet is a reply?* (This doesn't fit very well with the rhetorical framing of the opening question.) Or could he possibly have said he loves W.? (Remembering that for one man to say that he loves another in Shakespeare's day did not presume an amorous relationship.) No matter—this is the first mention we have of Y.M. loving anyone (even if it is mentioned as a negative). The characters are coming into focus.

----

* Helen Vendler makes this suggestion, but in relation to people in general, not to a particular woman. Vendler, *The Art of Shakespeare's Sonnets*, 85.

10

For shame deny that thou bear'st love to any
Who for thy self art so unprovident;
Grant if thou wilt, thou art belov'd of many,
But that thou none lov'st is most evident.
For thou art so possess'd with murd'rous hate,
That 'gainst thy self thou stick'st not to conspire,
Seeking that beauteous roof to ruinate
Which to repair should be thy chief desire.
O change thy thought, that I may change my mind,
Shall hate be fairer lodg'd than gentle love?
Be as thy presence is, gracious and kind,
Or to thy self at least kind hearted prove.
 Make thee another self for love of me,
 That beauty still may live in thine or thee.

6 *thou stick'st not* you do not hesitate **7** *roof* house (your body); *ruinate* ruin **9** *my mind* my opinion of you **10** *fairer* more beautifully **11** *presence* appearance **14** *still* always

Sonnet 10 sounds like a reply to Y.M.'s response to Sonnet 9. The first line implies that he has denied the charge made in the couplet of Sonnet 9 that he has no love toward others; and *unprovident* in the second line echoes the *unthrift* in that sonnet. The antitheses (*many/none, love/hate, ruin/repair*) carry such emotion that we don't even notice that Shakespeare says the opposite of what he means in line 1. It *should* say, "For shame deny that thou bear'st *not* love to any." The power of this line, especially the word *deny*, allows us to understand the sense despite the illogical syntax. What is W.'s reply in this sonnet? At first, he does hardly more than repeat the argument of Sonnet 9, replacing *murd'rous shame* with *murd'rous hate*.

The structure of Sonnet 10 is similar to Sonnet 9: premise in the first two lines, counterargument in the next six lines, new argument in the next four lines, then a two-line conclusion. It's the new argument that's different: "Change your mind about not having a child, which shows that you hate yourself. Everybody loves you, who are the most beautiful—should hatred come from someone more beautiful than love does? Be as kind as you appear—have a child to show you love me." (That explains the change from *shame* in Sonnet 9 to *hate* in Sonnet 10.) This gives us a clue to what Y.M.'s response to Sonnet 9 might have been. He might have said something like this: "How could you say I bear love to no one? Look at all the friends I have. I love all my friends, including you." W. responds by saying, "Please have a child. I can't think well of you if you don't. Let me think better of you, as you deserve. Do this for the love you say you bear me." Do we mind that it doesn't really make sense to suggest that Y.M. should have a child so that beauty will always live in his offspring or himself: *thine or thee?* The addition of *or thee* is required for both the meter and the rhyme, but not for the sense. I don't know how many times I read that before I noticed it. Now that I have, it doesn't bother me. We don't notice these inconsistencies in normal conversation—it's just as easy to miss them when Shakespeare adopts a conversational tone.

We started to hear a hint of care in Sonnets 5 and 6. Now with the first use of the word *me* that care has become certain—there is a loving relationship at some level between these two. After the stern opening of Sonnet 10, the gentle tone of the couplet comes as a welcome relief. Is this how Y.M. reacts to it? I wonder.

11

As fast as thou shalt wane so fast thou grow'st,
In one of thine, from that which thou departest,
And that fresh blood which youngly thou bestow'st,
Thou may'st call thine, when thou from youth convertest.
Herein lives wisdom, beauty, and increase,
Without this folly, age, and cold decay,
If all were minded so, the times should cease,
And threescore year would make the world away.
Let those whom nature hath not made for store,
Harsh, featureless, and rude, barrenly perish,
Look whom she best endow'd, she gave thee more,
Which bounteous gift thou shouldst in bounty cherish.
    She carv'd thee for her seal, and meant thereby,
    Thou shouldst print more, not let that copy die.

1-2 *thou grow'st ... departest* i.e., you gain in your child what you lose as you age **3** *youngly* in youth **4** *convertest* turn away **7** *times* generations of man **9** *for store* to breed **10** *featureless* ill-featured **11** *Look whom* whomever **13** *seal* stamp from which impressions are made

There's some more diction to explain in Sonnet 11. The first two lines contain parenthetical thoughts, but instead of interrupting the main idea, it's moved to the end of it. The main thought of these lines is: "As fast as thou shalt wane, so fast thou grow'st, in one of thine." This thought would normally be interrupted by the parenthetical phrase, *from that which thou departest* ("As fast as thou shalt wane, so fast thou growest, in one of thine.) Instead, that thought is placed at the end of the line. Just as Shakespeare often rearranges words to suit his needs, he has no compunction about doing the same thing with phrases. If we are prepared for that, the lines are understandable—if a bit contorted. Not quite stilted—the lines read smoothly enough—they're just difficult. Shakespeare reorders the phrases to get the proper meter and rhyme. Although this kind of interrupted thought to complete an idea is common in speech, I don't think anyone would speak the lines this way. Yet on reading the lines, they don't ruin the mood for me—I don't have to work too hard to find the meaning. ("As fast as you depart from life—as fast as you age—so fast will your child develop into a new life—a new embodiment of you.") I can almost hear W. saying them.

Note the lists in lines 5, 6, and 10. Shakespeare's contemporaries could use lists like these in the most boring ways to fill in lines. But these lists are anything but boring —*wisdom, beauty, increase; folly, age, decay; harsh, featureless, rude.* Simple antitheses in lines 5 and 6, yet that *cold decay* is startling! Sonnet 11 feels like a throwback to earlier sonnets with its detached tone and lack of emotion—except for that *cold decay* in line 6 and the *harsh, rude, barren* line 10. What's going on? Did the request in the couplet of Sonnet 9 offend Y.M.? Was the softening in Sonnet 10 insufficient to appease him? Is Sonnet 11 an attempt to mend fences? Even the meter is conciliatory, softened as it is with six feminine endings and otherwise regular lines—except for line 10.[*] But the harshness of line 10 is directed not toward Y.M. but toward others—those whose features are *not made for store.* Does W. succeed? Is Y.M. mollified? These are important questions. We have come to expect Y.M. to be someone who might need to be mollified by W. And we expect W. to be someone who wants not only to get him to marry and have a child, but to remain in his good graces— to please him. Let's read on and see how he makes out.

---

[*] The regularity of the first four lines, heightened even more by the feminine endings and the regular and symmetrical pauses after the fourth syllables of lines 2 and 4, is abruptly challenged by the multiple, irregular pauses of the following lines. The poem picks up its regularity again, only to crash against line 10: "**HARSH, FEA**tureless, and RUDE, **BAR**renly PER**ish**." The line seems to describe itself. One might be tempted to read the initial foot as a regular iamb, de-emphasizing *harsh*, but the commas will not allow such a banal line to exist. This is a sonnet of contrasts: feminine lines, regular lines; regular feet, irregular line 10; no midline pauses, multiple midline pauses; waning, growth, beauty, harshness, life and death, beginning and end.

12

When I do count the clock that tells the time,
And see the brave day sunk in hideous night,
When I behold the violet past prime,
And sable curls all silver'd o'er with white;
When lofty trees I see barren of leaves,
Which erst from heat did canopy the herd
And Summer's green all girded up in sheaves
Borne on the bier with white and bristly beard,
Then of thy beauty do I question make
That thou among the wastes of time must go,
Since sweets and beauties do themselves forsake,
And die as fast as they see others grow;
    And nothing 'gainst Time's scythe can make defense
    Save breed to brave him, when he takes thee hence.

1 *tells* counts **2** *brave* splendid **4** *sable* golden brown **6** *erst* formerly
7 *Summer's green* i.e., fresh grain **8** *bier* handbarrow **9** *question make*
consider **14** *breed* offspring; *brave* defy

We have heard the theme of this sonnet before: "Other things may grow with time, but beauty will eventually die—unless you have a child." There are distinct echoes of previous sonnets: *hideous* (Sonnet 5), *barren* (Sonnet 11), *wastes* (Sonnets 1 & 9), *grow* (Sonnet 11). But the tone is the gentlest we have heard. W. has nothing bad to say about Y.M. in Sonnet 12. He waits until line 9 to question his beauty, and then only in the context of concern about its impermanence. Dramatically, we hear the word "I" for the first time, in line 1. This makes the sonnet personal right at the outset. In Sonnet 10, only after the usual detached discussion about the potential outcome of Y.M.'s continued singleness did W. inject that little touch of personalness: *for love of me.* Here, the first twelve lines are devoted to telling Y.M. how W. feels. He doesn't actually let his feelings be known until line 9—that his thoughts of time passing and things fading remind him that Y.M.'s beauty will die unless he has a child. He teasingly delays this detail with the repeated refrain "When I," subtly varied every two lines from *When I do count* to *When I behold* to *When lofty trees I see,* that last variation especially helpful to keep the verse from getting boring.

Note how despite the gentle tone, the impending doom is also made more personal in this sonnet. Although W. questions *thy beauty,* it is not Y.M.'s beauty that must go *among the wastes of time,* it is Y.M. himself ("thou...must go"). Similarly, in the couplet, Time's scythe does not come after beauty, he *takes thee hence.* The alliteration emphasizes this point. All those words that start with *b,* some of them a bit unusual. Swarming around the all-important *beauty* and *beauties* we find these: *brave, behold, barren, borne, bier, bristly, beard, breed,* and *brave.*

Things have gotten much more personal in Sonnet 12. W. wants Y.M. to know how *he* feels, not just what the world might think of him (we had a glimpse of that in Sonnet 10 with *change thy thought, that I might change my mind*—here it feels much stronger). There was only one little "me" in Sonnet 10; the word "I" appears four times in Sonnet 12. Now we feel that W. wants Y.M. to know that it is *he* who cares about remembering him after he dies.

13

O that you were your self, but love you are
No longer yours, than you your self here live,
Against this coming end you should prepare,
And your sweet semblance to some other give.
So should that beauty which you hold in lease
Find no determination, then you were
Your self again after your self's decease,
When your sweet issue your sweet form should bear.
Who lets so fair a house fall to decay,
Which husbandry in honor might uphold,
Against the stormy gusts of winter's day,
And barren rage of death's eternal cold?
  O none but unthrifts, dear my love you know,
  You had a Father, let your Son say so.

5 *in lease* i.e., for a term **6** *determination* end **10** *husbandry* good management **12** *barren rage* fierce cruelty that causes barrenness **13** *unthrifts* prodigals

There's a lot packed into the first line of Sonnet 13. This looks like another response to something Y.M. has said. I imagine something like this: "I understand what you are saying. You think marriage and children are important. Perhaps it's right for you. But that's you—I am my own self and maybe that's not for me." W. then expands on the meaning of *self* to prove Y.M.'s folly. His self, he explains, is not his, he is only borrowing it, along with his beauty, from Nature. The only way to keep his lease from expiring is by having a child. This repeats the arguments of Sonnets 4 through 6. References to other sonnets include *husbandry* from Sonnet 3, *house*, which calls back the image of *roof* from Sonnet 10, and *barren*, the image from Sonnets 11 and 12. What has changed? It's hard to miss the term of address in line 1. Until now, Y.M. has been a tender churl, an unthrifty loveliness, a beauteous niggard, music to hear, and most often, *thou*. Here, he is *love* and in line 13 *my love*. As important as this change is we should not read these terms in a modern sense. (Edmond Malone notes, e.g., the use of the term "my lover" several times in addresses from soldiers to generals and that Ben Jonson signed letters to John Donne, "Your ever true Lover."* I will assume throughout that an expression of a loving relationship between two men in *The Sonnets* not necessarily imply homosexuality.) You may have also noted that W. has changed pronouns from "thou" and "thine" to "you" and "your." Shakespeare sometimes uses these to distinguish differences in levels of intimacy or respect, but there was a good deal of variation at the time, especially in poetry. In *The Sonnets,* it's difficult to say it represents anything more than poetic convenience.

We also have something new in Sonnet 12: W. raises concern about Y.M.'s father. We have heard about the world, about Nature, about his mother—now it's an appeal to doing for himself what he has done for his father. Isn't this a bit surprising? Shouldn't this have been the primary concern along—perpetuating the father's line? Why has this taken so long? Was it the elephant in the room? Note the difference in tenses between this sonnet and Sonnet 3. In Sonnet 3, W. said to Y.M., *thy **art** thy mother's glass,* meaning that she is still alive. Here, he says, *You **had** a father,* implying he is no longer alive. I imagine W. saying, in effect, "I really didn't want to say this, but if you don't do something, what would your father think of you!" And he seems to say it reluctantly.

---

* See Boswell, *Plays and Poems,* 20:256. For a further discussion, see Atkins, *Sonnets,* 14-16.

14

Not from the stars do I my judgment pluck,
And yet me thinks I have Astronomy,
But not to tell of good, or evil luck,
Of plagues, of dearths, or seasons' quality;
Nor can I fortune to brief minutes tell,
Pointing to each his thunder, rain and wind,
Or say with Princes if it shall go well
By oft predict that I in heaven find.
But from thine eyes my knowledge I derive,
And, constant stars, in them I read such art
As truth and beauty shall together thrive
If from thy self, to store thou wouldst convert;
   Or else of thee this I prognosticate:
   Thy end is Truth's and Beauty's doom and date.

1 *judgment* opinion; *pluck* derive **2** *Astronomy* astrology **5** *fortune ... tell* i.e., foretell the events of every moment **6** *Pointing* appointing; *his* its **7** *Or ... well* or say whether all will go well with princes **8** *By ... find* by what I see in the stars often predict **10** *art* learning, science **11** *As* that (I can tell that) **12** *store* increase; *convert* turn **14** *doom and date* prescribed end

I find an odd mixture in this sonnet. Strangely beautiful, yet distant. It doesn't have the same flow as earlier sonnets. The diction is convoluted, yet understandable—as long as you look out for those inverted phrases and are forgiving about the grammar. Shakespeare seems to have gone out of his way to invert those phrases to preserve the rhyme. The sonnet sounds deliberately stilted, matching its distant tone.

The theme is unchanged in Sonnet 14, but the argument is different. We have to untwist the phrases to understand some of the lines (5, 7 and 8). Starting with line 3, we can read them this way to make sense:

> But not to tell of good, or evil luck
> Of plagues, of dearths, or seasons' quality,
> Pointing to each his thunder, rain and wind;

> Nor can I tell fortune to brief minutes,
> Or say if it shall go well with Princes
> By that [what] I in heaven find oft predict

All this to lead up to the argument: "I read such knowledge in your eyes, those constant stars, (more constant than Astronomy) that I predict that truth and beauty will survive if you have a child and that if you don't, your death will be their doom." This is the first mention of *truth*, a word packed with meaning in Shakespeare's day (honesty, righteousness, faithfulness, loyalty). The only words to remind us of earlier sonnets (other than *beauty*) are *convert* (Sonnets 7 and 11) and *store* (Sonnet 11).

I find the same reluctance in the rhythm of Sonnet 14 as I do in its convoluted syntax and its distant tone.* The same reluctance I heard in Sonnet 13. On first reading, Sonnet 14 seems to have returned to the more distant relationship of the earlier sonnets. But has it?

---

* There's a varying rhythm to this poem, slowing down as stressed beats pile up against each other. It moves quickly along the first quatrain, slows down at the beginning of the second, pausing with the spondee in "Nor CAN i FORtune to BRIEF MINutes TELL," then hurrying through the flow of the start of line 6 ("POINting to EACH") to point out with regularity the thunder, rain and wind. The third quatrain slows again, first to pause on Y.M.'s eyes ("But FROM THINE EYES"), then to allow W. to "READ SUCH ART" in them. Line 13 is then slowed down by a trochee followed by a four-syllable word: "of THEE THIS i progNOStiCATE." The last line is all monosyllables except for the two-syllable *beauty*.

15

When I consider every thing that grows
Holds in perfection but a little moment,
That this huge stage presenteth naught but shows
Whereon the Stars in secret influence comment;
When I perceive that men as plants increase,
Cheerèd and check'd even by the self-same sky,
Vaunt in their youthful sap, at height decrease,
And wear their brave state out of memory,
Then the conceit of this inconstant stay,
Sets you most rich in youth before my sight,
Where wasteful time debateth with decay
To change your day of youth to sullied night,
    And all in war with Time for love of you
    As he takes from you, I ingraft you new.

(Double sonnet with Sonnet 16.)

4 *influence* an astrological term, the supposed flowing from stars of ethereal fluid acting upon the destiny of men **6** *Cheerèd and check'd* encouraged and stopped **7** *Vaunt* exult **8** *brave* splendid; *out of memory* until it is forgotten **9** *conceit* idea; *stay* duration **11** *debateth* deliberates

16

But wherefore do not you a mightier way
Make war upon this bloody tyrant time?
And fortify your self in your decay
With means more blessèd than my barren rhyme?
Now stand you on the top of happy hours,
And many maiden gardens yet unset,
With virtuous wish would bear your living flowers,
Much liker than your painted counterfeit.
So should the lines of life that life repair
Which this (Time's pencil or my pupil pen)

Neither in inward worth nor outward fair
Can make you live your self in eyes of men.
  To give away your self, keeps your self still,
  And you must live drawn by your own sweet skill.

5 *on the top* at the peak **6** *unset* unplanted **7** *wish* desire **8** *counterfeit* portrait **9** *lines of life* living lineaments (of children) **10** *Which...pen* since this poem, the product of my inexpert writing, which paints a picture of you for all time; *pencil* paintbrush; *or* in other words **11** *fair* beauty **13** *give away yourself* i.e., transfer yourself into children (by giving yourself to a woman)

These two sonnets make another pair that must be read as one poem (like Sonnets 5 and 6). Sonnet 15 is incomplete without Sonnet 16 and Sonnet 16 lacks sense without its predecessor. This becomes obvious once we come upon the first word of Sonnet 16: *But.* The pair introduces for the first time the theme of W.'s ability to immortalize Y.M. in verse. The importance of Sonnet 16 is that it makes that theme secondary to the power of procreation.

Sonnet 15 is filled with evocative phrases: *presenteth naught but shows, the Stars in secret influence, the conceit of this inconstant stay, you most rich in youth, wasteful time debateth with decay, day of youth,* and *sullied night.* The imagery in Sonnet 15 is also more mature than any in previous sonnets. The syntax is clear as the images change subtly, starting with things that grow, moving to the world as a stage, influenced by the stars (referring us back to Sonnet 14), everything *Cheerèd and check'd,* by the same sky. We think of an audience cheering actors, yet in the next line the *youthful sap* draws us back into a garden.

With the same technique as Sonnet 13, but at a slower tempo, Shakespeare introduces the first two quatrains with *When I,* setting up the premise of the third quatrain: "All this makes me think how rich you are to me and how Time will *change your day of youth to sullied night.*" The conclusion of the couplet is even more personal than that of Sonnet 13 (the one that first introduced "I" and called Y.M. "love"). After the very distant Sonnet 14, we now find W. isn't asking Y.M. to have a child *for love of me,* he's declaring war on Time itself *for love of you*. But wait…there's another sonnet just around the corner. And it starts with a "but."

Sonnet 16 is less complex. The main metaphor here is a simple and conventional one.* W. paints a word picture of Y.M. with his verse (the *painted counterfeit*), which explains the phrase about the pencil and the pen in line 10. In Shakespeare's day, *pencil* was another word for *paintbrush*.† Here it's used as a metaphor for the painter's art. It's compared to a pen, a metaphor for the poem being written. It's *Time's pencil* because, as W. said in Sonnet 15, his verse will immortalize Y.M. for all time (the poem is Time's paintbrush). The *pupil pen* is our familiar condensed adjective: "the pen of a pupil, which is therefore inexpert." This exaggerated humility is another convention on the part of W. We mustn't take this seriously (Y.M. wouldn't have).

The beginning of line 10 is a bit confused. The grammar demands "Since this" instead of "Which this." ("The lines of life should repair that life, *since* this poem, neither in inward worth nor outward beauty, can make your true self seen by the eyes of men.") *Which* sounds like the same problem we saw in Sonnet 1, typical of everyday speech. The straightforward thought is "which this poem cannot," but the verse needs to be filled in with the *pupil pen*, the "neither…neither" construction, and that final line that needs the change in grammar. The grammar gets left behind, but the meaning survives.

What are we to make of all this? What do we imagine Y.M. makes of it? Fourteen lines proclaiming W.'s ability to immortalize Y.M. in his verse. Immediately followed by: "Oh no, don't pay any attention to that sonnet, there's a much better way. Rather than rely on my poor verse, my painted counterfeit that can only mimic you, I have a much better way (you'll never guess)— give yourself to a woman and draw an image of yourself by having a child." Does this sound sincere? Is W. truly backing away

---

* There is much controversy about the reading of line 10—unnecessary to my mind. I am very satisfied with my reading, which I discuss fully in my article, Atkins, "The Application of Bibliographic Principles," 507-9.

† The modern meaning is not found before 1612.

from his claim of Sonnet 15? Or is it just a feeble attempt to continue the procreation theme? Do those last few words in the couplet tell us anything: *drawn by your own sweet skill?* Is this just flattery?

17

Who will believe my verse in time to come
If it were fill'd with your most high deserts?
Though yet heav'n knows it is but as a tomb
Which hides your life, and shows not half your parts.
If I could write the beauty of your eyes,
And in fresh numbers number all your graces,
The age to come would say "this Poet lies,
Such heav'nly touches ne'er touch'd earthly faces."
So should my papers (yellowed with their age)
Be scorn'd, like old men of less truth than tongue,
And your true rights be term'd a Poet's rage,
And stretchèd meter of an Antique song.
      But were some child of yours alive that time,
      You should live twice, in it and in my rhyme.

6 *numbers* verses **12** *stretchèd meter* poetic license **13** *that time* in that future time

Shakespeare now lets his wordplay go all out. With *in fresh numbers number all your graces* (line 6) he uses the repetition of the same word or root in different senses, a favorite Elizabethan device. He does almost the same thing in line 8 with just one word in between (*heavenly touches ne'er touch'd*, as he did in Sonnet 5: *that unfair which fairly*). Some may find this device too clever. I find it charming. The *numbers* (verse) *number* (enumerate) Y.M.'s graces, which are disbelieved: such *heav'nly touches* (strokes of art) could never have *touch'd* (been applied to) a mere mortal. This wordplay adds to the sonnet's light, carefree tone. There are no grave exhortations, no prophesies of doom, simply a disarming, humble assessment of the inadequacy of W.'s verse to show the true nature of Y.M. Of course, this is a sonnet: convention requires both the humility and the praise to be exaggerated.

Note the intertwining of two conceits at once in the second and third quatrains: (1) that no one will believe W.'s verse because Y.M.'s graces are so great as to be unbelievable, and (2) nobody will believe a poet anyway. The use of *will* in the first line is necessary for the first conceit. The change in tenses then lead us to expect that this verse *would* be believed *if* it *were* or *could* something. Instead, we get the second conceit: it *should* be scorned as the words of a mere poet. The playfulness of the verse helps make it recognizable as a device. This has the effect of making the poet seem clever and the compliment showier. Future readers may not be expected to believe the verse, but W. expects Y.M. to believe every word.

The conclusion of Sonnet 17 says more. Even as W. imagines the scorn heaped on his *papers (yellowed with their age)*, rather than suggesting Y.M. ignore the value of his worth in favor of having a child, he suggests instead—in what reads like a delightful surprise in the couplet—why not have the best of both worlds, my verse *and* your child? W., it seems, is moving a step further away from the steady procreation narrative he has been harping on. The story goes on.

18

Shall I compare thee to a Summer's day?
Thou art more lovely and more temperate,
Rough winds do shake the darling buds of May,
And Summer's lease hath all too short a date.
Sometime too hot the eye of heaven shines,
And often is his gold complexion dimm'd,
And every fair from fair sometime declines,
By chance, or nature's changing course untrimm'd.
But thy eternal Summer shall not fade,
Nor lose possession of that fair thou ow'st,
Nor shall death brag thou wand'rest in his shade,
When in eternal lines to time thou grow'st.
    So long as men can breathe or eyes can see,
    So long lives this, and this gives life to thee.

4 *lease* allotted time; *date* duration **7** *fair from fair* beautiful thing from beauty **8** *untrimm'd* divested of adornment **10** *ow'st* own **12** *lines* verse; *to time thou grow'st* you will become part of time

Sonnet 18 brings the most dramatic change we have seen. For seventeen sonnets we have had the same theme, "get a child to perpetuate your beauty," with varying arguments. The last three sonnets introduced the idea that W.'s verse could do the same—first, only in an inferior way, then as a coequal. Sonnet 18 abandons the procreation theme completely, proclaiming W.'s verse to be the key to immortality. We also saw the gradual shift from concerns about the general (the world, Nature, others) to the personal (me, I)—a more caring tone. The tone of Sonnet 18 is *passionately* personal. This—at last—sounds like a love poem. The effect is similar to a change of acts in the plays.

I get the sense of a longer lapse between Sonnet 17 and Sonnet 18 than between any of the previous sonnets. Something very different is going on. A lot must have happened. There has been a discussion, perhaps. We don't know what, though. An understanding? ("OK, I really wasn't serious about the procreation idea, I just care about you, let me just tell you how I feel.") A request? ("Could you please just forget about the child thing? It's not going to happen. But I really like your sonnets. Could you write some more?") A declaration? ("Let's stop kidding ourselves, we love each other, we enjoy each other's company, let's celebrate that.") We can't tell what caused the change, only that something has changed.

This seems a good time to discuss the issue of love in *The Sonnets* a bit more. Sonnet 18, read on its own, sounds to a modern reader as if it were written by a man to a beautiful young woman. We take our cues from the words *lovely, fair, gold complexion, summer*, not words we would traditionally apply to a man. But these *were* words used to apply to handsome (beautiful, in Elizabethan terms) young men in Shakespeare's day. Remember the reference to *my love*? It's difficult to shake that term. But it's important to put this sonnet in perspective. It was first printed in 1609. We have to change our frame of reference to understand it in context. The modern reader must make a mental adjustment to think of a young Elizabethan gentleman described as being *more lovely and more temperate* than a summer's day. Shakespeare's readers would have had no such problem—it would have seemed natural. But that doesn't mean that we can't appreciate it out of context as well. One of the beauties of Sonnet 18 is how fluidly it can be applied to love of any sort (well, almost—we'll get to that much later). For the modern reader, what is hardest to imagine is any two lovers reading this sonnet and finding it does *not* apply to them. It is just an expression of love.

But more than love, Sonnet 18 expresses a change in the relationship between W. and Y.M. No longer is W. a supplicant, asking him to change his mind, to do the world a favor—to do *him* a favor. W. is now an adoring fan. He admires Y.M. and will immortalize him in verse *as a favor to him*. The roles have changed.

19

Devouring time blunt thou the Lion's paws,
And make the earth devour her own sweet brood,
Pluck the keen teeth from the fierce Tiger's jaws,
And burn the long liv'd Phoenix in her blood,
Make glad and sorry seasons as thou fleet'st,
And do what e'er thou wilt swift-footed time
To the wide world and all her fading sweets;
But I forbid thee one most heinous crime:
O carve not with thy hours my love's fair brow,
Nor draw no lines there with thine antique pen,
Him in thy course untainted do allow,
For beauty's pattern to succeeding men.
    Yet do thy worst old Time despite thy wrong,
    My love shall in my verse ever live young.

4 *Phoenix* a legendary bird which lives for hundreds of years and then propagates itself from its own ashes; *in her blood* in her vigor
10 *antique* (1) pranksterish (2) making old

What's going on here? In Sonnet 18 we had a change in theme, a change in tone, a change in relationships. Now we have

52

a dramatic change in style. Shakespeare mimics the style and thought of the poet, Ovid, reaching back to ancient Rome. One might call it grandiloquent. Maybe even bombastic. Why this style? Why now? Perhaps Y.M. was quite pleased with the adoration of Sonnet 18. Perhaps he asked, "I really like your sonnets—could you write some more?" Is this the result? Like throwing gasoline on a fire?

Yet we can't help noting another dramatic change—the difference between the first twelve lines and the couplet. The quatrains are devoted to a plea to Time to do his worst, but to spare Y.M.'s *fair brow*. It's interesting, too, that as opposed to the procreation sonnets, in Sonnet 19, Time is not asked to spare Y.M. from death but to spare him from aging—he is to *draw no lines* in his brow and allow him to go along time's course *untainted*. The couplet changes course. "Never mind," it says, "go ahead, do your worst, I've got you beat—my love will live young forever in my verse."

I keep going back to read this sonnet and each time I get different takes on it. My first impression was that W. was encouraged by Y.M. and wound up trying too hard. The couplet sounded weak to me—not strong enough to counter all the bombast of the preceding twelve lines. Then I felt the gentle couplet was meant to be a statement of the strength of W.'s verse against Time's worst—with that emphasis placed so strongly on *ever*.[*] But now I wonder. Is the sonnet a little joke? Is there a smirk to go along with the couplet? There's something jarring about that *Yet do thy worst old Time* after all the protestations about *not* doing his worst. It sounds like W. is saying, "Ha, ha, only kidding. I really don't care what you do, I can do better!" After all, what else could he have been thinking? Twelve lines begging Father Time not to age Y.M. How was that going to work? The suspense was building, what were we to expect? Not, "Spare him, he's going to have a child." We gave that up. What then?

---

[*] The word *ever* begins a foot with a trochee immediately after the midline pause, giving it a very strong emphasis: "My LOVE shall IN my VERSE | **EVer** live YOUNG."

"Spare him, make him a god?" Not likely. Or "Spare him because I love him?" That doesn't seem to work out too well for
most people. The couplet must have been a surprise. I think a
smile just might have been expected.

20

A woman's face with nature's own hand painted,
Hast thou the Master Mistress of my passion,
A woman's gentle heart but not acquainted
With shifting change as is false women's fashion,
An eye more bright than theirs, less false in rolling;
Gilding the object whereupon it gazeth,
A man in hue all *Hues* in his controlling,
Which steals men's eyes and women's souls amazeth.
And for a woman wert thou first created,
Till nature as she wrought thee fell a-doting,
And by addition me of thee defeated,
By adding one thing to my purpose nothing.
    But since she prick'd thee out for women's pleasure,
    Mine be thy love and thy love's use their treasure.

2 *Master Mistress* the focus of attention (what is aimed at, a term
from an Elizabethan bowling game) **5** *rolling* looking about **7** *A
man...controlling* i.e., A man whose appearance affects all kinds **11**
defeated disappointed **12** *one thing* i.e., a penis

This sonnet always makes me laugh. Even funnier, are the
comments of a famous 18th century editor who reads this "ful-
some panegyric" with "an equal mixture of disgust and
indignation."* Absolutely no sense of humor when it comes to
penises. But for the story, what is most important is the dramatic
pause inserted by Sonnet 19, separating these very different parts
of the story. The change in style in Sonnet 19 now seems stark,
with the reversion to a more natural style in Sonnet 20. There is
a clean break. No more talk of immortality, just praise and love.
The theme is completely different. "Your face is as beautiful as

---

* The editor is George Steevens. See Boswell, *Plays and Poems*, 20:241.

any woman's, your heart as gentle, but you aren't false like women, even though you appear to have been first created to be one. Alas, Nature goofed and added something that made you an object for women's pleasure, not mine. But that's ok, let them use you, I have the treasure of your true love." This sonnet is a statement of the asexual love between W. and Y.M.—a love that is superior to sensual love. This sonnet introduces a new theme into our series.

There are four lines that deserve mention.* Line 7 is admittedly difficult, but it looks like an example of a compressed thought explained more fully in the next line. *Hues* always means "color," but color is often used metaphorically to mean "appearance" or "type," as in "what color of thing is that?" And we can't pass by line 4 without discussing the reference to *false women*. Do we excuse this simply on the grounds that we should not expect an enlightened attitude about women from an Elizabethan male? There are too many strong female characters in Shakespeare's plays for this to sit well with me. And too many false men. It sounds flip. The other explanations that come to my mind are: (1) exaggerated praise, and (2) foreshadowing. This second possibility is strengthened by two other lines, 8 and 13, which note that Y.M. *steals men's eyes and women's souls amazeth* and was pricked out *for women's pleasure*. In all those sonnets begging Y.M. to get married and have a child, did he even seem to be interested in women at all? Wasn't there less a sense of, "Please pick one of your lovely lady friends and marry her," than "Go find a wife and have a child"? In Sonnet 20, Y.M., is expected to be interested in women—or at least they are expected to be interested in him. Perhaps too interested? Will those eyes of *his* prove *false*

---

* I should also give credit to Martin Friedman ("Shakespeare's 'Master Mistris'") for the gloss for *Master Mistress* in line 2. He explains that both "Master" and "Mistress" were used interchangeably as the name for the ball thrown out at the beginning of the game of bowls for the players to aim at. Here, they are used as a metaphor as an object that is the center of attention or of "passionate interest." Stephen Booth makes passing note of Friedman's gloss as one possibility (so passing that other editors, including myself, missed it). Booth, *Sonnets*, 163.

in rolling?

21

So is it not with me as with that Muse,
Stirr'd by a painted beauty to his verse,
Who heav'n itself for ornament doth use,
And every fair with his fair doth rehearse,
Making a couplement of proud compare
With Sun and Moon, with earth and sea's rich gems;
With April's first born flowers and all things rare,
That heaven's air in this huge rondure hems.
O let me true in love but truly write,
And then believe me, my love is as fair,
As any mother's child, though not so bright
As those gold candles fix'd in heaven's air:
    Let them say more that like of hear-say well,
    I will not praise that purpose not to sell.

2 *Stirr'd…beauty* inspired by artificial beauty **4** *every…rehearse* compares every beauty to his beloved **5** *couplement* combination; *compare* comparison **8** *rondure* sphere; *hems* encloses **12** *gold candles* the stars **13** *that…well* i.e., that are fond of gossip **14** *that purpose not to sell* i.e., since I am not a huckster

Is this a reply sonnet? Has Y.M. complained that W.'s verse doesn't praise him as highly as other poets praise their subjects? If he has, the response is a conventional one, insisting that W.'s praises are sincerer than the extravagant nature symbolism of other poets. But it's the sonnet's tone that is most notable. Is it a gentle rebuke, or a bit of condescension—or even annoyance? Is this directed at other poets who fail to conventionally repudiate convention, or to Y.M., who fails to see the difference between just praise and mere flattery?

In the first two quatrains W. ironically shows just how well he can use nature symbolism as he denounces it. And while the second quatrain encourages us to think of all the precious things in the world, we tend to pass over concerns about how a young man's fairness may be compared with *earth*, or what gems might be found in the sea.

And what do we think of the repetition of *heaven's air*, in lines 8 and 12? In line 8, it is a beautiful image, the *huge rondure* of the Earth gently hemmed in by the air of heaven. In line 12, the repetition makes us recognize the artificiality of the phrase. We wouldn't notice the repetition of *heaven* (also present in line 3), which by itself only reminds us of the scope and theme of the sonnet, but the uniqueness of the phrase *heaven's air* makes its repetition obvious. Some have thought it sounds pointless or hollow. I find it emphasizes the difference between W.'s truth and all the drivel of extravagant comparisons summed up by that phrase.

W. waits until the last line to state his defense. "I am no coarse salesman," he says. "I have no need to hawk *my* wares." This seems rather bland for a reply to a complaint. The emotion has been taken down considerably from the last two sonnets. Perhaps this is not a reply sonnet, just a simple statement, structured in the manner we have usually seen: premise, argument, counterargument. This would make the decrease in emotion more reasonable. We see the same dramatic effect in Shakespeare's plays: intense passages followed by less intense ones with alternation of emotional strength. This is one of the features of Shakespeare's dramatic art that sets him apart even from his great contemporaries, such as Christopher Marlowe.

22

My glass shall not persuade me I am old,
So long as youth and thou are of one date,
But when in thee time's furrows I behold,
Then look I death my days should expiate.
For all that beauty that doth cover thee,
Is but the seemly raiment of my heart,
Which in thy breast doth live, as thine in me,
How can I then be elder than thou art?
O therefore love be of thy self so wary,
As I not for my self, but for thee will,
Bearing thy heart which I will keep so chary
As tender nurse her babe from faring ill.
      Presume not on thy heart when mine is slain,
      Thou gav'st me thine not to give back again.

1 *glass* mirror **2** *of one date* the same age **4** *expiate* end **6** *seemly* becoming **11** *chary* carefully **13** *Presume not on* make no presumptions about

In Sonnet 22, W. refers to Y.M. as *love*, as he did in Sonnet 13, but the relationship has changed—he now describes him in the most glowing terms. But is this a direct negation of the statement we just heard in the couplet of Sonnet 21, that "I will not praise that purpose not to sell"? Is W. saying, "OK, you want some flattery? I'll give you flattery!" If so, the flattery comes wrapped in a conventional conceit—the exchange of lovers' hearts. That the exchange is imagined as a physical one—we can feel Y.M.'s heart being tugged back and forth from breast to breast, child to nurse, lover to lover—is also conventional. What isn't conventional is the little joke at the end. You have to follow the circuitous workings of the Elizabethan mind to get this joke.

There are two conventions Shakespeare is toying with here. Added to the exchange of lovers' hearts is the exaggerated age of W. compared to Y.M. He combines these into a compliment of Y.M.'s beauty (which makes the supposedly old W. feel young because it covers his heart as it covers Y.M.'s, the two being interchangeable). There is nothing too suspicious in the first two quatrains, but the third quatrain starts the set up with a new argument. "You better watch out for yourself (as I will watch out for you) since our hearts are the same."[*] So far it still sounds like a compliment, especially with the added image of the tender nurse and baby. Very caring. The joke is in the couplet. The heart, usually taken to be the embodiment not just of love but of the soul, is conventionally represented by sonneteers also in its physical sense (with references to the breast or blood, for example) to emphasize the dependence of the lovers on each other. In the couplet, the heart is taken also in its physiological sense as the organ upon which life itself depends. Now it's clear that the joke started with the third quatrain. "I am old, therefore beware. Our hearts are one, so I feel no older than you. I feel like I will not die until you are old (since our hearts are one, we must be the same age). You gave me your heart (as I gave you mine) and I won't ever give it back—even when I die. And since the heart is the seat of life as well as the soul, you better take care of my heart (as I will take care of yours) to make sure *you* don't die young." The joke is on those other poets. The *coarse salesmen* of Sonnet 21 who *like of hear-say well.* Just as their *proud* comparisons to nature were mocked as insincere in the previous sonnet, conventional poets are more subtly mocked in this one by showing the absurdity of taking the literal exchange of hearts too far.

How do we picture Y.M. reacting to Sonnet 22? Is he disarmed by the subtle dig at convention? Does he laugh at the joke? Or is there anything deeper going on? Do we remember those rolling eyes of Sonnet 20? Is there some need for Y.M. to be cautioned to be *of thy self so wary?* Is there a nervousness to Y.M.'s laugh?

---

[*] The meter does give a clue that something funny's going on. The initial trochee of line 4 puts the emphasis on *Then*, instead of *death*, where it would have been had it been blandly written in iambic pentameter ("Then death look I...). Only when Y.M. turns old, will W. look to death. Now we recognize how odd that statement was, how out of place to speak of welcoming death as Y.M. ages.

23

As an unperfect actor on the stage,
Who with his fear is put besides his part,
Or some fierce thing replete with too much rage,
Whose strength's abundance weakens his own heart
So I for fear of trust, forget to say,
The perfect ceremony of love's rite,
And in mine own love's strength seem to decay,
O'ercharg'd with burthen of mine own love's might.
O let my looks be then the eloquence,
And dumb presagers of my speaking breast,
Who plead for love, and look for recompense,
More than that tongue that more hath more express'd.
    O learn to read what silent love hath writ,
    To hear with eyes belongs to love's fine wit.

2 *put besides* forgets **3** *rage* passion **4** *heart* courage, vigor; *Whose...heart* the abundance of which passion weakens his strength **5** *for...trust* fearing to trust myself **7** *decay* weaken **8** *O'ercharg'd* overloaded; *burthen* burden **10** *dumb presagers* silent messengers **12** *more express'd* more often expressed **14** *wit* intelligence

W. appears to be on the defensive again. The story has continued: it seems from lines 5, 6 and 12 that Y.M. has been showered with verbal expositions of love by *that tongue that more hath more express'd* while W. has forgotten *to say the perfect ceremony of love's rite.* The flowing lines combine with the imagery to describe a scene so vividly that I can see it before my eyes. I picture W. dumbstruck in front of Y.M., just as he describes himself. Like an untrained actor, standing stock still in the footlights, unable to remember his part because of stage fright. He compares the effect of his overabundance of love on his inability to say what he should to a *fierce thing* who is so excited with passion it loses strength to fight.

Other than lines 3 and 4 (whose image is easier to sense than to explain), there is no complicated syntax or metaphor to

AMONG HIS PRIVATE FRIENDS

obscure the meaning in this sonnet. The argument is stated simply, as if it were important that it should be quite clear.* W. has been accused of being inadequate in his praise. He excuses himself on ancient principle, rephrasing the words of Petrarch: "He who can say how he burns, burns little."† W. tells Y.M. to use love's fine wit to hear with his eyes the love he expresses in his looks. Is this just the abject lover pleading forgiveness? Does Y.M. buy the excuse? Is Y.M. getting tired of excuses? Is W. weary of complaints? Is there a hint of chiding in that last line? I wonder.

---

* The common emendation *looks* for *books* in line 9 is controversial. I stand firmly by this emendation, which I defend in detail in Atkins, *Sonnets*, 78-80.

† The quotation is from *Rime Sparse*, Number 170. The Italian reads: "chi po dir com' egli arche è 'n picciol foco." Durling, *Petrarch's Lyric Poems*, 317. The English translation is by Donald Frame from his edition of Montaigne's Essays, which I think captures the sense well. Montaigne, *Complete Essays*, 7.

24

Mine eye hath play'd the painter and hath stell'd
Thy beauty's form in table of my heart,
My body is the frame wherein 'tis held,
And pérspectíve is it best Painter's art.
For through the Painter must you see his skill,
To find where your true Image pictur'd lies,
Which in my bosom's shop is hanging still,
That hath his windows glazèd with thine eyes.
Now see what good-turns eyes for eyes have done:
Mine eyes have drawn thy shape, and thine for me
Are windows to my breast, where-through the Sun
Delights to peep, to gaze therein on thee.
    Yet eyes this cunning want to grace their art:
    They draw but what they see, know not the heart.

1 *stell'd* portrayed **2** *table* surface on which a picture is painted **4** *it* its **7** *still* always **8** *his* its; *glazèd* paned with glass **13** *this cunning want* lack this skill

If Sonnet 24 is any indication, Y.M. was having none of W.'s excuses of Sonnet 23. W., in turn, seems to have *no fear of trust* in himself in this sonnet— over the top might be a reasonable description of it. The diction is relatively straightforward, but the conceit of the second and third quatrains can be confusing if one tries to fit everything to a single physical reality.

Shakespeare is playing with two conventions which can be best understood if we think of W.'s heart as being in two places at once. The conventional *windows* to the heart (or breast) are the eyes, but here Shakespeare substitutes Y.M.'s eyes for W.'s. This relies on the additional convention of the identity of lovers' hearts and souls—Y.M.'s eyes are the windows to his own heart, but since he and W. are as one, they are also the windows to W.'s heart. This allows the sun to *peep* through Y.M.'s eyes to see W.'s heart on which the beauty of Y.M. is painted. (That the sun should be delighted to peep at Y.M.'s image is a typically exaggerated compliment.) Of course, the sun could see Y.M.'s beauty directly, and convention demands that W.'s own eyes should be able to function as windows to his own heart just as well as Y.M.'s. However, the circuitous path by which *thy beauty's form* is seen makes it seem grander. Y.M.'s beauty is seen through the lover's eyes, painted on the lover's heart, which is seen through the loving eyes of Y.M., the windows to Y.M.'s heart, which is identical to the lover's heart. Whew! How's that for a *ceremony of love's rite?*

But the sonnet doesn't end with the quatrains, it ends with the couplet. This is an example of a couplet that reverses the sentiment of the sonnet it completes. It turns out that those eyes that were supposed to be such valuable windows to the heart are unable to appreciate all of Y.M.'s glory, they *draw but what they see, know not the heart.* It is W., by implication, through his own heart and soul, who is fully cognizant of Y.M.'s worth. All the high-flown praise is just too meager for the object of love in an Elizabethan sonnet sequence. I say score one for W. on this round.

25

Let those who are in favor with their stars,
Of public honor and proud titles boast,
Whilst I whom fortune of such triumph bars
Unlook'd for joy in that I honor most;
Great Princes' favorites their fair leaves spread,
But as the Marigold at the sun's eye,
And in themselves their pride lies burièd,
For at a frown they in their glory die.
The painful warrior famousèd for might,
After a thousand victories once foil'd,
Is from the book of honor rasèd quite,
And all the rest forgot for which he toil'd.
    Then happy I that love and am belovèd
    Where I may not remove, nor be removèd.

4 *unlook'd for* unexpectedly; *that* what **6** *But* only; *as the Marigold* which opens and shuts under the influence of the sun **9** *painful* toilsome **11** *rasèd* erased

The diction of this sonnet is fairly simple, little to puzzle over. Only the gardening metaphor in the second quatrain needs some explanation. The English marigold closes up at night, opening again when exposed to the sun. This is compared to the pride of princes' favorites (represented as their spreading leaves), which instantly die back at the princes' frowns. W. says he may not be a prince's favorite or a famous warrior, but those are only passing glories that may disappear in a moment.

But we have to read the end of this sonnet before we find out what has been going on in our story. We have heard of W.'s love toward Y.M. It now appears that Y.M. also loves W. We can't tell whether this has been a given all along and just unstated, or whether the relationship has evolved. We only know that W. is now comfortable proclaiming their mutual love. A love, that he says, will never change—for either of them (and therefore better than those passing glories).

Is it significant, then, that this is the first sonnet to suggest the inferiority of W. compared to Y.M.? This is a recognized sonnet convention, but does it tell us anything about our story? If there has been a first declaration that their affection is mutual, this would be an appropriate moment for W. to express his relative lowliness as a way of showing his gratitude. Or the relationship between the men could have been understood all along and only the openness of expression may have changed. But there could also have been some doubt about the reciprocity, now resolved. The difference in stature between the men may be nothing more than a poet's exaggeration for effect. Or there could be enough social distance to have kept W. in doubt about Y.M.'s feelings until a definite statement was made. We can't tell. We are only listening in on a portion of the dialogue. We're not meant to know more.

And what do we make of that declaration of mutual immutability that closes Sonnet 25? It's common enough for a lover to declare his undying love, but is it presumptuous for him to say that the one who loves him will also do so undyingly? Does it seem presumptuous to Y.M.? Or is it taken for granted as the nature of true love? At the heart of this question is the nature of the relationship between the two men at this point. How recip-rocal is it? Are they on the same page? We are left in the dark. The relationship itself is like a third character whose place in the story we must puzzle out.

26

Lord of my love, to whom in vassalage
Thy merit hath my duty strongly knit;
To thee I send this written ambassage
To witness duty, not to show my wit.
Duty so great, which wit so poor as mine
May make seem bare, in wanting words to show it,
But that I hope some good conceit of thine
In thy soul's thought (all naked) will bestow it;
Till whatsoever star that guides my moving,
Points on me graciously with fair aspèct,
And puts apparel on my tottered loving,
To show me worthy of thy sweet respect.
   Then may I dare to boast how I do love thee,
   Till then, not show my head where thou mayst prove me.

3 *ambassage* message conveyed by an ambassador 6 *bare* meager; *wanting* lacking 7 *conceit* thought 8 *(all naked)...bestow it* will give it lodging despite its nakedness 9 *my moving* i.e., what happens in my life 10 *aspèct* astrological influence 11 *tottered* tattered, i.e., poorly clothed 14 *prove* bring me to the test

Sonnet 26 returns to the themes of Sonnets 21 and 23. We might imagine Y.M. asking, "Why do you not tell your love for me with greater wit and showiness?" W. answers, "Because, right now, my wit is inadequate to your great worth, and I must wait until the stars are better aligned to write words that will do you justice. Until then, I will write to show you my duty." The duty that he shows is, without being stated, his love. Despite the lord/vassal terminology, it's the speaker's inadequate wit, not his social position, that makes his duty seem *bare* (that is, inade-quate). The conceit of the beloved as a lord and the lover as his vassal is a sonnet convention tired enough to have been mocked by sonneteers.*

The diction of this sonnet is easy to understand. The structure is also simple but different from the usual. Instead of the premise /argument /counterargument with contrasts between quatrains and couplet, we have a single idea running through all 14 lines. There are no changes in tone, just one voice all the way through. I imagine W. on one knee, with head bowed as I read these lines.†

What does this sonnet tell us about the relationship between W. and Y.M.? What's going on in the story? Is this just a return to earlier themes? It reads more like one long apology. Did Y.M. think W. was being presumptuous in Sonnet 25? Is there a question about how much he reciprocates W.'s love? Or is W.'s love reciprocated, but Y.M. has a different idea about commitments? Is this a lovers' spat?

27

Weary with toil, I haste me to my bed,
The dear repose for limbs with travail tired,
But then begins a journey in my head
To work my mind, when body's work's expired.
For then my thoughts (from far where I abide)
Intend a zealous pilgrimage to thee,
And keep my drooping eyelids open wide,
Looking on darkness which the blind do see.
Save that my soul's imaginary sight

---

* See, for example, Sonnet 9 of John Davies's "Gulling Sonnets," in which the sonneteer wonders why love should keep his wit in the "yoke of wardship," finally concluding that "he hath another Title got, / And holds my wit now for an Idiot." Evans, M., *Elizabethan Sonnets,* 198. (I have modernized the spelling.)

† This is the first sonnet that clearly suggests it was written and sent to Y.M. to be read. Other sonnets will also make references to being read. However, I don't think we need to take these references literally and I therefore disagree with Edmondson and Wells, who consider this sonnet an example of Shakespeare's personal correspondence (Edmondson and Wells, *All the Sonnets of Shakespeare,* 152).

Presents thy shadow to my sightless view,
Which like a jewel (hung in ghastly night)
Makes black night beauteous, and her old face new.
　　Lo thus by day my limbs, by night my mind,
　　For thee, and for myself, no quiet find.

(Double sonnet to be read with Sonnet 28.)

2 *travail* (1) journeying (2) travail **6** *intend* set out upon **9** *imaginary* fanciful **10** *shadow* image

28

How can I then return in happy plight
That am debarr'd the benefit of rest?
When day's oppression is not eas'd by night,
But day by night and night by day oppress'd.
And each (though enemies to either's reign)
Do in consent shake hands to torture me,
The one by toil, the other to complain
How far I toil, still farther off from thee.
I tell the Day to please him thou art bright,
And dost him grace when clouds do blot the heaven;
So flatter I the swart complexion'd night:
When sparkling stars twire not thou gil'st the even.
　　But day doth daily draw my sorrows longer,
　　And night doth nightly make grief's length seem stronger.

6 *shake hands* unite **7** *to complain* by making me complain **11** *swart* dark **12** *twire* peek; *gil'st the even* gilds the evening

This double sonnet is written in a light mood. It offers comic relief after the more serious sonnets preceding it. The conventional themes—the separation of lovers, sleepless nights, dreams of the beloved—do not detract from its charm. I find something amusing about the drooping eyelids being kept open only to see darkness—except for the brightness of the vision of Y.M. (the brightness is compared to a jewel because some gemstones were thought to be able to be seen in the dark by producing their own light). Day oppressing night, night oppressing day, both consenting to torture W. Yet W.'s attempts to distract his torturers with tales of Y.M.'s wonders fail—both day and night just get worse for him. All giving W. the opportunity to compliment Y.M., once again. Extravagantly.

The syntax of the sonnets makes them easily approachable, designed to highlight the poet's cleverness. Part of the flattery is the showing off of the poet's brilliance—the better he is, the more his praise flatters Y.M. The sparks fly so fast they barely have a chance to register. W. travels far from his loved one only to have his thoughts perform a *zealous pilgrimage* back. His wide-open eyes see no more than the blind, except for the vision of Y.M., seen without sight. The night is simultaneously ghastly, black and beauteous, old made new. Antithesis is used differently in these sonnets than it was in previous ones. Then the contrast was dramatic. Here it's comical. His limbs keep him up during the day, his mind at night. He finds no quiet by day or night. The couplet says he finds no quiet for himself or Y.M. This makes no more sense than beauty living *in thine or thee* in Sonnet 10. But who cares? This sonnet is too much fun.

The fun continues in Sonnet 28 with the mortal enemies, Day and Night, making a pact by shaking hands, just to torture W. That handshake removes any seriousness from what follows. And that's a good thing because the plan that W. will stop his oppressors by flattering them with the idea that Y.M. makes them look better when they would otherwise be at their worst (the day blocked by clouds, the night devoid of stars) could only be uttered with tongue placed firmly in the cheek. The conclusion—abject failure—sounds like a deflated balloon. Well, what could he expect? Of course, he remains grief stricken—he's still far from where he wants to be.

Our sense of story has made a leap. We feel a large gap in our knowledge about what's going on. We don't know how much time has elapsed, why there's a separation, how long it's been, how long it will be, whether it has anything to do with the relationship between W. and Y.M. We are in as much darkness as the blind.

29

When in disgrace with Fortune and men's eyes,
I all alone beweep my outcast state,
And trouble deaf heav'n with my bootless cries,
And look upon my self and curse my fate,
Wishing me like to one more rich in hope,
Featur'd like him, like him with friends possess'd,
Desiring this man's art, and that man's scope,
With what I most enjoy contented least.
Yet in these thoughts my self almost despising,
Haply I think on thee, and then my state,
(Like to the Lark at break of day arising)
From sullen earth sings hymns at Heaven's gate.
 For thy sweet love rememb'red such wealth brings,
 That then I scorn to change my state with Kings.

1 *in disgrace* out of favor **3** *bootless* useless **6** *like him, like him* i.e., like another, like still another **7** *art* skill; *scope* power **10** *Haply* perchance **12** *sullen* gloomy, dark

OK, the fun is over. This is a serious poem. Yes, the theme of the melancholy lover whose spirits are uplifted at the mere thought of his beloved is a longstanding sonnet convention.* But Shakespeare's treatment of it is different. Just the fact that it is a love between men with no sexual overtones adds a different dimension to it. (Sonnet 20 specifically took sex off the table. When we get to some later sonnets, the lack of sexual overtones in these earlier ones will be even more obvious.)

Right away, Sonnet 29 sounds more powerful, more personal than previous sonnets. This is a sonnet of emotions. W. is no longer telling Y.M. how his beauty graces the world, or why it requires him to have a child, or how he can make it live on in verse—instead he tells Y.M. how he makes him *feel.* The emotions are carefully orchestrated throughout the sonnet. In the first quatrain, W. is *all alone*, weeping. Heaven is *deaf* to his *bootless*

---

* See, for example, Sir Philip Sidney's *Astrophel and Stella*, Sonnet 64, which has strong echoes to this poem. (Evans, M., *Elizabethan Sonnets*, 28).

cries. His cries for help echo his crying over his *outcast state*—they *trouble* heaven, reminding us of his troubles as he goes on to *curse his fate.*

The second quatrain brings in comparisons of all the things W. could hope for—good looks, *friends, art,* power—but doesn't have. And lacking these, he enjoys what he has less, he says. Until we get to the third quatrain, which starts with *Yet.* Instead of waiting for the couplet, the sonnet changes at line 9 (with its important qualifier *almost despising)*, taking a full six lines to build the reversal of emotion. W., thinking of Y.M., compares himself to the lark who starts from *sullen earth,* ascends to the sky *at break of day* to *sing hymns at Heaven's gate.** (I find the image unfolding before my eyes like the lark's wings.) This leads to the couplet's statement: forget all those things I mentioned before, they're worth nothing to me. *For thy sweet love rememb'red such wealth brings, / That then I scorn to change my state with Kings.* If that doesn't melt Y.M.'s heart, I don't know what will.†

We get a sense of a change in the relationship in Sonnet 29. It feels like something has gone on in our story. Has absence made the heart grow stronger? Or has there been a lapse of time? Enough for the relationship to—evolve? Develop? Mature? I'm not sure what the right word is. I don't think we have enough details to find the right word.

---

* Line 11 has given a few editors some problems, but only because they didn't trust the punctuation. The culprit is the word *from* in line 12, which those who ignore the punctuation read as attached to the verb *arising.* But the parentheses show us what is meant.

† This is my wife's favorite sonnet. Pretty good choice, don't you think?

30

When to the Sessions of sweet silent thought,
I summon up remembrance of things past,
I sigh the lack of many a thing I sought,
And with old woes new wail my dear time's waste;
Then can I drown an eye (unus'd to flow)
For precious friends hid in death's dateless night,
And weep afresh love's long since cancell'd woe,
And moan th' expense of many a vanish'd sight.
Then can I grieve at grievances foregone,
And heavily from woe to woe tell o'er
The sad account of fore-bemoanèd moan,
Which I new pay as if not paid before.
    But if the while I think on thee (dear friend)
    All losses are restor'd, and sorrows end.

1 *Sessions* sittings, as of a court **3** *sigh* lament with sighing **4** *new wail* newly bewail **6** *dateless* endless **7** *cancell'd* fully paid **8** *expense* loss; *sight* (1) sight; (2) sigh **9** *foregone* former **10** *tell o'er* recount

The theme has stayed the same in Sonnet 30. As we saw with the procreation sonnets, the argument has shifted, but there's also something different about the approach. I get the impression not of a response to an indifferent young man but of a writer who feels his wit has been *so poor* he must make up for his *wanting words*. The language reminds me of those words from Sonnet 26, with Thought taking the role of the Lord of the Manor presiding over his court and assessing the condition of his estate's resources.* W. summons his remembrances to the sessions of Thought's court (crying over his old woes as if they were fresh as he recalls them), counting up all his lost friends and his precious years gone by (not his waste of time, but his *loss* of precious time). Some explanation is needed to understand line 8. *Sight* was an old form of *sigh* and in Shakespeare's day it was thought that every time you sighed you lost some of your vital

---

* I owe this analogy to the manorial court to Ingram and Redpath, *Sonnets*, 74.

spirit. There seems to be a pun on "expending your spirit with sighs" (i.e., losing your health) over "those who are now lost to sight" (i.e., dead).

Then all of a sudden, everything is reversed in the couplet. W. thinks of his *dear friend* and *all losses are restored and sorrows end*. I get a completely differently feeling compared to Sonnet 29, with its grand swings down to *sullen earth* and up to *heaven's gate*. Instead, Sonnet 30 has a steady, gentle rhythm right through to that reversing couplet. That's also different from the reversing couplets of the procreation sonnets that often had a sense of drama or surprise. Sonnet 30's couplet is restrained, quiet. We expect that couplet after Sonnet 29, but not the way we expected the recurring theme of the procreation sonnets. Those created tension, this creates relief.

But there's no motion in our story. Nothing has changed with Sonnet 30. It's a restatement of Sonnet 29 in sentiment, demeanor, and maturity, as well as in theme.

31

Thy bosom is endearèd with all hearts,
Which I by lacking have supposèd dead,
And there reigns Love and all Love's loving parts,
And all those friends which I thought burièd.
How many a holy and obsequious tear
Hath dear religious love stol'n from mine eye,
As interest of the dead, which now appear,
But things remov'd that hidden in there lie.
Thou art the grave where buried love doth live,
Hung with the trophies of my lovers gone,
Who all their parts of me to thee did give,
That due of many, now is thine alone.
    Their images I lov'd, I view in thee,
    And thou (all they) hast all the all of me.

1 *endearèd* enriched **2** *by lacking* because of missing them **3** *there* i.e., in thy bosom **5** *obsequious* devoted, as a dutiful mourner **6** *religious* steadfast **7** *interest of* what is owed to; *which* who **8** *remov'd* absent; *in there* in thy bosom **10** *trophies* memorials; *lovers* loved ones **11** *parts* shares **12** *That due of many* what was due to many **14** *all they* all that they were

The language is not easy in this sonnet. The word order of the first quatrain can make it difficult to understand until you get to the last line and realize that W. is saying that all his lost loves (hearts) are now regained within the all-encompassing love of Y.M. The equivalence of heart, bosom and love have to be understood and the vagueness of the lost loves—whether friends or lovers, lost or dead—has to be accepted. The religious language is a convention used to make the sonneteer's love seem more serious. This explains the terms *religious love* and *holy*. There may also be a religious reference in line 10 to the custom of hanging wreaths upon monumental statues.* These complexities give the sonnet a mystical feel to me that heightens its effectiveness.

Although it has the same theme and sentiment as the previous two sonnets it sounds very different. The key to this sonnet is not beauty, or love, but *allness*. We find *all* seven times in Sonnet 31, three times in the beautiful last line: *And thou (all they) hast all the all of me*. It's the comparison of Y.M. with *all* that is good that gives this poem its emotional power. In thirteen lines, all those formerly held dear are now embodied—entombed and memorialized—within Y.M. with the eulogy to him in the last line. W.'s love for him encompasses all past loves.

We now have three sonnets that say essentially the same thing: "No matter how sad I am or what sorrows I endure, I think of you and would not change my state with kings, you make all my sorrows go away, you are everything to me." The first built gradually to the conclusion, the second came to it suddenly at the end, the third encompassed the concept from the very start. There is still no motion in our story. The relationship seems stable through these three sonnets. The only sense we get is a greater strength of assurance with each successive sonnet as

---

* I owe the note on line 10 to Massey, *Sonnets*, 168.

to the truth of the sentiment. There was a reminder in Sonnet 30 of the inadequacy of W.'s ability to show his love with his poetry. There's none of that in Sonnet 31's all-encompassing love.

32

If thou survive my well contented day,
When that churl death my bones with dust shall cover,
And shalt by fortune once more re-survey
These poor rude lines of thy deceasèd Lover,
Compare them with the bett'ring of the time,
And though they be out-stripp'd by every pen,
Reserve them for my love, not for their rhyme,
Exceeded by the height of happier men.
Oh then vouchsafe me but this loving thought,
"Had my friend's Muse grown with this growing age,
A dearer birth than this his love had brought
To march in ranks of better equipage;
    But since he died and poets better prove,
    Theirs for their style I'll read, his for his love."

1 *well contented* agreed upon **3** *fortune* chance **5** *bett'ring* progress **7** *Reserve* preserve; *rhyme* poetic skill **8** *height* eminence; *happier* more gifted **11** *dearer* more precious **12** *march in ranks of better equipage* stand well with those with finer skills

Following right after a sonnet with a funeral march for lost loves (all found again in the love for Y.M.), Sonnet 32 comes along with a funeral for W. It brings back the conventional theme of the lack of importance of the poet's skill compared to the love it expresses. With calmness, W. imagines his own mortality (*When that churl death with dust my bones shall cover*) and Y.M.'s future assessment of his *poor rude lines*. He asks Y.M., with conventional humility, to save his poems *for my love* even though they are not as good as those by better poets (although perhaps he could have written better if he had a chance). The couplet is unusual in that it repeats the same statement made earlier in line 7. Is W. piling it on?

There's not much difficulty with the language in Sonnet 32. There are just a few well-worn metaphors: *lines* for poetry, *pen* for those who write with one (i.e., poets), *rhyme* for poetic skill, *dearer birth* for better creation, and *march in ranks of better equipage* for stand well with those with finer skills (a conventional use of a military metaphor). Once these are understood, the diction is straightforward.

What's going on? We've seen a lot of ups and downs since the procreation sonnets. Declarations of love, intimations of reciprocity, proclamations of the ability to immortalize Y.M. in verse, apologies for inadequate praise, comic relief, an expression of deep love that erases all losses (with professed humility). And now we have a sonnet that returns to prior themes: the humble poet whose skill is *outstripp'd by every pen,* but whose love is steadfast, asking only to be remembered. This is a dramatic turn after the seriousness of the previous three sonnets. It feels like a cooling off. Like Y.M.'s response was not quite as expected and W. felt the need to back off. Is there something behind this?

33

Full many a glorious morning have I seen
Flatter the mountain tops with sovereign eye,
Kissing with golden face the meadows green,
Gilding pale streams with heav'nly alchemy;
Anon permit the basest clouds to ride
With ugly rack on his celestial face,
And from the forlorn world his visage hide,
Stealing unseen to west with this disgrace.
Even so my Sun one early morn did shine
With all triumphant splendor on my brow,
But out alack, he was but one hour mine,
The region cloud hath mask'd him from me now.
    Yet him for this, my love no whit disdaineth,
    Suns of the world may stain, when heav'n's sun staineth.

2 *with sovereign eye* with a royal glance of the sun **5** *Anon* yet at the next moment; *basest* darkest **6** *rack* piling up (of clouds) **7** *forlorn* forsaken, wretched **11** *out alack* alas **12** *region cloud* high clouds

Sonnet 33 is arranged as an allegory in the first two quatrains, a specific example of the allegory in the third quatrain and a conclusion in the couplet. As we might expect from an allegory, the language is difficult. As cloudy as the topic. There is some confusion between the subject of the sentence, morning, and the part that is the subject of the allegory, the Sun, which is not even mentioned in the first two quatrains. We have to hold onto the image that everything relating to the morning does so only in its representation of the Sun. And it's critical to read the first two quatrains as a single sentence: "I have seen many a glorious morning flatter mountain tops, kiss meadows, gild streams, and yet at the next moment permit clouds to pile up and hide his face from the world as he slinks off to set in the west." The transition to the third quatrain then seems more natural. Even the couplet takes some work to get through Shakespeare's diction. Once you get used to it, reading "Yet him for this..." may not be that difficult to reconstruct as "Yet my love no whit disdaineth him for this" (but it does take getting used to).

Something has happened that we can only guess at. Y.M. is being compared to a blotted sun. The words *disgrace* and *stain* are hard to miss. This paragon of beauty, the dear friend, the love that could banish all sorrows has committed some fault. All we can tell from this sonnet is that W. is disappointed in something that Y.M. has done. And what's really interesting is that it's not addressed to Y.M. It's as if W. were meditating about a problem and just thought he'd let Y.M. know how he felt. It's written almost like a soliloquy in a play. The tone of the sonnet is of mild reproach. The last line may be interpreted either as forgiving, or as accepting the general existence of imperfection. We'll need to read further to learn more.

34

Why didst thou promise such a beauteous day,
And make me travel forth without my cloak,
To let base clouds o'er-take me in my way,
Hiding thy brav'ry in their rotten smoke?
'Tis not enough that through the cloud thou break,
To dry the rain on my storm-beaten face,
For no man well of such a salve can speak,
That heals the wound, and cures not the disgrace.
Nor can thy shame give physic to my grief,
Though thou repent, yet I have still the loss,
Th' offender's sorrow lends but weak relief
To him that bears the strong offense's cross.
  Ah but those tears are pearl which thy love sheeds,
  And they are rich, and ransom all ill deeds.

3 *base* contemptible **4** *brav'ry* splendor; *rotten smoke* unwholesome vapors **8** *disgrace* offense **9** *physic* remedy **13** *sheeds* sheds

We have no doubt that this sonnet discusses the same event as referred to in Sonnet 33. The imagery of the beautiful day turned sour, the shared words, *cloud* and *disgrace,* and the mention of a *strong offense* all support this assumption. The language is straightforward now. No beating around the bush. But the story is filled out only a bit more. Y.M. has *wounded* the speaker; the wrong is a personal one. And the harm cannot be undone—the wound may be cured, but a scar (*the disgrace*) will remain. There are much stronger negatives in Sonnet 34 than in the previous sonnet: *base, rotten, shame, offender, cross*. The manner of this sonnet is even more reproachful than its predecessor. However, its couplet is a clear and beautiful statement of forgiveness: *those tears are pearl*. There is so much in just those four words! The shape of the tears is echoed in the pearls, which reflect their preciousness to W. for the sentiment they express. And that sentiment, that show of love, *ransoms all ill deeds*.

Love has come to the rescue. But Y.M. is now put on the defensive. What will follow this?

35

No more be griev'd at that which thou hast done,
Roses have thorns, and silver fountains mud,
Clouds and eclipses stain both Moon and Sun,
And loathsome canker lives in sweetest bud.
All men make faults, and even I in this,
Authórizing thy trespass with compare,
My self corrupting, salving thy amiss,
Excusing thy sins more than thy sins are.
For to thy sensual fault I bring in sense,
Thy adverse party is thy Advocate,
And 'gainst my self a lawful plea commence;
Such civil war is in my love and hate,
    That I an accessory needs must be,
    To that sweet thief which sourly robs from me.

4 *canker* worm that preys upon blossoms **6** *Authórizing* justifying; *compare* comparison **8** *Excusing...are* i.e., I am like all men, who make too much of their own sins when excusing them **9** *to...sense* I bring in my feelings to excuse your fault

Sonnet 35 adds some more to our understanding of what Y.M. has done to earn W.'s reproaches of the previous two sonnets. We learn that Y.M. has trespassed, sinned, committed a *sensual fault*—robbed W. of something. A sexual transgression is implied but the details are still obscure. W. distances himself emotionally by referring to proverbial truths. We find these old saws in sayings from Shakespeare's contemporaries: "The sweetest rose hath his prickle"; "In the fairest rose is soonest found a canker"; "No man is without his faults."[*] The forgiveness is more bitter than it was before though, making W. an *accessory* to a crime, *corrupting* himself, forcing him to feel both love and hate.

The language of this sonnet is as difficult as the subject matter. The overall sense of W. excusing Y.M.'s sin more than he should is clear, corrupting himself in the process, but line 8 is a puzzler. It should be confirming that sense, but what does W. mean by *more than thy sins are?* My gloss is nothing more than a guess.[†] When I read the line, I feel it more than I understand it. It's as if the last word were followed by an ellipsis: "more than thy sins are..." I feel it's up to me to fill in the blank. ("Are worth being excused?") The next two lines explain what's going on: "Though my judgment blames your fault, my feelings take your side."

There's a gradual progression in Sonnet 35 from forgiveness to fault, reversing the sudden progression of Sonnet 34. But the fault in Sonnet 35 is two-edged, turned against both Y.M. and W. There's almost a return to the humility of some of the earlier sonnets, with W.'s love attempting to raise Y.M. above censure. But the relationship is no longer as simple as it was before. Things have changed. *The offender's sorrow lends but weak relief to him that bears the strong offense's cross.* W. wants to forgive and have only love for Y.M., but the *trespass* (and we still don't know quite what that entailed) was so hurtful, W. is left

---

[*] Tilley, *A Dictionary of Proverbs,* 576, 80, 410, respectively.

[†] Even worse, the original text reads, "Excusing *their* sins more than *their* sins are." Most editors choose the emendation I have adopted here, but others have been proposed, including leaving the text as is. (The printing of *their* when *thy* was the intended word is a frequent error in *The Sonnets*, probably owing to an unusual manuscript abbreviation used by Shakespeare for *their* often misread by the compositor as the abbreviation for *thy*. See note by Edmond Malone in Boswell, *Plays and Poems,* 20:249.)

with a *civil war*, not just in that he both loves Y.M. and hates what he did, but hating himself for forgiving *that sweet thief that sourly robs from me.*

36

Let me confess that we two must be twain,
Although our undivided loves are one;
So shall those blots that do with me remain,
Without thy help, by me be borne alone.
In our two loves there is but one respect,
Though in our lives a separable spite,
Which though it alter not love's sole effect,
Yet doth it steal sweet hours from love's delight.
I may not evermore acknowledge thee,
Lest my bewailèd guilt should do thee shame,
Nor thou with public kindness honor me,
Unless thou take that honor from thy name:
    But do not so, I love thee in such sort,
    As thou being mine, mine is thy good report.

1 *twain* separated **5** *respect* essence **6** *separable spite* spiteful separation **7** *sole* unique **10** *bewailèd* lamented **14** *report* reputation

There's an interesting turn of events here. We've gone from W. sharing part of Y.M.'s guilt in Sonnet 35 to taking all of it in Sonnet 36. It sounds in line 1 that a physical separation is being proposed to solve the *civil war* of the previous sonnet. Instead, it's a social separation that's proposed to ensure that *those blots that do with me remain* (without any *help* from Y.M.) are *borne alone* by W. This is what causes the *separable spite* (the spite of Fortune that makes us separable, or "a separating spite"). Is this just a selfless sonneteering lover, willing to sacrifice himself for his beloved? But then what sort of *trespass* could allow for a guilt so easily transferred? What could Y.M. have done that could be so shameful for both himself and W. and at the same time could be claimed by W. to be his fault alone? And how can W. ask Y.M., with apparent sincerity, not to do him any public honor because it would dishonor himself? "No," he says, "my love for you is such that since you are mine, your good reputation is my good reputation." Trespass, guilt, honor, love, reputation. A confusion of lover's logic. And we still lack the key.

37

As a decrepit father takes delight,
To see his active child do deeds of youth,
So I, made lame by Fortune's dearest spite,
Take all my comfort of thy worth and truth.
For whether beauty, birth, or wealth, or wit,
Or any of these all, or all, or more,
Entitled in thy parts, do crownèd sit,
I make my love engrafted to this store.
So then I am not lame, poor, nor despis'd,
Whilst that this shadow doth such substance give,
That I in thy abundance am suffic'd,
And by a part of all thy glory live.
    Look what is best, that best I wish in thee,
    This wish I have, then ten times happy me.

3 *dearest* most grievous **4** *of* from **5** *wit* intelligence **7** *Entitled in thy parts* yours by title **8** *engrafted* fastened; *store* treasure **10** *shadow* idea; *substance* reality **13** *Look what* whatever

In Sonnet 37, W. compares himself to a *decrepit father* who enjoys watching his *active child* prance around while he is unable to himself. So even though he has been slighted by Fortune (*made lame*), his love allows him to enjoy the *abundance* of Y.M.'s *store* of blessings and, as he tells him, *by a part of all thy glory live.*

The theme of this sonnet echoes the couplet of Sonnet 36. "No matter how worthless I am, because of my love (for you) I judge my worth by yours." But everything else about the sonnet is different. There is no mention of guilt, or shame in Sonnet 37, only a return to the conventional lowliness of the sonneteer that reminds us of an earlier time in the relationship between W. and Y.M. The diction of this poem also feels less mature— three lines with lists of items, a line with *all* twice that says virtually nothing (line 6), and a repetitious couplet—*best, best, wish, wish*—

with another blast from the past, *ten times* (repeated so often in Sonnet 6). It sounds half-hearted, like W. is deliberately trying to put the *transgression* behind him, to forget it ever happened. Except for that one word in line 3: *spite*. The lone reminder of the *separable spite* that can't quite be forgotten.

The diction is unabashedly Shakespearean, contorted. No need for clarity here. Metaphors, phrase inversions, verboseness—anything will do to distract attention from what went on before.

38

How can my Muse want subject to invent
While thou dost breathe that pour'st into my verse
Thine own sweet argument, too excellent
For every vulgar paper to rehearse.
Oh give thy self the thanks if aught in me
Worthy perusal stand against thy sight,
For who's so dumb that cannot write to thee,
When thou thy self dost give invention light?
Be thou the tenth Muse, ten times more in worth
Then those old nine which rhymers invoke,
And he that calls on thee, let him bring forth
Eternal numbers to outlive long date.
    If my slight Muse do please these curious days,
    The pain be mine, but thine shall be the praise.

1 *want* lack **4** *vulgar paper* common composition **5** *in me* of mine **6** *stand against thy sight* meet your eyes **8** *invention* imagination **10** *invoke* invoke **12** *numbers* verses; *long* a distant **13** *curious* particular **14** *pain* labor, effort

What are we to make of this sonnet? Y.M.'s faults have disappeared. There are echoes from prior sonnets: *Muse, dumb, ten, numbers.* Are those reminders of former times? We have returned to the all-out praise and flattery we heard earlier (as in Sonnets 15 and 21). The argument is simple. "It's easy to write poetry about you. Anyone could do it—you're like a tenth muse. If my poems are pleasing, I'll take credit for the work of writing them, but you deserve the praise for inspiring them." But that's just the argument. We have to decide what this sonnet *says*. If I try to read it seriously as nothing but praise, it reads over-the-top to me. Treacly I would say, especially after the last three sonnets. The verse doesn't seem very convincing—as if it isn't trying very hard. There's a certain clumsiness to it that feels deliberate to me. I find myself preferring to read the sonnet with an undertone of irony with a subtle difference especially in how I say *every vulgar paper, give thy self the thanks*, and *my slight muse*.

I hear Y.M. saying after reading the previous sonnet, "That's lovely. How do you manage to be so inventive?" Perhaps not recognizing the sacrifice and restraint W. required to forgive him, oblivious to the hurt he had inflicted, accepting too easily W.'s excuses for him. OK, W. thinks, I'll oblige you with more praise and ignore your obtuseness. But I won't do it willingly. Will you even notice how cheaply I hand you your praises this time around?

39

Oh how thy worth with manners may I sing,
When thou art all the better part of me?
What can mine own praise to mine own self bring,
And what is't but mine own when I praise thee?
Even for this, let us divided live,
And our dear love lose name of single one,
That by this separation I may give
That due to thee which thou deserv'st alone.
Oh absence what a torment wouldst thou prove
Were it not thy sour leisure gave sweet leave
To entertain the time with thoughts of love,
Which time and thoughts so sweetly dost deceive;
   And that thou teachest how to make one twain,
   By praising him here who doth hence remain.

1 *with manners* with decency **5** *for* because of **6** *name* appellation **8** *That due* what is owing **11** *entertain* occupy **12** *Which...dost deceive* which...thou (absence) dost cheat (by making time go faster) **13** *twain* two

We have turned back with Sonnet 39 to the theme of the trespass, although it's not explicitly discussed. The transition is a gentle one, starting once again with praises. But the second quatrain goes right back to the same answer to the problem that was proposed in Sonnet 36: *we must be separated.* The word *absence* in line 9 gives an even stronger sense of a physical separation than initially given by Sonnet 36—a sense amplified by the rest of the sonnet. But if we remember Sonnet 36 and read Sonnet 39 in that context, there's every reason to read this sonnet as a restatement of Sonnet 36—the need for a social separation. The shared words and word roots support this reading: *undivided/divided; separable/separation; twain/twain.* What has changed is what surrounds the separation. In Sonnet 36: *blots, bewailed guilt, honor;* in Sonnet 39: *praise, torment, sour leisure, sweet leave, deceive.* Praise is prominent in Sonnet 39, repeated three times, but all those other words and phrases contain negative images.

There's an interesting dynamic in this sonnet. The first quatrain sounds like we're going to hear nothing but compliments about Y.M. Then the second quatrain unexpectedly brings back the talk of separation, reminding us that the relationship is not doing so well. But it's the third quatrain that is the most arresting, the most beautiful. It has a bittersweet touch, the absence that *wouldst* prove a *torment* but doesn't because of the *sour leisure* that gives *sweet leave* to think of love, and so deceives time, making it go faster. Yet even though the negatives are presented as positive (absence that doesn't torment, sour leisure that's sweet) the negative images persist—adding a sour taste to the sweet praise. The wound is healing, but the scar remains.

40

Take all my loves, my love, yea take them all,
What hast thou then more than thou hadst before?
No love, my love, that thou mayst true love call,
All mine was thine, before thou hadst this more.
Then if for my love, thou my love receivest,
I cannot blame thee, for my love thou usest,
But yet be blam'd, if thou this self deceivest
By willful taste of what thy self refusest.
I do forgive thy robb'ry, gentle thief,
Although thou steal thee all my poverty,
And yet love knows it is a greater grief
To bear love's wrong, than hate's known injury.
    Lascivious grace in whom all ill well shows,
    Kill me with spites yet we must not be foes.

1 *my loves, my love* throughout this sonnet, "my love" alternately means my lover, my love for you, or refers to Y.M. **6** *for* because; *thou usest* you enjoy (in the sexual sense) **7** *this self* i.e., W.; *deceivest* cheat **8** *By…refusest* by deliberately taking my lover because she rejected you (and you then seduced) **10** *steal thee* steal for thyself; *poverty* poor stuff **12** *known* expected **13** *Lascivious grace* you who are lascivious, yet full of grace

This sonnet is disorienting on several levels. The word *love* or *loves* appears ten times, meaning alternately a lover, Y.M., the emotion, or love in the abstract. It's difficult to keep track of which one W. is referring to at any one time. In line 6, it's not at all clear. Along with the alternation of meaning of this single word is the alternation of feeling. W. *cannot blame* in line 6, but then *will blame* if Y.M. is frivolously cheating him, but then *forgives him* in line 9 no matter what he steals from him, *although* to bear love's wrong is known to be a *greater grief than hate's injury* in line 12. Line 8 is infuriatingly vague (what does *thy self* refuse, or what refuses *thy self*?) and we can barely tease out a meaning from a story we must piece together. The couplet sums up the disorientation of the sonnet in half lines: outburst (*Lascivious grace*), cold reason (*in whom all ill well shows*), pathos (*Kill me with spites*), forgiveness (*yet we must not be foes*).

I find I have trouble deciding how to read this sonnet. Some days I read it quietly, plaintively. Other days, I read it dramatically, explosively. Both readings are there—they depend on my mood, on how I've been reading *The Sonnets* up to then, how I feel about Y.M. and W. How does this fit in with the story of *The Sonnets?* Either reading is compatible with the same story. We have a better idea about what has caused the problem—Y.M. seems to have stolen W.'s lover. His best friend's girl? I imagine W. had adjusted to the theft, and the change in the relationship between himself and Y.M. Things were different. Y.M. had committed a trespass, he had faults, but W. still loved him. W. decided to make a sacrifice for the sake of Y.M.'s honor. He accepted the need for a greater degree of separation between them. In some ways their relationship had grown. It was probably just a passing thing. Or so he thought. Now, it seems Y.M. had done it again. A new trespass had occurred. He hadn't expected this. It was callous. He could not pretend it hadn't happened. He had to say something more. *My love, my love, my love, I cannot blame you—unless—but still I forgive you. Lascivious grace, we must not be foes.* But how does he say this? Calmly? Angrily? Maybe both ways.

41

Those pretty wrongs that liberty commits,
When I am sometime absent from thy heart,
Thy beauty, and thy years, full well befits,
For still temptation follows where thou art.
Gentle thou art, and therefore to be won,
Beauteous thou art, therefore to be assailed.
And when a woman woos, what woman's son,
Will sourly leave her till he have prevailed?
Aye me, but yet thou migh'st my seat forbear,
And chide thy beauty, and thy straying youth,
Who lead thee in their riot even there
Where thou art forc'd to break a two-fold truth:
    Hers by thy beauty tempting her to thee,
    Thine by thy beauty being false to me.

1 *pretty* considerable; *liberty* improper freedom **4** *still* always **5** *Gentle* kind **9** *migh'st* mightest; *my seat forbear* forgo the place belonging to me **11** *riot* debauchery **12** *truth* troth

Sonnet 41 reverses the method of Sonnet 40. Instead of starting with blame and ending with forgiveness, this sonnet starts with eight lines of excuses and ends with six lines of blame. The story is made fairly clear: Y.M. has stolen the affections of a woman W. cares about. The language suggests he has had an affair with her (he has been *assailed, wooed* and he has *prevailed, strayed,* had no *forbearance*). We are still in the dark about the lady, though. Who is she? W.'s girlfriend? His mistress? His fiancèe? His wife? Surely not the last—that would hardly allow for the eight lines of excuses. Even a fiancèe seems far-fetched. All we know is that W. was attached enough to the woman to feel that Y.M.'s actions represented a betrayal of trust. This was a serious breach of their relationship. *Ay me, but yet thou migh'st my seat forbear*—that line always makes me gasp. "Couldn't you forbear for my sake," he asks? And not only did he cause harm to their relationship, he caused harm to the woman. By tempting her, he made her be false as well.

The couplet is an odd sort of back-handed compliment: "You are so beautiful, no woman could resist you, so my lover's betrayal of me is your fault. And as I am bound to love you for your beauty, your betrayal of me is a break of trust that cannot be undone by my loss of love for you." W. seems to be saying, "You are so beautiful, you can get away with anything."

42

That thou hast her it is not all my grief,
And yet it may be said I lov'd her dearly,
That she hath thee is of my wailing chief,
A loss in love that touches me more nearly.
Loving offenders thus I will excuse ye,
Thou dost love her, because thou know'st I love her,
And for my sake even so doth she abuse me,
Suff'ring my friend for my sake to approve her.
If I lose thee, my loss is my love's gain,
And losing her, my friend hath found that loss,
Both find each other, and I lose both twain,
And both for my sake lay on me this cross.
    But here's the joy, my friend and I are one,
    Sweet flatt'ry, then she loves but me alone.

3 *of my wailing chief* my chief lament **7** *abuse* mistreat **8** *approve* prove, try **9** *my love's* the one I love's **12** *cross* burden

This is a sonnet of resolution. W. tried to resolve the rift in his friendship in Sonnet 35 through social separation; in Sonnet 42 he tries to resolve it with indifference. He has her, she has him, and W. loses both. He is fine with this, he says, but he seems sad, left only with the *joy* of *sweet flattery*. A woman he cares about loves Y.M. and he finds this flattering. Is the flattery anywhere but in W.'s imagination? There is something about the couplet, with its sudden reversal of argument and shift in tone at the same time that rings false. It feels like W. is having a hard time even convincing himself of what he is saying.

Note the words that tie Sonnet 42 to the earlier sonnets

dealing with the event: *grief, loss, cross, twain.** The sonnet also tries to resolve our understanding of what's gone on. Y.M. has stolen the affections of a woman who had a relationship with W. W. was hurt and angry, but he's conflicted. He makes clear in this sonnet that he values his friendship with Y.M. more than he does his relationship with the woman—but he does value both. There's something so pathetic about the last line: *Sweet flattery, then she loves but me alone.* It seems so obviously wrong. Could W. be that naïve, that infatuated? Or is it so blatant it's actually meant as a sting to the conscience of Y.M.? I can't decide. Would Y.M. have the same difficulty deciding?

43

When most I wink then do mine eyes best see,
For all the day they view things unrespected,
But when I sleep, in dreams they look on thee,
And darkly bright, are bright in dark directed.
Then thou whose shadow shadows doth make bright,
How would thy shadow's form, form happy show
To the clear day with thy much clearer light,
When to unseeing eyes thy shade shines so?
How would (I say) mine eyes be blessèd made,
By looking on thee in the living day,
When in dead night thy fair imperfect shade,
Through heavy sleep on sightless eyes doth stay?
    All days are nights to see till I see thee,
    And nights bright days when dreams do show thee me.

1 *wink* close my eyes **2** *unrespected* unnoticed **4** *darkly...directed* seeing clearly in the dark, are directed toward what is bright (i.e., you) **5** *shadow* image; *shadows* darkness **6** *shadow's form* actual body; *form happy show* create a delightful appearance **8, 11** *shade* image

---

* Most editors accept the emendation in Sonnet 34 of *cross* for *loss* in line 12 of Sonnet 34, making the echo of these two sonnets very strong. Few would argue that Shakespeare intended to rhyme *loss* with itself in Sonnet 34. See Atkins, *Sonnets*, 105.

(imperfect because it is not real) **14** *show thee me* show you to me

A lot seems to have happened between Sonnet 42 and Sonnet 43. We don't know how much time has elapsed. The breach in the relationship seems to be forgotten. And Sonnet 43 implies a physical separation between W. and Y.M. (he can only see him in his imagination). We don't know why they are apart and whether it has anything to do with the breach, but the tone is light, carefree. This difference in tone and unknown leap in time are dramatically similar to the changes seen in Shakespeare's plays at the beginning of a new act.

This sonnet returns to convention, the contrast between the *day* of Y.M.'s presence and the *night* of absence (reminiscent of Sonnets 27 and 28). Shakespeare throws an entire rhetorical repertoire into this sonnet in a dizzying whirlwind: antithesis, alliteration, oxymoron and a slew of others. The convoluted wordplay of line 4 is complicated by Shakespeare's love of paradox and inversion of word order. I read the line to mean: "Because my eyes are directed to your brightness in the dark (when they are closed) they can see clearly in darkness." But the cleverest thing about Sonnet 43 is its use of repetition. It's as if W. challenged himself: "How many ways can I tell Y.M. that, being away from him, I'm most happy when I'm asleep because I get to see him in my dreams?" It's hard to separate all the images, but I count eight. And in the process, repetition is prominent. Whether it's mirror images of words (*darkly bright, are bright in dark*), or the repetition of a word with a different sense (*thou whose shadow shadows doth make bright*), or repetition with a different ending (*To the clear day with thy much clearer light*), they all add to the notion that W. is repeating himself.* And, to me, they

---

* The technical terms for these techniques include: diaphora (the repetition of a word in a different sense), epizeuxis (the repetition of a word with no other words between), diacope (the repetition of a word with one or a few other words between), polypton (the repetition of words from the same root but with different endings), and chiasmus (the reversal of words in parallel clauses). See Booth, *Sonnets*, 203, who uses some different terminology for

enhance the sense of happiness that he expresses at seeing Y.M.
in his dreams. W. seems to be having fun.

The couplet reinforces the change that has occurred. Whatever the reason for the separation, there's an expectation that W.
and Y.M. will be reunited (*All days are nights to see till I see thee*).
This is not an enforced separation that must be endured to solve
a problem. It's just a temporary inconvenience.

44

If the dull substance of my flesh were thought,
Injurious distance should not stop my way,
For then despite of space I would be brought,
From limits far remote, where thou dost stay.
No matter then although my foot did stand
Upon the farthest earth remov'd from thee,
For nimble thought can jump both sea and land,
As soon as think the place where he would be.
But ah, thought kills me that I am not thought
To leap large lengths of miles when thou art gone,
But that so much of earth and water wrought,
I must attend time's leisure with my moan,
    Receiving naught by elements so slow,
    But heavy tears, badges of either's woe.

(Double sonnet to be read with Sonnet 45.)

1 *dull* slow **4** *limits* bounds; *where* to where **9** *ah, thought* ah, the
thought **11** *earth and water* two of the four elements making up
the universe, the other two being air and fire (see Sonnet 45);
wrought fashioned **12** *attend* wait for

---

some of the devices. If you're interested, Paul Ramsey has a nice discussion
of the use of rhetoric in *The Sonnets* (Ramsey, *The Fickle Glass,* Chapter 5, 99-
116).

45

The other two, slight air, and purging fire,
Are both with thee, wherever I abide,
The first my thought, the other my desire,
These present absent with swift motion slide.
For when these quicker Elements are gone
In tender Embassy of love to thee,
My life being made of four, with two alone,
Sinks down to death, oppress'd with melanch'ly;
Until life's composition be recured,
By those swift messengers return'd from thee,
Who even but now come back again assured,
Of thy fair health, recounting it to me.
    This told, I joy, but then no longer glad,
    I send them back again and straight grow sad.

1 *slight* insubstantial **4** *present absent* now here and immediately gone **8** *melanch'ly* (thought to be induced by an excess of humors composed of the heavy elements, earth and water) **9** *recured* restored to proper balance **10** *messengers* i.e., fire and air, desire and thought

Sonnets 44 and 45 (the grammar makes it obvious they are meant to be read as a pair) continue the same light tone of Sonnet 43. They reinforce the story begun in the previous sonnet of W.'s separation from Y.M. and eager desire for their reunion. There's no indication that any time has passed nor that anything new has occurred. The sense I get is of a rapid succession of missives dashed off by the restless W. before any possibility of an answer could be received.

There are some wonderful phrases in these sonnets, as light as they are. The *injurious distance* that separates them takes on a mock-serious tone because of the hyperbole of the solution W. proposes. He presents for us the image of his foot standing on a remote shore, from which, as *nimble thought,* he can leap across ocean and land to reach Y.M. W. then mocks himself, bemoaning his inability to *leap large lengths* like Thought, teasing himself with the paradox that it is thought itself (thinking) that makes him realize this. He imagines himself alternately (*present absent*) drained and resupplied with half his body's elements. (This is based on Ovid's philosophy that the world was made of four elements: earth, water, air, and fire. Shakespeare, in keeping with sonnet convention, treats thought and desire as equivalent to air and fire, respectively.)[*] He is either *oppress'd with melanch'ly* when he sends off his *tender Embassy of love* (losing two of his elements, thought and desire) or joyful again when he receives assurance of Y.M.s good health. The hyperbole sets up the joke, reserved, as usual, for the final couplet. Here, we are teased through twenty-six lines until we get to the end of Sonnet 45. The last two lines give us a comic image of the speaker vacillating rapidly between joy and sorrow as his thoughts and desires slide with the swiftness of those light elements (compared to the heavy barriers caused by earth and water, flesh and tears) between himself and Y.M.

When will W. get a response from Y.M.? What will we learn when he does?

---

[*] See Lee, *"Ovid and Shakespeare's Sonnets,"* 471. Ovid took this worldview from Aristotle. Although differing from our atomic theory, it closely mirrors our current view of the phases of matter: solid, liquid, gas, and energy (the last requiring Einstein's theory, $E=mc^2$).

46

Mine eye and heart are at a mortal war,
How to divide the conquest of thy sight,
Mine eye, my heart thy picture's sight would bar,
My heart, mine eye the freedom of that right.
My heart doth plead that thou in him dost lie,
(A closet never pierc'd with crystal eyes)
But the defendant doth that plea deny,
And says in him thy fair appearance lies.
To side this title is impanellèd
A quest of thoughts, all tenants to the heart,
And by their verdict is determinèd
The clear eye's moiety, and the dear heart's part.
　　As thus, mine eye's due is thy outward part,
　　And my heart's right, thy inward love of heart.

2 *conquest of thy sight* i.e., spoils, consisting of the sight of you 3 *thy picture's sight* the sight of your image 6 *closet* private room 9 *side* decide 10 *quest* jury; *tenants to* vassals of

What's going on in Sonnet 46? The theme is a conventional one, an argument between the heart and the eye to determine who has better claim to see the truest vision of the beloved. The eye says that the heart cannot see Y.M.'s beauty—that function is reserved to the eye. The heart argues that the eye can't really see Y.M. because he is enclosed within the heart's impenetrable depths. The problem is resolved in the final couplet. There's a certain steady drumbeat to Sonnet 46. It moves on with determination from the first line to the last. The verdict was set from the beginning—the thoughts, under the control of the heart, had no doubt how things would turn out.

But what is this sonnet doing here? Are W. and Y.M. still separated? Is W. able to see Y.M. or only a picture of him, as the heart can only see an imagined picture? The light tone, with the friendly verdict of the couplet dividing the spoils of war, keeps this sonnet within the same frame as the preceding three. What rescues this sonnet from silliness is the parenthetical line 6: (*A closet never pierc'd with crystal eyes*). In the middle of this conventional sonnet, distanced from emotion by its dry, legal language, we find this unexpected definition of W.'s heart, filled with things that cannot be seen by the most piercing eyes—locked up, impenetrable.

But we have not yet heard from Y.M. W. continues blithely on. Our story has not advanced.

47

Betwixt mine eye and heart a league is took,
And each doth good turns now unto the other,
When that mine eye is famish'd for a look,
Or heart in love with sighs himself doth smother;
With my love's picture then my eye doth feast,
And to the painted banquet bids my heart;
Another time mine eye is my heart's guest,
And in his thoughts of love doth share a part.
So either by thy picture or my love,
Thy self away, are present still with me,
For thou not farther than my thoughts canst move,
And I am still with them, and they with thee.
    Or if they sleep, thy picture in my sight
    Awakes my heart, to heart's and eye's delight.

1 *a league is took* an agreement is reached **5, 9, 13** *picture* image **6** *painted banquet* visual feast **10, 12** *still* always

Sonnet 47 puts Sonnet 46 in context. Having determined the appropriate domains belonging to the eye and the heart, Sonnet 47 now proceeds to show how they may join together to bring joy to W. even when Y.M. is absent. It's the antidote to Sonnet 42.

The grammar and the imagery of this sonnet are simple. There are no stilted phrases; the sonnet sounds conversational.*

---

* In line 10, the usual grammar would demand, "Thou self away, *art* present." Many editors choose to emend, but I side with those who think

I find Sonnet 47 as charming as it is simple. Its simplicity is an essential part of its charm. There's the image of the heart smothering itself in sighs and the eyes *feasting* on Y.M.'s picture, which they both then share. A banquet of sights and sighs. And then we have Y.M. always present, unable to get away from W.—he's either in his heart, his eyes, or in his dreams. Nothing about this sonnet is elaborate. It's all about eyes and pictures, hearts and thoughts. And love. Very straightforward.

But we still haven't heard from Y.M. What does he think? Is he charmed by the couplet? Does he feel the same way about W.? What's going on back home?

48

How careful was I when I took my way,
Each trifle under truest bars to thrust,
That to my use it might unusèd stay
From hands of falsehood, in sure wards of trust?
But thou, to whom my jewels trifles are,
Most worthy comfort, now my greatest grief,
Thou best of dearest, and mine only care,
Art left the prey of every vulgar thief.
Thee have I not lock'd up in any chest,
Save where thou art not, though I feel thou art,
Within the gentle closure of my breast,
From whence at pleasure thou mayst come and part,
　　And even thence thou wilt be stol'n I fear,
　　For truth proves thievish for a prize so dear.

1 *took my way* set out on my journey **2** *under...thrust* to secure in the safest places **3** *my use...stay* remain unused by anyone except me **4** *hands of falsehood* thieves; *sure wards of trust* trustworthy hands **5** *to* in comparison with **8** *vulgar* common **11** *closure* enclosure **14** *truth proves thievish* honesty itself turns thief

---

Shakespeare preferred the grammatical mismatch to the discordant sound of the clashing consonants, *t* and *p*. We find the same issue elsewhere in *The Sonnets*.

The tone has changed in Sonnet 48. It's more somber, reflective. This is not as dramatic a change as the one we saw in Sonnet 43. It's more similar to a change of scenes in the plays. From concerns about seeing Y.M. (in his heart, in an image, or on his return), we move to concerns about the vulnerability of those things held most dear—including Y.M.

This sonnet gives us a portrait of the dualities of life. The antitheses are insistent: *use/ unused; hands of falsehood/ wards of trust; jewels/ trifles; comfort/ grief; best of dearest/ vulgar thief; thou art not/ thou art; come/ part.* The simile in line 5, "thou art to jewels as jewels are to trifles," gives way in line 6 to "thou who art my worthy comfort art now my greatest grief." This may mean no more than W. has the greatest fears about what he most treasures. But can we read this without thinking about the betrayal of trust that occurred in Sonnets 40 to 42? Could Y.M. read those words without a pang of conscience? Do we detect a trace of bitterness in W.'s voice?

Sonnet 48 is sensitive to context. Had we no reason to suspect Y.M., the couplet could sound like a perfectly innocent compliment. But even ignoring the concept of a sonnet story, making no assumption that the sonnets about the breach in the relationship have any relation to this one, just having read those sonnets make double meanings become more evident. Placed before Sonnet 32, the darker side would still be there, but instead of implying W.'s bitterness, it would suggest W.'s prescience of the bitterness that life brings as we enjoy its sweetness. If we place the sonnet in a sequence of love poems that speak only of praise and devotion, the bitterness would only reflect the *reader's* knowledge of the world. Read by itself, Sonnet 48 changes subtly with the perspective of the reader. It can be bitter, it can be sweet, or it can be bittersweet.

What has happened between Sonnet 47 and 48? Has W. become more reflective? Has he become impatient with the lack of response from Y.M.? Has he had a response that suggested a cooling of Y.M.'s feelings toward him? Or has W. heard something? Are there rumors going around? Surely, we're going to hear more.

49

Against that time (if ever that time come)
When I shall see thee frown on my defects,
When as thy love hath cast his utmost sum,
Call'd to that audit by advis'd respects,
Against that time when thou shalt strangely pass,
And scarcely greet me with that sun thine eye,
When love converted from the thing it was
Shall reasons find of settled gravity.
Against that time do I ensconce me here
Within the knowledge of mine own desert,
And this my hand, against my self uprear,
To guard the lawful reasons on thy part.
    To leave poor me, thou hast the strength of laws,
    Since why to love, I can allege no cause.

1, 5, 9 *Against* in provision for **3** *When as* when; *cast his utmost sum* made its final reckoning **4** *advis'd respects* well-considered reasons **5** *strangely* like a stranger **8** *of settled gravity* for courteous coldness (like a nodding acquaintance) **9** *ensconce me* fortify myself **10** *desert* merit **12** *guard* defend **14** *allege no cause* make no case

The most important words in Sonnet 49 are enclosed within parentheses in line 1: *if ever that time come*. This makes me wonder: why is this possibility being raised? Haven't we been told this was a love everlasting? I find myself asking the same questions I did with the previous sonnet. Is W. concerned because he hasn't heard from Y.M.? Has Y.M. finally replied in terms less warm than anticipated? Has W. heard something? The tone of this sonnet argues against a direct reply from Y.M. Suspicion seems more likely.

With its legal metaphors and its conventional pose of the humble, undeserving sonneteer, hardly worth the notice of the beloved, Sonnet 49 seems unsurprising—until we get to the third quatrain. The first two quatrains merely state the expected idea that W. has faults that would give reason to Y.M. to stop loving him. The third quatrain starts out sounding as if it is going to be a typical counterargument. W. comforts himself with *the knowledge of mine own desert*. We expect this to lead to a defense for W. to come to his own rescue. Instead, he raises his hand *against himself* to guard the *lawful reasons* not on his own part, but on Y.M.'s part. The couplet humbly states that Y.M. has every reason to leave him since W. himself can come up with no reason why he should love him.

There is great beauty and subtlety leading up to this unexpected outcome. W.'s love casts *his utmost sum*. His audit is not unconsidered—it's called by *advis'd respects*. We find both a chill and a warmth to that time that he fears *when thou shalt strangely pass, / And scarcely greet me with that sun thine eye*. And against those reasons of *settled gravity* W. can only *ensconce me here*.

Taken as an isolated sonnet, this looks like exaggerated humility intended as a compliment to the loved one. But in the context of our story it must give us pause. Is this a test? Is W. begging the question, trying to get Y.M. to reply? After all, as far as we know, it's only Y.M. who has defects that merit his being *scarcely greeted*. What will happen next?

50

How heavy do I journey on the way,
When what I seek (my weary travel's end)
Doth teach that ease and that repose to say
"Thus far the miles are measur'd from thy friend."
The beast that bears me, tired with my woe,
Plods dully on, to bear that weight in me,
As if by some instinct the wretch did know
His rider lov'd not speed being made from thee.
The bloody spur cannot provoke him on,
That sometimes anger thrusts into his hide,
Which heavily he answers with a groan,
More sharp to me than spurring to his side,
    For that same groan doth put this in my mind:
    My grief lies onward and my joy behind.

(Double sonnet to be read with Sonnet 51.)

1 *heavy* sadly **3** *Doth teach...to say* only tells me that **6** *dully* slowly

51

Thus can my love excuse the slow offense
Of my dull bearer, when from thee I speed,
From where thou art, why should I haste me thence,
Till I return of posting is no need.
O what excuse will my poor beast then find,
When swift extremity can seem but slow,
Then should I spur though mounted on the wind,
In wingèd speed no motion shall I know.
Then can no horse with my desire keep pace,
Therefore desire (of perfects love being made)
Shall weigh no dull flesh in his fiery race,
But love, for love, thus shall excuse my jade:
    Since from thee going he went willful slow,
    Towards thee I'll run, and give him leave to go.

1 *slow offense* offense of slowness **2** *dull* slow **4** *posting* speedy traveling **6** *swift extremity* extreme swiftness **8** *know* recognize **10** *perfects* perfectest **11** *weigh* carry **12** *jade* worn-out horse **13** *willful* stubbornly **14** *go* walk

Sonnets 50 and 51 (another pair) return to the lightheartedness of Sonnets 43 to 46. The sullen tone of Sonnet 50 is lightened by a joke. It depicts W. as a miserable rider, worn out by travel and saddened by being separated from Y.M. The horse turns out to have more sense than his rider. W. imagines that his horse goes slowly because he is fatigued by his master's woe and instinctively knows there's no reason to hurry since his rider is traveling away from where he wants to be. (Perhaps the horse thinking, "Oh, get a life!") In frustration, the rider spurs his horse on, only to be reminded of his own predicament by the horse's groan (the horse undoubtedly enjoying the irony). In Sonnet 51, the rider takes the horse's point of view and finds excuses for him. The entire spirit of the sonnet is lifted as it speeds up with thoughts of the return to Y.M. The joke is saved for the couplet—the rider impatiently jumping off his horse and running ahead with the speed of desire, much faster than his horse could carry him (reminding us of the speedy messengers of Sonnet 45). The change in tempo is important—the speediness of the joke makes the slowness of everything before it seem more amusing.

The grammar of the first quatrain in Sonnet 50 is confused. The problem is the phrase *that ease and that repose* in line 3, which refers to *my weary travel's end* in line 2. The quatrain says, "How heavy I journey when what I seek teaches what I seek to say [to me]..." It would make more sense if it said, "How heavy I journey when what I seek *teaches me* to say..." or "when what I seek *only says* [to me]..." Shakespeare probably had these thoughts in his head and needed the line as written to fill out the meter and match the rhyme, ignoring the grammatical lapse.

There's a lot of playing around with words in Sonnet 51 that adds to the suspicion that a joke is coming. We have the two condensed adjectives, *slow offense* (line 1), for offensive slowness, and *swift extremity* (line 6), for extreme swiftness. There's the paradox of *wingèd speed* (line 8) that knows no motion, and the word repetition in line 12. Line 12 is difficult. What exactly is the meaning of *But love, for love?* The first *love* is probably Love personified. Does *for love* mean "for love of you?" Does this really add anything to the sense? I'm not sure we need to understand the phrase beyond the obvious *for love of something*. We just need to get through this line to get to the joke in the couplet. (Does Y.M. laugh? He must!)

It seems that the momentary doubts of Sonnets 48 and 49 have passed. Perhaps W. has received some reassurance from Y.M. More likely, given the resemblance of Sonnets 50 and 51 to the sonnets preceding 48 and 49, W. has just moved on. Let's keep reading and see how far he gets.

52

So am I as the rich whose blessèd key
Can bring him to his sweet up-lockèd treasure,
The which he will not every hour survey,
For blunting the fine point of seldom pleasure.
Therefore are feasts so solemn and so rare,
Since seldom coming in the long year set,
Like stones of worth they thinly placèd are,
Or captain Jewels in the carconet.
So is the time that keeps you as my chest,
Or as the wardrobe which the robe doth hide,
To make some special instant special blest,
By new unfolding his imprison'd pride.
    Blessèd are you whose worthiness gives scope,
    Being had to triumph, being lack'd to hope.

4 *For blunting* for fear of blunting **5** *solemn* formal **6** *seldom* rarely **8** *Or* that is to say (like); *captain* chief; *carconet* jeweled collar **9** *as* like **10** *wardrobe* dressing room (often for costly garments); *the robe doth hide* doth hide the robe **12** *his* its

In this sonnet, Y.M. is compared to a chest full of treasure, a joyous feast, a special jewel, and a fine garment. Each image is brought up with the vividness of a brief scene: with a gloating miser, a joyous celebrant, a jeweler and proud gentleman. What would seem to be the most trifling item, the fine garment, is presented with a wealth of specialness that dwarfs the rest, unfolding its *imprison'd pride*. The point of the sonnet is summed up in the memorable line 4, the reason it's best not to overdo a good thing: *For blunting the fine point of seldom pleasure.*

Taken on its own, this sonnet might read as an excuse for W. being unable to spend as much time as he would like with Y.M. Without the previous references to being physically apart, the impression is of a need to share Y.M.'s time with others. Also ignoring the sonnets about the breach in the relationship, the impression I get is of a busy man of state, or perhaps a popular gentleman. But in the context of this sonnet sequence, having just been reading about the physical separation of W. from Y.M., the simple statement of the couplet is, "When I am with you I triumph, when we are apart, I hope I will see you again soon." But still, that breach is there in the background. And we are reminded of it by those two sonnets with darker tones (48 and 49) that raised questions of rumors and suspicions. Does that change the way we read the couplet? Is there some anxiety in that word *hope*? "I *hope* I will see you again soon...[will I *ever*]?" Sometimes I feel it changes the tenor of the whole sonnet. Is W. like an anxious miser, a stingy host, a frugal jeweler, each treasuring what he has but fearing he will lose it? How do we think Y.M. would read this sonnet? Does he read only the compliment or does he also sense some anxiety?

53

What is your substance, whereof are you made,
That millions of strange shadows on you tend?
Since every one, hath every one, one shade,
And you, but one, can every shadow lend.
Describe Adonis and the counterfeit
Is poorly imitated after you,
On Helen's cheek all art of beauty set,
And you in Grecian tires are painted new.
Speak of the spring and foison of the year,
The one doth shadow of your beauty show,
The other as your bounty doth appear,
And you in every blessèd shape we know.
    In all external grace you have some part,
    But you like none, none you for constant heart.

1 *whereof* of what **2** *strange shadows* images foreign to you, not your own; *on you tend* wait on you **3** *shade* spirit (with play on shadow cast by light) **4** *you...lend* you, although but one person, can lend your image to everyone **5** *counterfeit* word-picture **7-8** *On...new* use all of art to portray Helen's beauty and we have an image of you dressed in Grecian attire **9** *foison* rich harvest **10** *shadow* only a part

The tone shifts again in Sonnet 53. The history of the relationship between the two men has faded further into the distance. Did W. ever beg Y.M. to marry and have children? Was there ever a *sensual fault*? Have they been separated? Did W. suffer sleepless nights? Have they been reunited? We can tell none of this from Sonnet 53. It speaks only of praise of Y.M. And its conventionality and allusions to classic Greece make it sound so formal. The couplet especially sounds amnesiac. We may not be surprised to hear W. praise Y.M. extravagantly—we're used to that. But to say that he is unequaled in constancy of heart—what are we to make of that? There are a few possibilities. Perhaps W. has finally heard from Y.M. and received reassurance of his continued love for him. Perhaps this is W.'s way of saying Y.M.'s transgression, although irksome, means nothing as long as their loving friendship continues, which he has no doubt remains constant. Or perhaps it's a plea: "My love for you remains constant. I have forgotten about the past. May I not assume your love for me is constant, too?"

Remember Sonnet 21, "So is it not with me as with that Muse…"? The conclusion of that sonnet was, "I will not praise that purpose not to sell." Hmm. This sonnet sounds a lot like the kind of hucksterism W. promised not to use in Sonnet 21. But that should not surprise us, should it? *This is a sonnet cycle. Contradictions are part of the tradition and W. is no exception.* The premise of Sonnet 53 relies on the Platonic theory popular in Shakespeare's day that what we perceive is a reflection (or shadow) of some underlying reality. He plays with this using the puns on *shadow* and *shade* meaning either an image or the blocking of the sun. The syntax is particularly tortured in the first quatrain. The meaning is, "Who are you, of what are you made that you have so many shadows? Everyone makes only one shadow [cast by the sun] but you [the embodiment of all beauty] lend your shadow [the image of beauty] to all others who have any beauty." All this is further elaborated in the next two quatrains that explain that every external beauty, male, female and natural, is but a shadow of Y.M.

But why does this sonnet sound so distant?

54

Oh how much more doth beauty beauteous seem,
By that sweet ornament which truth doth give,
The Rose looks fair, but fairer we it deem
For that sweet odor, which doth in it live.
The Canker blooms have full as deep a dye
As the perfumèd tincture of the Roses,
Hang on such thorns, and play as wantonly,
When summer's breath their maskèd buds discloses.
But for their virtue only is their show,
They live unwoo'd, and unrespected fade,
Die to themselves. Sweet Roses do not so,
Of their sweet deaths, are sweetest odors made.
    And so of you, beauteous and lovely youth,
    When that shall vade, by verse distills your truth.

2 *By* by means of; *truth* righteousness **5** *Canker blooms* dog-roses **7** *wantonly* frolicsomely **8** *maskèd* hidden **9** *for* because **10** *unrespected* neglected **14** *vade* fade; *distills your truth* your truth (righteousness, essence) is distilled

Sonnet 54 continues in the same tone as Sonnet 53. The same adulation, expressed within the same conventional idea of beauty and the reality it represents. It expands on this theme with the Renaissance concept that unites outward beauty with inward good ("truth," in the sense of honesty or righteousness). By this thinking, those who were outwardly beautiful, by nature, must have inner beauty, too. The sonnet spends ten lines on the metaphor of the rose and its perfume. It's not until the couplet that it returns to the earlier theme of the power of W.'s verse to immortalize Y.M.'s truth. This reverses the thought of Sonnet 53—instead of Y.M.'s beauty being an image of all the beauty of the world, W.'s verse is an image of the *truth* that Y.M.'s beauty merely represents.

The syntax of Sonnet 54 is easy to understand through the three quatrains, keeping the metaphor clear. The only line presenting any difficulty is the last one, with the final phrase of the couplet *by verse distills your truth*. This is typical of Shakespeare's diction. The line as written is required for the meter and the rhyme. It's a compression of two thoughts, with a change in word order and mixed grammar. We have a combination of "by verse your truth is distilled" and "verse distills your truth." I read it as equivalent to "by verse is your truth distilled." I think it can be understood as such and fits with the indefinite mood of the rest of the sonnet.*

But this is just the surface of Sonnet 54, praising Y.M., maintaining a restrained distance through convention, returning to the theme of W.'s ability to immortalize him in verse. However, running through the sonnet is the antithesis to the sweet rose: the canker rose. And so we hear such words as *thorns, wantonly, unwooed, unrespected, fade, die, deaths.* These sound like veiled, ugly forebodings, not unlike those we heard in the procreation sonnets. The statement in those earlier sonnets was, "These bad things will happen unless you get an heir." In Sonnet 54, the statement is, "These bad things *would* happen when you die, *except that* my verse will keep your truth alive." Is this just saying, "You are worthy of my great praise, which will live on in this verse for years to come"? Or is it saying, "You will die unrespected *unless* my verse is there to sing your praises after your death. *I can give you immortality. You need me.*" I can't escape these darker undertones when I read this sonnet. I feel something brewing.

---

* Some editors choose to emend "by" to "my," but I prefer the original text, which is paralleled by a similar construction in *Comedy of Errors* 2.1.112-13: "and no man that hath a name / By falsehood and corruption doth it shame" (i.e., a man shames himself, or is shamed, by falsehood and corruption).

55

Not marble, nor the gilded monuments
Of Princes shall outlive this powerful rhyme,
But you shall shine more bright in these contents
Than unswept stone, besmear'd with sluttish time.
When wasteful war shall *Statues* overturn,
And broils root out the work of masonry,
Nor *Mars* his sword, nor war's quick fire shall burn
The living record of your memory.
'Gainst death, and all oblivious enmity
Shall you pace forth, your praise shall still find room,
Even in the eyes of all posterity
That wear this world out to the ending doom.
    So till the judgment that your self arise,
    You live in this, and dwell in lovers' eyes.

2 *rhyme* poem **3** *these contents* what is here contained **4** *Than* than in; *stone* memorial tablet; *sluttish* unkempt **6** *broils* battles **7** *Nor Mars his sword* neither Mars's sword **9** *oblivious enmity* hateful oblivion **10** *still* always **12** *That wear* who last; *doom* judgment **13** *judgment* judgment day; *that* when

The theme of Sonnet 55 picks up on the couplet of Sonnet 54, the immortalization of Y.M. in W.'s verse. The differences are enough, though, to cause a dramatic change in feeling. The style is more formal, similar to the ancient Latin poet, Ovid (as we heard back in Sonnet 19). This adds a further distance between this sonnet and the relationship between the two men. And the word *beauty* is nowhere to be found.

Although the point of the sonnet is to compliment Y.M., it says more about poetry than it does about Y.M.'s virtues. The sonnet claims it will make Y.M. *shine bright, pace forth;* his praise will *find room* among *all posterity* until judgment day; he will *live in* this sonnet for all lovers to see. All this despite the hazards of *sluttish time, unswept stone, wasteful war, overturned statues, Mars's sword, fire, death,* and *oblivion.* Sonnet 55 says nothing about what there is to praise about Y.M. It says a great deal about the power of poetry. When I read this sonnet, I feel that power is a stronger force than the praise. I hardly feel the presence of love. That has receded in the distance like so much else.

Why this change, I wonder? Is W. emboldened, feeling comfortable about emphasizing his value to Y.M.? Or is he anxious about their relationship? Is he worried about the mutual love he proclaimed to be everlasting in Sonnet 25? Or could he be subtly mocking the poets who proclaim the power of their verse? Could Shakespeare even be parodying himself, mocking the poet who is so convinced of his own power over time?

56

Sweet love renew thy force, be it not said
Thy edge should blunter be than appetite,
Which but today by feeding is allayed,
Tomorrow sharpened in his former might.
So love be thou, although today thou fill
Thy hungry eyes, even till they wink with fullness,
Tomorrow see again, and do not kill
The spirit of Love, with a perpetual dullness.
Let this sad *Int'rim* like the Ocean be
Which parts the shore, where two contracted new,
Come daily to the banks, that when they see
Return of love, more blest may be the view.
    As call it Winter, which being full of care,
    Makes Summer's welcome, thrice more wish'd, more rare.

1, 5 *love* spirit of love **4** *sharpened in his* sharpened into its **6** *wink* shut in sleep **9** *sad Int'rim* unfortunate interval **10** *parts the shore* divides the shores; *contracted new* recently betrothed **11** *banks* seashore **12** *love* the loved one **13** *As call* call

Something has happened. For the first time, W. has cause to defend his love for Y.M. He addresses this sonnet not to Y.M., but to his own *sweet love*. He asks his love to renew its force, not to be dulled like a sated appetite. He speaks of a *sad interim*, which he compares to an *ocean* separating lovers, which when relieved will be as welcome as *summer* is after the cares of *winter*. We are reminded of Y.M.'s faults, but now the fault lies squarely with W. Has he grown weary of the lack of attention from Y.M. and failed somehow to show his love as he had before? Has Y.M. detected a difference in tone in his sonnets and called him to task? Or maybe W. repeated a rumor he heard, causing Y.M. to take offense and leading to a rift in the relationship? Or could W. have been paying more attention to someone else, making Y.M. jealous of his attention? Then again, could someone else have been paying more attention to Y.M., making W.'s attentions pale in comparison? We don't know the answers to these questions, only that this sonnet raises them. The answers may await us.

I read this sonnet with gentle plaintiveness. If the verbs are read too forcefully (*renew...be so...do not kill...Let*) the verse sounds overblown and out of tune with the gracefulness of the final couplet. If we take our cue from the couplet and read the entire poem with the gentleness of those two lines, we may find it sounding less like Ovid's imperial Rome of Sonnet 55 and more like the sweet English summer welcomed in by the last line. I hear not just a change of heart or an excuse in Sonnet 54, but an apology.

57

Being your slave what should I do but tend
Upon the hours, and times of your desire?
I have no precious time at all to spend,
Nor services to do till you require.
Nor dare I chide the world without end hour,
Whilst I (my sovereign) watch the clock for you,
Nor think the bitterness of absence sour,
When you have bid your servant once adieu.
Nor dare I question with my jealous thought,
Where you may be, or your affairs suppose,
But like a sad slave stay and think of naught
Save where you are, how happy you make those.
    So true a fool is love, that in your Will,
    (Though you do any thing) he thinks no ill.

5 *world without end* tedious, everlasting **10** *suppose* imagine **12** *Save where* except wherever

We've gone from a gentle apology in Sonnet 56 to abject subservience in Sonnet 57. Has Y.M. said something in response to the apology? Perhaps: "Is that all you have to say for yourself?" W. must dig deeper. He is a *slave*, a *servant*, whose time belongs only to his *sovereign*. Although the sonneteer as slave/servant is conventional, just as there were undertones in Sonnet 54, they are unmistakably present here as well. He dare not *chide* the hour that seems to have no end, while he watches the clock, nor think the *bitterness of absence sour*, nor question with his *jealous thought* where he may be. But how could bitterness be anything but sour? And why are his thoughts jealous? Where *has* Y.M. been? Is W. chiding the tedious time or Y.M.? And then there's the couplet. The obvious pun on *your Will* (what you choose to do/your William) leads to double meanings for *love* and *fool* (love is so fond of its object of desire it will forgive anything/I, who love you, am such a fool, I will forgive anything).[*]

Each time I come upon this sonnet I never know how I'm going to read it. Is it a quiet, plaintive sonnet, accepting what is, loving unreservedly? Or is it an angry sonnet, filled with irony and regret? The words are carefully orchestrated. W. tends upon the *hours, and times* of Y.M.'s *desire*. He has *no precious time at all to spend* until Y.M. requires it and *dare* not *chide* the *hour* that will not end while he watches *the clock* for his return. He won't even think *the bitterness of absence sour*. I wonder how he manages that? And though his thoughts are *jealous* he, once again, *dare* not question Y.M.'s whereabouts. He admits one other thing—while Y.M. is making others *happy*, W. is a *sad slave*. How does Y.M. read this sonnet? Is he proud enough that he reads only subservience? Or does he note some sense of irritation?

---

[*] "Wait a minute," I hear you ask, "if 'will' is a pun on William, doesn't that imply that *The Sonnets* are autobiographical?" No, it doesn't. Remember that it was conventional for poets to write sonnets as if telling their own story. Shakespeare is just using his own name for the main character in his sonnet story. That doesn't make the story an autobiography—any more than a novel written in the first person (even if the author uses his own first name for his protagonist).

58

That God forbid, that made me first your slave,
I should in thought control your times of pleasure,
Or at your hand th' account of hours to crave,
Being your vassal bound to stay your leisure.
Oh let me suffer (being at your beck)
Th' imprison'd absence of your liberty,
And patience tame, to sufferance bide each check,
Without accusing you of injury.
Be where you list, your charter is so strong,
That you your self may privilege your time
To what you will, to you it doth belong,
Your self to pardon of self-doing crime.
    I am to wait, though waiting so be hell,
    Not blame your pleasure be it ill or well.

2 *in thought control* want to control **3** *th' account of hours* an accounting of how you spend your time **4** *stay* wait for **6** *Th'…liberty* i.e., I who am imprisoned by the absence that your liberty brings **7** *And…check* and let me tame my patience, and hold back each lack of forbearance **9** *list* please; *charter* acknowledged right **10** *privilege* give privilege to **13** *I am to* I must

I imagine Y.M. having replied to Sonnet 57: "What did you say?" Not quite sure how to take W.'s words, he asks for clarification. Sonnet 58 repeats the thought of Sonnet 57 in stronger terms. The bitter undertones are also stronger. Even the first three words are ambiguous: *That God forbid.* Is this serious or sarcastic? The answer sets the tone of the entire sonnet. On its surface, it's more subservient than Sonnet 57. But the subservience is stated with even stronger negatives. Look at the words running through this sonnet: *suffer, imprison'd, tame, sufferance, accusing, injury, pardon, crime, hell, blame.* We can either read this as, "Despite all this, I recognize your privilege and wait on your pleasure." Or, "Yes, you are within your rights and I wait on your pleasure (but don't think for a minute I am enjoying this and remember that you're putting me through hell)." Y.M. might be pleased with the subservience and ignore the undertones. Or perhaps he might read those undertones and be fine with them. "OK," he might think, "go right ahead and feel as injured as you like, as long as you recognize where we stand." On the other hand, does he feel remorse?

If the grammar of lines 1-3 seems confusing, it's because it's a bit tricky. Line 1 compresses two ideas in one: "That God that made me first your slave" and "That God forbid." The sense is, "The God that made me first your slave, *that* God forbid." As for line 3, to parallel line 2 we would expect line 3 to read "should crave" instead of "to crave." But I think, *I should in thought* just means "I should want to." The three lines then say, "That God forbid I should want to control your thoughts or to crave an accounting of your hours from you." The grammar reflects the condensed thoughts, not the sentence structure.

59

If there be nothing new, but that which is
Hath been before, how are our brains beguil'd,
Which laboring for invention bear amiss
The second burthen of a former child?
Oh that recórd could with a backward look,
Even of five hundreth courses of the Sun,
Show me your image in some antique book,
Since mind at first in character was done,
That I might see what the old world could say,
To this composèd wonder of your frame,
Whether we are mended, or where better they,
Or whether revolution be the same.
    Oh sure I am the wits of former days,
    To subjects worse have giv'n admiring praise.

1 *which is* which exists now **3** *invention* something new **4** *burthen* burden **5** *recórd* written evidence **6** *hundreth* hundred **7** *your image* a picture of you in words **8** *Since...done* since thought was first expressed in writing **10** *composèd wonder* wonderful composition **11** *mended* improved; *where better they* in what respects they are better **12** *revolution be the same* one cycle repeats another

The fuss seems to be over. All appears to be forgiven and W. once again praises Y.M. in typical sonnet fashion. Sonnet 59 returns to ancient Rome, adopting not only Ovid's style, but his concept of the world. To understand this sonnet, we have to know that Ovid believed that everything in the world was indestructible and merely changed form recurrently over the eons, a process referred to by Shakespeare as *revolution* (like that of the sun). The same philosophy is reflected in *Ecclesiastes* 1:10, "there is nothing new under the sun."

Despite the simplicity of the theme, Sonnet 59 is linguistically complex. Lines 3-4 say: "If there is really nothing new in this world, our brains are just mistakenly 're-inventing the wheel' when try to say something new to praise you," comparing it to having a second labor (with a pun on *labor*) to bear a child who's already been born (a bizarre image, when you think about it, apparently just to get in that pun on *labor*). Lines 7-8 say: "Show me some description of you in an ancient book, written anytime since men first began to put their thoughts into words." The use of the old form, *hundredth,* looks like a deliberate attempt to make the poem feel antique.* The *image* is a metaphor for an evocative written description (a throwback to Sonnet 16), as is made clear by the quatrain that follows. In line 10, *composed wonder* is typical Shakespearean diction, making the adjective and noun change places to compress the idea of "wonderful composition." Finally, in line 11, instead of repeating *whether* three times, Shakespeare substitutes *where* in the middle, compressing in that one word the thought "in what respects," and, typically leaving out the verb "are," which is easily understood from the context.

Simple, conventional theme, complicated language, uncomplicated relationship. No sign of anything that's gone on before—or of any emotion.

---

* "Burthen" is Shakespeare's usual spelling for "burden," so I don't count that as an antique spelling.

60

Like as the waves make towards the pebbled shore,
So do our minutes hasten to their end,
Each changing place with that which goes before,
In sequent toil all forwards do contend.
Nativity, once in the main of light,
Crawls to maturity, wherewith being crown'd,
Crooked eclipses 'gainst his glory fight,
And time that gave, doth now his gift confound.
Time doth transfix the flourish set on youth,
And delves the parallels in beauty's brow,
Feeds on the rarities of nature's truth,
And nothing stands but for his scythe to mow.
    And yet to times in hope, my verse shall stand,
    Praising thy worth, despite his cruel hand.

4 *sequent* successive **5** *Nativity* the new-born babe; *once in the main of light* once it is exposed to the sea of light, i.e., once born **6** *wherewith* with which **7** *Crooked* malignant **8** *confound* destroy **9** *transfix* make motionless, as if pierced through, i.e., stop **11** *nature's truth* true nature **13** *to times in hope* in future times

Like the previous sonnet, Sonnet 60 is conventional, written in the style of Ovid and borrowing his view of the world. The language is even more complicated. Time is compared to the ocean's waves, always moving forward, each wave taking the place of the one before it. The sonnet returns to themes we've heard before: Time as the destroyer of youth and beauty, and the power of verse to immortalize. What's different about Sonnet 60 is its emotional power. The power builds from the first quatrain to the third, until it dramatically reverses with the couplet. Quietly, in those two lines, the poet declares Time to be unequal to his verse. Beautiful imagery, dramatic, powerful.

The second quatrain is best understood as a shifting image. It starts with a baby (*nativity* in the abstract, being used to represent the concrete result of it) that, after birth (*main* being a metaphor for the open ocean), matures (with the play on *crawls*)

until the peak of adulthood (the *crown* of achievement) after which Time takes away everything it gave. Note the different manifestations of Time's power: it *eclipses, confounds* (destroys, or eats up—the usual meaning in Shakespeare's work), *transfixes, delves parallels* (digs trenches), *feeds,* and *mows* with his *scythe.* Note also the objects of Time's destruction: the *flourish set on youth, beauty's brow,* the *rarities of nature's truth* (true nature, or the truth that nature embodies, an example of condensed thought)— nothing is left standing. Except W.'s verse. *That* will stand the test of time. It will remain for future times (*to times in hope,* or in hoped for times, not just the future, but a better future) to praise *thy worth.*

What do we remember most when we read this sonnet? The power of Time dominates the quatrains. Time is overcome by W.'s verse in the couplet. But in all fourteen lines, Y.M. is allowed only two words in the very last one: *thy worth.* There was a shift in Sonnet 55 toward an emphasis on the power of verse as opposed to praise of Y.M. In comparison to Sonnet 60, that sonnet seems filled with his praises. Sonnet 60 makes him almost disappear from view. It sounds like a poet praising his own verse, not the supposed object of it. It has to make you wonder what's going on in the relationship.

61

Is it thy will thy Image should keep open
My heavy eyelids to the weary night?
Dost thou desire my slumbers should be broken,
While shadows like to thee do mock my sight?
Is it thy spirit that thou send'st from thee
So far from home into my deeds to pry,
To find out shames and idle hours in me,
The scope and tenure of thy Jealousy?
O no, thy love, though much, is not so great,
It is my love that keeps mine eye awake,
Mine own true love that doth my rest defeat,
To play the watchman ever for thy sake.
    For thee watch I, whilst thou dost wake elsewhere,
    From me far off, with others all too near.

4 *shadows* images produced by the imagination **8** *scope* reach; *tenure* (1) hold (upon the speaker) (2) tenor **11** *defeat* destroy

Something interesting has happened since Sonnet 60. The emotional distance has closed—no more ancient Roman verses with cool praises. Instead we have the return of *love* (mentioned three times) with no question about its being reciprocated. At the same time, we have the re-opening of a physical distance between the two men. Y.M. is now *far from home* while W. is plagued with sleepless nights. It's not clear whether or how these two changes are connected, nor how long a span of time has occurred. But the change is dramatic.

The similarity to the earlier sonnets about absence and sleepless nights (27 and 28) is unmistakable. Even the playful, charming tone is the same. But those sonnets came before the sonnets about Y.M.'s trespass. They were all innocence. It's impossible to read this sonnet the same way. There's something else different about Sonnet 61. How can we read the word *jealousy* and not think of W.'s reason for feeling jealous? Or the suspicions raised about whether Y.M. might have his own cause for jealousy? Even line 9 (*O no, thy love, though much, is not so great*) that earlier in the sequence would be nothing but a sign of the joke to come, here must at least make us think "My love is greater than yours." And if we think it, does Y.M.? And that last line: *From me far off, with others far too near.* Although it *can* be read innocently as a compliment, a sign of how much W. loves Y.M., it's hard to erase the memory of Y.M. being too close to someone W. dearly wished he hadn't.

The language of Sonnet 61 isn't difficult, with only an extended parenthetical thought in the second quatrain that's not very hard to follow. The main idea is the question, "Is it thy spirit, that is the scope and tenure of thy jealousy?" The rest of the quatrain modifies Y.M.'s spirit *that thou send'st from thee / So far from home into my deeds to pry, / To find out shames and idle hours in me.* We don't even notice the mashed up grammar that borrows "that" from *that thou send'st* to fill in for "that is the scope" (dropping the verb "is").

62

Sin of self-love possesseth all mine eye,
And all my soul, and all my every part;
And for this sin there is no remedy,
It is so grounded inward in my heart.
Me thinks no face so gracious is as mine,
No shape so true, no truth of such account,
And for my self mine own worth do define,
As I all other in all worths surmount.
But when my glass shows me my self indeed,
Beated and chopp'd with tann'd antiquity,
Mine own self love quite contrary I read
Self, so self loving were iniquity,
    'Tis thee (my self) that for my self I praise,
    Painting my age with beauty of thy days.

5 *gracious* pleasing **8** *As* as though; *other* others **9** *glass* mirror **10** *Beated* battered; *chopp'd* chapped; *antiquity* old age

The physical separation of Sonnet 61 is no longer mentioned. It seems to have been a brief jaunt, used as an occasion

119

to re-introduce the style of earlier sonnets. Exaggerated praise in conventional sonnet fashion, with typical Shakespearean playfulness. Sonnet 62 continues this mood. The convention in this case is the comparison of the loved one's youth to the poet's advanced age, common among poets even under the age of 40.* We also find a recurrence of the theme of the identity of W.'s self with that of Y.M. (as in Sonnets 22 and 36). But the most obvious comparison is to Sonnet 31, the sonnet of *allness*. That sonnet mentioned *all* seven times; Sonnet 62 uses the word five times. Sonnet 31 borrowed religious language to make W.'s love seem more serious. In Sonnet W., the same technique (with the use of *sin, soul, iniquity*) adds mock seriousness that heightens the humor of the joke that's waiting in the couplet. The playful trick of making it appear that W. is referring to his own graciousness in the first two quatrains (truth, worth, and "self" love) makes us wait for the setup in the third quatrain for the revelation in the couplet. At last we learn that, through the identity of his self with Y.M.'s, he was referring to Y.M. all along.

That similarity between Sonnet 62 and Sonnet 31 helps tie them together emotionally. Although they are opposite in tone, they share a depth of feeling. That *allness* is inescapable. W. is all in. I sense that Y.M. is expected to enjoy the compliment offered by Sonnet 62 and get a good chuckle at the same time. Do we think it works? What's going on with their relationship? Are they on the best of terms? Or are things a bit shaky?

63

Against my love shall be as I am now
With time's injurious hand crush'd and o'erworn,
When hours have drain'd his blood and fill'd his brow
With lines and wrinkles, when his youthful morn
Hath travail'd on to Age's steepy night,
And all those beauties whereof now he's King
Are vanishing, or vanish'd out of sight,
Stealing away the treasure of his Spring.

---

* See discussion in Rollins, *New Variorum*, 1:167.

For such a time do I now fortify
Against confounding Age's cruel knife,
That he shall never cut from memory
My sweet love's beauty, though my lover's life.
   His beauty shall in these black lines be seen,
   And they shall live, and he in them still green.

1 *Against* in face of the time when **2** *o'erworn* worn out **5** *travail'd* traveled; *steepy* steep, difficult **9** *fortify* build defenses **10** *confounding* destroying **14** *still green* always young

Sonnet 63 is similar to Sonnet 60. It repeats the theme that W.'s verse will immortalize Y.M.'s beauty. And it's written in the same high style of Ovid. But there are differences. Sonnet 63 has a few personal touches—the mention of Y.M.'s wrinkled forehead of the future and the time when *all those beauties whereof now he's King* have vanished. Yet there's still that sense that the immortality of verse is more important than Y.M.'s beauty. (W. says his beauty will be immortalized because of the verse, not that the verse will immortalize him because of his beauty.) More striking is that Sonnet 63 is not addressed to Y.M. This has been true of only a few previous sonnets. Some were addressed to Time or Love. Others (like Sonnets 23 and 25) were not addressed to anyone in particular but were obviously intended for Y.M. He may be mentioned in the third person, as in Sonnet 33, but he isn't so intimately involved in the subject matter. In Sonnet 33, I would say his is addressed glancingly. Sonnet 63 is different. Its audience appears to be everyone. It sounds like a soliloquy. This may be nothing more than a way of turning a compliment into a grand gesture: "I have said this to you before, but now I declare it to the world!" But along with the Ovidian style, it sounds remote. Especially after lines 10 and 11, the most sensitive in the poem, *My sweet love's beauty* seems like a surprise. So much so that, to me, the couplet sounds lifeless, cold. I get the sense that there's something on W.'s mind. He still loves Y.M., I feel, but the exuberance of the earlier days of their relationship isn't there. He still finds him sweet, lovely, beautiful, but...

64

When I have seen by time's fell hand defaced
The rich proud cost of outworn buried age,
When sometime lofty towers I see down rased,
And brass eternal slave to mortal rage.
When I have seen the hungry Ocean gain
Advantage on the Kingdom of the shore,
And the firm soil win of the wat'ry main,
Increasing store with loss, and loss with store.
When I have seen such interchange of state,
Or state it self confounded, to decay,
Ruin hath taught me thus to ruminate,
That Time will come and take my love away.
    This thought is as a death which cannot choose
    But weep to have, that which it fears to lose.

2 *cost* costly things **3** *sometime* formerly **4** *brass eternal* long-living brass; *mortal rage* deadly ravages of Time **8** *Increasing...store* i.e., one gaining by the other's loss, one losing by the other's gain **10** *confounded* consumed **14** *to have* because it has

Sonnet 64 continues the Ovidian style and the theme of Time the Destroyer. The imagery is powerful, the verbs are active. The first two lines set the tone: Time doesn't just erase the past, it's *fell hand* defaces the *outworn, buried age* that was so *rich, proud* and costly. The *hungry Ocean* eats up the shore, the soil wins against *the wat'ry main*. More results in less, less results in more. In an *interchange of state*, state itself is consumed to ultimate *decay*. All this ruin reminds W. of Y.M.'s death.

But the sonnet abandons the argument of immortalization by verse. Instead, Sonnet 64 becomes much more personal. First person pronouns appear six times in this sonnet. The addressee is again indefinite, but it feels like W. doesn't care about anyone but Y.M. when we read this. In contrast to the previous sonnet, the repeated use of the pronoun *I* throughout the quatrains softens the tone, making the couplet a culmination of the poem's sentiment. For the first time in a while, W. sounds emotional—

like he cares.

In one way, though, the couplet of Sonnet 64 is surprising. After all the previous sonnets about the ravages of Time, this couplet has a new response. At first, the answer was to get a child. Then W. assured Y.M. that no matter what Time did, he (or his beauty) would last forever in his poet's verse. Sonnet 64 is no longer concerned about how Y.M. will deal with the effect of Time. It concerns itself only with how W. will deal with it— Time that will inevitably separate him from the one he loves. Yes, it's still a compliment to Y.M., but it's a very personal one that exposes W.'s deepest feelings. This is new. And the feelings are so strong that W. doesn't just say that he weeps at the thought of losing Y.M., but that he weeps *for the joy of having* that which he fears to lose. He also doesn't say that he fears death, or even the death of his lover, only that *Time will come and take my love away.* It is this *thought* that is *as a death,* which makes him weep. This is the most powerful sonnet we've read in a long time. Has something happened? Or is W. just tired of playing the game? Does he just want to get it all out, once and for all? What does Y.M. think of this display of emotion?

65

Since brass, nor stone, nor earth, nor boundless sea,
But sad mortality o'er-sways their power,
How with this rage shall beauty hold a plea,
Whose action is no stronger than a flower?
O how shall summer's honey breath hold out,
Against the wrackful siege of batt'ring days,
When rocks impregnable are not so stout,
Nor gates of steel so strong but time decays?
O fearful meditation, where alack,
Shall time's best Jewel from time's chest lie hid?
Or what strong hand can hold his swift foot back,
Or who his spoil of beauty can forbid?
    O none, unless this miracle have might,
    That in black ink my love may still shine bright

1 *Since* since there is neither **2** *sad* grave **3** *rage* violence; *hold* maintain **4** *action* case **6** *wrackful* destructive **12** *spoil* plunder **14** *still* always

Sonnet 65 takes a step back, returning to the approach of Sonnet 63, or even close to that of Sonnet 60. The style remains Ovidian, the theme continues to harp on Time the Destroyer and returns to the power of verse to negate it. The personal touches are not as strong as in Sonnet 63, with only the single first person pronoun, *my*, in the last line. But beauty is mentioned twice, and that *fearful meditation* of line 9 makes us consider *W.'s* meditations.

Although the sonnet has no specific addressee, it sounds less like a soliloquy than Sonnet 63. There's something about the struggle between beauty and Time that runs through this sonnet. *Sad mortality, rage, wrackful siege,* and *spoil* are pitted against *beauty, summer's honey breath,* and *time's best jewel.* That last, especially, personalizes the sonnet, making it clear that the meditation is *fearful* because of concern about where Y.M.'s beauty can be kept hid from Time's all-encompassing chest (it is full of fear, anxious, not fearsome).* The couplet states this explicitly. (The word *un-less* is obviously rhetorical. We are not to question whether Y.M. will shine bright in W.'s verse. We have been told it will and we accept the *miracle* as a given.) The intended audience for the sonnet's little tug-of-war drama seems to be Y.M.

66

Tir'd with all these for restful death I cry,
As to behold desert a beggar born,
And needy Nothing trimm'd in jollity,
And purest faith unhappily forsworn,
And gilded honor shamefully misplac'd,
And maiden virtue rudely strumpeted,
And right perfection wrongfully disgrac'd,
And strength by limping sway disablèd,
And art made tongue-tied by authority,
And Folly (Doctor-like) controlling skill,
And simple Truth miscall'd Simplicity,
And captive good attending Captain ill.
    Tir'd with all these, from these would I be gone,
    Save that to die, I leave my love alone.

2 *As* such as, for instance; *desert* worth, merit; *a beggar born* having to beg for what it deserves **3** *needy…jollity* i.e., the indigent nobody festively attired **4** *unhappily forsworn* maliciously renounced **8** *limping sway* incompetent leadership **9** *art* learning, science **10** *Doctor-like* with the air of one who knows **11** *Simplicity* folly **12** *captive…ill* the good, subdued and subservient to the bad

Well this is different. We've not seen anything like this before.† W. starts out with a death wish, goes on to list the ills of the world, repeats his wish, withdrawing it only in the last line for fear of leaving Y.M. alone. What are we to make of this? The first thing we note is the shift from the theme of the

---

* So Tucker, *Sonnets*, 141.

† The form is that of the Provençal *enueg*, which is composed of a list, an initial repetition and some sign of annoyance.

immortalization by verse to something much more caring. "The world's troubles weigh on me so much I would gladly die and be rid of them—except that I love you and don't want *you* to be alone in this world without me." This does fit the conventional framework of the sonneteer complimenting the beloved, but this is a somber compliment. We might imagine, instead of saying he doesn't want to leave his love alone, he might say he simply doesn't want to leave his love. True, the former is more selfless, but the latter seems more emotional. Compare, for example, how we feel reading this sonnet, with our emotions reading Sonnet 29. In that sonnet, after listing all his personal woes, W. remembers Y.M.'s *sweet love* and then he scorns to change his state *with Kings*. In Sonnet 29, our spirits soar with W.'s. In Sonnet 66, we may feel comforted, but can we leave that last line without a sense of sadness? I can't.

Sonnet 66 is a total break from the previous sonnets. It makes us stop cold in the middle of a series that was going along with no sign of problems. We've had no indication of a reason for this unprecedented change in form. This has happened before in *The Sonnets*. And when it has, it has signaled a new episode, a dramatic change in events. Let's see what's around the corner.

67

Ah wherefore with infection should he live,
And with his presence grace impiety,
That sin by him advantage should achieve,
And lace itself with his society?
Why should false painting imitate his cheek,
And steal dead seeing of his living hue?
Why should poor beauty indirectly seek
Roses of shadow, since his Rose is true?
Why should he live, now nature bankrupt is,
Beggar'd of blood to blush through lively veins,
For she hath no exchequer now but his,
And prov'd of many, lives upon his gains?
   O him she stores, to show what wealth she had,

In days long since, before these last so bad.

(Double sonnet to be read with Sonnet 68.)

1 *wherefore* for what reason; *with infection* in an age of corruption **4** *lace* embellish **5** *false painting* cosmetics **6** *steal dead seeing...living hue* steal a lifeless appearance (of beauty) from his living complexion **7** *poor* inferior; *indirectly* by imitation **8** *Roses of shadow* falsely rosy complexions (made up with rouge); *his Rose* his complexion **10** *Beggar'd...veins* i.e., lacking the blood to blush naturally **11** *exchequer* treasure of beauty **12** *prov'd of many* tested and tried (successfully) many times before **13** *stores* preserves

68

Thus is his cheek the map of days outworn,
When beauty liv'd and died as flowers do now,
Before these bastard signs of fair were born,
Or durst inhabit on a living brow;
Before the golden tresses of the dead,
The right of sepulchers, were shorn away,
To live a second life on second head,
Ere beauty's dead fleece made another gay.
In him those holy antique hours are seen,
Without all ornament, it self and true,
Making no summer of another's green,
Robbing no old to dress his beauty new,
　　And him as for a map doth Nature store,
　　To show false Art what beauty was of yore.

1 *days outworn* times past **3** *bastard signs* i.e., cosmetics; *fair* beauty **5** *tresses of the dead* i.e., wigs (made from the hair of dead persons) **6** *The right of* belonging properly to **9** *antique hours* ancient times **10** *all* any **11** *green* greenery **13** *as for* to act as; *store* preserve

As with previous sonnet pairs, the first word of Sonnet 68 makes it clear that these two sonnets make up one poem. The pair sticks to sonnet convention, using the Elizabethan disdain for cosmetics, wigs, and falseness in general, as an excuse for complimenting Y.M. "Why," the sonnet asks, "should Y.M.

have to live in the company of such false beauty and corruption?" His beauty is natural, others' must be embellished. The answer is that Y.M. represents the vestige of Nature's former glory days, when all beauty was like his, genuine, unadorned, true. Nature requires that he show those pretenders what true beauty was really like (again relying on Ovid's philosophy of the world, as in Sonnet 59). Not only does Y.M.'s beauty surpass all others' now, but it represents the paragon of beauty as in Nature's golden days.

This extravagant praise, extending through two sonnets, comes right after a sonnet listing the ills of the world and a wish to leave it, ending not with praise of Y.M. that might cancel all those ills, but only the sad thought that W. wouldn't want to leave him alone. In that context, I find the pile of negatives running through these sonnets disturbing. They are describing *others*, but the antithesis of Y.M.'s goodness seems weak in comparison. The words I remember after reading these sonnets are *infection, impiety, sin, false, dead, poor, bankrupt, beggar'd, bad, outworn, bastard, sepulchers, robbing*. What positives do we have to match these? *His rose is true, his gains, beauty* (which lived and died as flowers do, whose dead fleece made another gay, robbing no old to dress itself, and showing false Art what it was of Yore), *holy antique hours, true*. There is scarcely a positive without mention of a negative and many more negatives in these poems. These are not happy sounding poems any more than Sonnet 66 was. They give me a chill. I have a sense of foreboding.

69

Those parts of thee that the world's eye doth view
Want nothing that the thought of hearts can mend;
All tongues (the voice of souls) give thee that due,
Utt'ring bare truth, even so as foes Commend.
Thy outward thus with outward praise is crown'd,
But those same tongues that give thee so thine own,
In other accents do this praise confound
By seeing farther than the eye hath shown.
They look into the beauty of thy mind,

And that, in guess, they measure by thy deeds,
Then, churls, their thoughts, (although their eyes were kind)
To thy fair flower add the rank smell of weeds.
    But why thy odor matcheth not thy show,
    The soil is this, that thou dost common grow.

2 *Want* lack; *thought of hearts* heart's desire **4** *as foes Commend* i.e., sparingly **6** *thine own* your due **7** *confound* ruin **10** *in guess, they measure* they estimate **14** *soil* ground, origin

Those simmering negatives of Sonnets 67 and 68 have burst out in Sonnet 69. No mincing words in this sonnet! Yes, our Y.M. is still the paragon of beauty, everyone admits that. But now W. doesn't just complain of personal injury that he can go on to excuse. He does more than harbor suspicions and fears and worry about getting less attention than he could wish for. For the first time, W. says that others have looked beyond Y.M.'s beauty into his deeds and decided that, well, he stinks. And rather than come to his defense, he *agrees* that Y.M. has grown *common*. That's not something we can imagine him saying earlier in their relationship. Something dreadful must have caused him to say this without fear of rebuke. It could only be taken as an insult—unless Y.M. were unable to refute the claim. Even so, there's no going back from here. The relationship has changed forever.

This sonnet is filled with allusions, using parts of human anatomy to represent aspects of people in general. What praise is offered is given sparely, only to have more taken away. We start with the *world's eye*, what everyone sees, lacking nothing in Y.M. that could be desired. *All tongues*, their voices, give him the due he deserves for his beauty, seemingly heightened by their elevation to *the voice of souls*. But that praise is only given as *bare truth* (as if barely able to be uttered), no greater than the praise a foe is forced to give a worthy enemy. And those same people whose tongues could barely praise Y.M.'s beauty see beyond what the eye can see. We hear of the *beauty* of his mind, but find that instead of beautiful flowers, their thoughts are more churlish than their kind eyes. They look at his deeds and find only rank weeds. W. says the cause, and what makes it grow (the *soil*), is that he has become common. Where can we possibly go from here?

70

That thou are blam'd shall not be thy defect,
For slander's mark was ever yet the fair,
The ornament of beauty is suspect,
A Crow that flies in heaven's sweetest air.
So thou be good, slander doth but approve,
Thy worth's the greater being woo'd of time,
For Canker vice the sweetest buds doth love,
And thou present'st a pure unstainèd prime.
Thou hast pass'd by the ambush of young days,
Either not assail'd, or victor being charg'd,
Yet this thy praise cannot be so thy praise,
To tie up envy, evermore enlarg'd.
    If some suspect of ill mask'd not thy show,
    Then thou alone kingdoms of hearts shouldst owe.

1 *defect* fault **3** *ornament* artificial adornment (like a "beauty mark"); *suspect* suspicion **5** *So* provided that; *slander…approve* slander only commends you **6** *Thy…time* you are all the more worthy since you are wooed by your contemporaries (and thus prone to slander) **7** *Canker* cankerous, malignant **10** *Either…charg'd* i.e., either not tempted, or if tempted emerging victorious **12** *tie up envy, evermore enlarg'd* i.e., silence malice, which is always at liberty **13** *mask'd not thy show* did not obscure your appearance **14** *owe* own

Sonnet 70 offers what we might have expected in Sonnet 69 but saw no hint of. After condemning Y.M. along with his accusers, W. now reverses course and offers excuses for him. It starts by falling back on proverb, the theme of slandered beauty born of envy. The metaphor of line 4 is interesting, comparing a beauty mark to a crow flying in *heaven's sweetest air*. The blackness and unsightliness of a crow breaking up a beautiful sky is presented as an image of something to be aimed at by those who are envious of beauty. There's an odd mixed message there. The second quatrain also makes us pause. Aside from the difficult language[*]—the meaning of *approve* is not clear in the context, and *being woo'd of time* is a real puzzler—it starts with a phrase that begs the question: *So thou be good.* Is Y.M. good? That doesn't seem to be taken for granted in this line (the first word could just have easily been *since*, but that's not what it says). It's not until the last line of the quatrain that Y.M. is vindicated. Does that make it sound half-hearted? "As long as you are *good*, slander is a compliment to your worth, it shows your value. And you *are pure and unstained*. Right?" The third quatrain elaborates. "We all risk being ambushed by youth. You managed to get through either without temptation or, having been tempted, coming out the *victor*. Right again?" But this is not enough praise to keep others from envying Y.M. Even he must always expect *some suspect of ill* (do those words sound like some everlasting curse?) If this were not the case, he would own *kingdoms of hearts*. In this couplet, I can't help feeling W. is damning Y.M. with faint praise. Line 13 sounds like damnation itself and line 14 like praise that he denies Y.M. Praise that we would have expected to be given earlier in the relationship. Why shouldn't Y.M. own kingdoms of hearts? We would have thought this no less extravagant a compliment than many others W. had showered on him.

Why is this sonnet here, why now? I imagine Y.M. deserving the brunt of Sonnet 69, but the effect on him of having his most ardent admirer fail to excuse him was a bit more than he could bear for long. Sonnet 70 is an attempt to soothe Y.M. without quite absolving him. Double meanings simmer through Sonnet 70 as much as the negatives simmered through Sonnet 68. And the sense I get is of a sensitive young man who hears what he likes to hear and a writer with enough wit to know exactly what he can get away with.

---

[*] Lines 5 and 6 have caused trouble for many editors. There is no consensus about how to read them. I decided to adopt an emendation I considered in my previous book, *worth's* for *worth* in line 6. See Atkins, *Sonnets*, 170.

71

No Longer mourn for me when I am dead,
Than you shall hear the surly sullen bell
Give warning to the world that I am fled
From this vile world with vildest worms to dwell.
Nay if you read this line, remember not
The hand that writ it, for I love you so,
That I in your sweet thoughts would be forgot,
If thinking on me then should make you woe.
O if (I say) you look upon this verse,
When I (perhaps) compounded am with clay,
Do not so much as my poor name rehearse,
But let your love even with my life decay,
    Lest the wise world should look into your moan,
    And mock you with me after I am gone.

4 *vildest* vilest 8 *make* cause 13 *wise* sane, not foolish; *moan* grief

The mood has changed. We're back in the world of love and compliments, but I read only sadness in Sonnet 71. There are *surly, sullen bells*, vile *worms*, forgotten thoughts, *woe, decay,* moans and even W. has only a *poor name*, all that is left once he is compounded with *clay* (how chilling, that phrase!). We could attribute all of this to the conventional sonneteer abasing himself for sake of his beloved, but we have to account for the surprising couplet. After the exhortations to Y.M. not to mourn W., we might expect any of a number of explanations at the end. The courtly lover might say: "I am too lowly for you to think of me after I am dead." The romantic lover's complaint might be: "I only want you to be happy, so don't be sad after my death." Or the religious lover might declare: "My spirit will always be with you, there is no need to mourn me after I die." Instead we hear: "Forget me when I am dead—someone might make fun of you because of me." Is this just an expression of the courtly lover's baseness or the romantic lover's self-abnegation? Or is it a complaint? I can imagine Y.M. making an offhand remark about being teased about his love for W. to which this sonnet is a response. Is Sonnet 71 a poke at Y.M.'s conscience?

72

> O lest the world should task you to recite,
> What merit liv'd in me that you should love,
> After my death (dear love) forget me quite,
> For you in me can nothing worthy prove.
> Unless you would devise some virtuous lie,
> To do more for me than mine own desert,
> And hang more praise upon deceasèd I,
> Then niggard truth would willingly impart.
> O lest your true love may seem false in this,
> That you for love speak well of me untrue,
> My name be buried where my body is,
> And live no more to shame nor me, nor you.
>> For I am sham'd by that which I bring forth,
>> And so should you, to love things nothing worth.

1 *task you* command you **6** *mine own desert* what I deserve **8** *niggard* miserly **10** *untrue* untruly **12** *nor me, nor you* neither me, nor you

At first glance, Sonnet 72 appears just to repeat the theme of Sonnet 71, asking Y.M. to forget W. after he is dead. But the couplet adds something different. Here, W. gives a reason why Y.M. might be mocked for loving him. W. claims he is worth nothing because he is *sham'd by that which I bring forth*. He says he's a bad poet! This could explain his excusing Y.M.'s exploits, so slandered by others. It sounds like someone has accused W. of being a lousy poet and Y.M. has repeated the accusations. Sonnets 71 and 72 would then be W.'s response. "You are told my talents as a poet are unworthy of you. Very well. Forget me when I am dead, I wouldn't want anyone to make fun of you for caring about me. Don't even speak well of me. That would be stretching the truth. I am ashamed of my meager poems and you should be ashamed of loving me."

Another difference in Sonnet 72 is the repeated suggestion that Y.M. *might* do well by W. He *might* devise some virtuous lie and hang more praise on W. than he deserves. He *might* (for love)

speak well of him. And I can't help but sense a bit of irritation in that *dear love* in line 3. Love is mentioned five times, but the sonnet tells Y.M. he should be ashamed to love someone as worthless as W.

There's not much to puzzle over in the language of Sonnet 72. The word juggling in line 4 (*For you in me can nothing worthy prove* instead of "For you can prove nothing worthy in me") is typical for Shakespeare. So, too, is the silent borrowing of the verb from line 13 to fill out line 14: "And so should you [be shamed], to love things nothing worth." Note that only the verb is borrowed, not the entire clause (Y.M. should be shamed, but not because of what *he* brings forth, only because of whom he loves). The metaphors are rich, though. Truth is a *niggard*, unwilling to the point of stinginess to spare a good word that's not deserved. Yet lies can be *virtuous* and *true love* may *seem false*. Y.M. would have to *hang* his praises on the *deceased* W. (I presume the image is intended to be of hanging memorial wreaths. But why do I see the deceased W. hanging from a gallows?) And in contrast to the preceding sonnet, W.'s name is not just forgotten, it's *buried*, dead along with his body.

We must decide the tone in which these sonnets are written. Are they humble, abject? Or are they ironic, provocative? How does Y.M. read them? We can't tell without hearing more of what's to come.

73

That time of year thou mayst in me behold,
When yellow leaves, or none, or few do hang
Upon those boughs which shake against the cold,
Bare ruin'd choirs, where late the sweet birds sang.
In me thou seest the twilight of such day,
As after Sunset fadeth in the West,
Which by and by black night doth take away,
Death's second self that seals up all in rest.
In me thou seest the glowing of such fire,
That on the ashes of his youth doth lie,
As the death bed, whereon it must expire,

Consum'd with that which it was nourish'd by.
This thou perceiv'st, which makes thy love more strong,
To love that well, which thou must leave ere long.

(Double sonnet to be read with Sonnet 74.)

4 *choirs* i.e., the parts of churches where choristers are placed; *late* lately **10** *his* its

74

But be contented when that fell arrest
Without all bail shall carry me away,
My life hath in this line some interest,
Which for memorial still with thee shall stay.
When thou reviewest this, thou dost review
The very part was consecrate to thee,
The earth can have but earth, which is his due,
My spirit is thine the better part of me.
So then thou hast but lost the dregs of life,
The prey of worms, my body being dead,
The coward conquest of a wretch's knife,
Too base of thee to be rememberèd.
　　The worth of that, is that which it contains,
　　And that is this, and this with thee remains.

1 *fell* cruel, deadly **2** *all* any **3** *line* verse; *interest* share, participation **4** *still* always **7** *his* its **13** *of that* of my body; *that which it contains* i.e., my spirit **14** *this* this poem

This pair of sonnets continues the theme of W.'s impending death, Y.M.'s reaction to it and to W.'s verse. But the argument is very different. There is no mocking or shame in these sonnets. Sonnet 73 is the opposite of Sonnet 72, praising the strength of Y.M.'s love, knowing W. is to die, rather than asking him to bury both him and his name. Sonnet 74's protestation of baseness may seem to resemble that of Sonnet 72, but it's specifically limited to W.'s body, unworthy in contrast to his spirit. The couplet of Sonnet 74 refutes Sonnets 71 and 72, asking Y.M. to retain W.'s poetry, the essence of his spirit, implicitly as a remembrance of him, rather than forgetting him entirely.

Something much more important is different in these two sonnets. They *sound* nothing like the two sonnets that preceded them. Comparing these four, the most generous assessment of the earlier two is that they were sad, quiet, humble. But if we read them with undertones, they were curt, angry, aggressive. This sonnet pair is like an elegy. These two sonnets make beautiful imagery out of the subject of death. The first twelve lines of Sonnet 73 contain image after image describing W.'s oncoming death in the gentlest way. Sonnet 74 then brings it to the spiritual plane, leaving earthly matters behind, the mere *prey of worms,* the *coward conquest of a wretch's knife.* It doesn't matter that Death is inevitable and need not involve any cowardice or wretchedness. That phrase perfectly evokes the worthlessness of the body compared to the spirit. This is a stark contrast to the earlier sonnets that compared the worthlessness of W. himself to...well, it's really not clear. Was he comparing himself to other poets? To other people? To Y.M.? It doesn't matter, now. In Sonnet 74, W. has *worth*, and it's contained in his poetry, his spirit.

Why this change? Has Y.M. said something? Did he catch the hurtful tone in the preceding two sonnets? Has he apologized? Or did they go over his head? Has W. forgiven some offhand remark and, being asked about the earlier sonnets did he say, "No, of course, I was only kidding, this is how I truly feel." Then he let out all the stops, showing Y.M. what a real poet could do.

75

So are you to my thoughts as food to life,
Or as sweet season'd showers are to the ground;
And for the peace of you I hold such strife,
As 'twixt a miser and his wealth is found.
Now proud as an enjoyer, and anon
Doubting the filching age will steal his treasure,
Now counting best to be with you alone,
Then better'd that the world may see my pleasure,
Sometime all full with feasting on your sight,

And by and by clean starvèd for a look,
Possessing or pursuing no delight
Save what is had, or must from you be took.
   Thus do I pine and surfeit day by day,
   Or gluttoning on all, or all away.

2 *sweet season'd* smelling of flowers, perfumed **3** *peace of you* peace obtained from you; *hold* endure **5** *anon* the moment after **6** *Doubting* fearing **8** *better'd* made happier **14** *Or…away* either taking all my pleasure in your presence, or in your absence having none

Sonnet 75 returns without reservation to praise of Y.M., bringing back from Sonnet 52 the image of the miser and his treasure. There is also a reprise of the comic tone of Sonnet 45, with its alternation of moods, as thought and desire swiftly changed places. In the first two quatrains, W. alternately enjoys the treasure of Y.M.'s company, wishing to show him off to the world, and fears so much to lose him that he wants to be alone with him all himself. How very much like a miser! The argument shifts in the third quatrain, when the metaphor turns to gluttony. Here W. complains that at one moment he is *full* from feasting on the sight of Y.M. and at the next, starving *for a look*. As the couplet explains, there is no middle ground for the poor glutton, he feasts until he is stuffed and then is hungry again, destined to *pine and surfeit day by day.*

I find the progression of these last seven sonnets interesting. We have gone from a sonnet that looked into the beauty of Y.M.'s mind, finding that he had grown common, to a sonnet that finds no delight except what is had from him. We went from dead poets and poetry to cowardly death and everlasting poetic spirit. And here we have praise, set to the tune of miserly, gluttonous love, evoking an earlier, simpler time in the relationship. The progression has been gradual enough that it has seemed natural. Is this a sonnet of healing, of reconciliation? Or perhaps of hopefulness?

76

Why is my verse so barren of new pride?
So far from variation or quick change?
Why with the time do I not glance aside
To new found methods, and to compounds strange?
Why write I still all one, ever the same,
And keep invention in a noted weed,
That every word doth almost tell my name,
Showing their birth, and where they did proceed?
O know sweet love I always write of you,
And you and love are still my argument;
So all my best is dressing old words new,
Spending again what is already spent,
    For as the Sun is daily new and old,
    So is my love still telling what is told.

2 *quick change* stylishness 3 *the time* fashion 4 *compounds strange* new compositions 5 *still* always; *all one* one way 6 *invention* poetic creation; *noted weed* distinctive garment 8 *where* whence 10 *still* always; *argument* theme 14 *still* always

Here's a new twist. After all the ups and downs of the relationship, W. pens another beautiful sonnet praising Y.M. In the first eight lines, W. is rhetorically repeating questions asked by Y.M.; they are answered in the last six lines.* Perhaps Y.M. thought he would show off his admiring poet to someone. Instead of appreciation, the response he received was disappointing. "Oh, that's just like all the others. They're all the same, aren't they? Can't your poet write anything different." Y.M. repeats the complaint to W. Sonnet 76 is W.'s reply.

The words of the first two quatrains don't seem to come easily. W.'s verse is accused of being *barren*. But of what? Of *new pride, variation, quick change*. He fails to *glance aside*. To what? *New found methods, compounds strange*. Instead, his verse stays in a *noted weed*, every word so familiar, they show where they come from,

---

* This technique was first pointed out by Roessner, "Double Exposure," 378, n. 10.

they *tell his name.* The metaphors shift around the shifty words—nothing sounds particularly pleasant in these eight lines. Why should anyone want a proud poet, or one who keeps glancing aside, changing quickly with the fashions, making strange compounds? Y.M. has asked this poet to explain why he is always the same, dressed in the same clothes. Aren't those repeated *whys* a bit annoying?

The last six lines sound much different. The language is pleasant and easy. *You and love, old words new, spending what is spent, the Sun daily old and new, telling what is told.* This is more than just a counterargument. It's more than justification. It sounds more like a lesson. The language of the first two quatrains sounds deliberately unpleasant. As if that's how the complaint felt to W. These lines sound condescending. "Oh, you want to know why my verse always sounds the same? Well—*sweet love*—if you need an explanation, here it is. I hope you find *that* satisfactory. *Sweet love.*"

77

Thy glass will show thee how thy beauties wear,
Thy dial how thy precious minutes waste,
The vacant leaves thy mind's imprint will bear,
And of this book, this learning mayst thou taste.
The wrinkles which thy glass will truly show,
Of mouthèd graves will give thee memory,
Thou by thy dial's shady stealth mayst know
Time's thievish progress to eternity.
Look what thy memory cannot contain,
Commit to these waste blanks, and thou shalt find
Those children nurs'd, deliver'd from thy brain,
To take a new acquaintance of thy mind.
    These offices, so oft as thou wilt look,
    Shall profit thee, and much enrich thy book.

1 *glass* mirror; *wear* exhibit themselves **2** *dial* sun-dial **3** *vacant leaves* blank pages **4** *of* from; *this learning* i.e., the wisdom brought by your own reflections **6** *mouthèd* open; *memory* reminder **8** *thievish* stealthy **9** *Look what* whatever **10** *waste blanks* blank pages **11** *nurs'd* fostered **13** *offices* actions

What have we here? Beauty, time, memory—these are themes that have been discussed before. But this sonnet's subject is unique. It's written about a blank book given as a gift to Y.M. (*this book* of line 4). The purpose of the sonnet is to explain the value of the gift, succinctly stated in the first quatrain. "Your mirror will show you how your beauties look (as if different aspects were worn as articles of clothing to be inspected—think of the expression "you wear that well"), your sundial will keep track of the time as you watch it slip away, and you will be able to write your thoughts down in the pages of this book and go back to read them again to learn from yourself." This is elaborated in the rest of the sonnet with some evocative imagery. Wrinkles showing *mouthed graves*, the dial's *shady stealth* (the stealthiness of the shadow) showing Time's *thievish progress* to eternity, *nurs'd children*, *deliver'd* from the brain to reawaken acquaintance. An excellent case is made for the *profit* of the book, taking into account the compressed Shakespearean diction of the couplet. I understand it to mean: "These offices [of putting your thoughts in the book and re-reading them], shall much enrich thy book and, so oft as thou wilt look [at the book it] shall profit thee."

But Y.M. is not offered eternal fame through verse. Nor is his beauty said to be the paragon of all beauty. And the gift is given to profit Y.M., not as a show of love—a word that is absent from this sonnet.

Why is this sonnet here? We had sonnets of praise, some nasty things said about Y.M., forgiveness, praise, aspersions cast on W.'s poetry and a snarky response. Now this. Is this an apology or just a pause in the action? Is it a new chapter in the relationship?

78

So oft have I invok'd thee for my Muse,
And found such fair assistance in my verse,
As every *Alien* pen hath got my use,
And under thee their poesy disperse.
Thine eyes, that taught the dumb on high to sing,
And heavy ignorance aloft to fly,
Have added feathers to the learnèd's wings,
And given grace a double Majesty.
Yet be most proud of that which I compile,
Whose influence is thine, and born of thee,
In others' works thou dost but mend the style,
And Arts with thy sweet graces gracèd be.
 But thou art all my art, and dost advance
 As high as learning, my rude ignorance.

3 *As* that; *Alien pen* other's pen, i.e., poet; *got my use* followed my practice **4** *under thee* i.e., with you as their Muse **5** *on high* aloud **6** *heavy* low **7** *added feathers* i.e., repaired **10** *influence* inspiration **11** *but mend* merely improve **14** *rude* crude

Sonnet 78 gives a clue to the reason for the complaint of

Sonnet 76: W. has competition. He's not the only one who is writing poetry about Y.M. He gets more specific in his attack. "I have written so often with you as my muse, anyone could see how easy it is to make beautiful verses by copying my example." This is more distinct than the complaints we heard in Sonnets 21 and 23 that W.'s praises may not have been extravagant enough. His defense is also more specific. "You may add to the art of other poets, but the art of my poetry is entirely due to you." I don't hear the reproachful undertones in this sonnet that I heard in Sonnet 76.

The language of Sonnet 78 poses a few problems for modern readers. There is the change from line 3, where *Alien pen* is treated as a singular noun (*hath got*), to line 4, where it is treated as plural (*their poesy*). This is standard Elizabethan fare. There's also the typical word reversal *aloft to fly* instead of "to fly aloft." We see this again in line 12, which in plain English would read, "And Arts be [i.e., are] with thy sweet graces, graced." Finally, the metaphor about adding feathers to wings (line 7) is from the sport of hawking. Damaged wings were repaired with added feathers, allowing hawks to fly better.

If we read the argument and counterargument of Sonnet 78, we might be tempted to think it's just about what it says. But if we look at how it goes about saying it, we find it's more complicated. This sonnet is filled with wordplay. There's antithesis (*dumb/on high*—i.e., *silent/aloud*; heavie/aloft—i.e., low/high), repeating words from the same root (*graces/gracèd*), and repetition of a word in different senses (*Arts...art...art*). They're not too obvious, a sign of the gracefulness with which Shakespeare uses them—emphasizing his superior *art*.

The couplet's advancement of W.'s *rude ignorance* to the level of *high learning* through Y.M., who is *all his art* is a statement of humility, but only in conventional terms. It's not meant to be taken seriously, it's just a compliment. It sounds like a return to the simpler language of earlier sonnets. But why has W. returned to this language, after all that's happened? Is he just taking a different tack, being less aggressive? Does he feel threatened and has decided he better play nice? Has Y.M. shown favor to another poet? Is this a reminder of the difference between flattery and love?

79

Whilst I alone did call upon thy aid,
My verse alone had all thy gentle grace,
But now my gracious numbers are decay'd,
And my sick Muse doth give another place.
I grant (sweet love) thy lovely argument
Deserves the travail of a worthier pen,
Yet what of thee thy poet doth invent,
He robs thee of, and pays it thee again.
He lends thee virtue, and he stole that word
From thy behavior, beauty doth he give
And found it in thy cheek: he can afford
No praise to thee, but what in thee doth live.
    Then thank him not for that which he doth say,
    Since what he owes thee, thou thy self dost pay.

2 *had all thy gentle grace* received all your favor **3** *numbers* verses **4** *give another place* give way to another **5** *thy lovely argument* the theme of your loveliness **11** *afford* offer **14** *owes* is obliged to give

There's been a subtle progression in the series of sonnets starting with 76. First there was a defense of W.'s poetry. Then a trifle, perhaps an apology—or a warning of more serious things to come. Then mention of competition in Sonnet 78. But here, in line 7, the problem has been focused down to a single Rival Poet.[*] The argument has also changed slightly from Sonnet 78 to Sonnet 79. In the previous sonnet, Y.M.'s virtues were said to add to the art of other poets in contrast to comprising all of W.'s art. Here, W. argues that the Rival Poet is simply lacking in invention. All that he has to offer is only what Y.M. has already

---

[*] Editors differ on which sonnet begins what is called, unsurprisingly, the Rival Poet series. Any suggestion that the Rival Poet reflects a contemporary of Shakespeare is out of keeping with my assumptions about *The Sonnets*. I am uninterested in that guessing game, anyway.

shown him. The unstated implication is that W.'s praises don't merely echo Y.M.'s virtues but reflect his love as well.

The language of Sonnet 79 reads easily. But I find something uneasy about the sonnet itself. It's that third quatrain. Those first three lines don't end with pauses, with the sense running on to the middle of the following lines, each with strong punctuation. Line 9 starts with a half-line and the quatrain continues with three full lines and a final half-line. It's balanced, but it seems deliberately designed to throw off the rhymes of the sonnet form. And this is the quatrain that details how the Rival Poet stole everything he invented from Y.M. Has W. stolen back the rhymes? Or is he demonstrating the effect the Rival Poet is having on *him*—as he noted in line 4—that his Muse is now *sick*? And I can't help hearing something odd whenever W. uses the term *sweet love*. Especially in line 5, so close to the word *lovely*: *I grant (sweet love) thy lovely argument*. The repetition seems too obvious. Is this irony? Condescension? Reproach? Or is it just love, despite everything?

80

O how I faint when I of you do write,
Knowing a better spirit doth use your name,
And in the praise thereof spends all his might,
To make me tongue-tied speaking of your fame.
But since your worth (wide as the Ocean is)
The humble as the proudest sail doth bear,
My saucy bark (inferior far to his)
On your broad main doth willfully appear.
Your shallowest help will hold me up afloat,
Whilst he upon your soundless deep doth ride,
Or (being wrack'd) I am a worthless boat,
He of tall building, and of goodly pride.
    Then If he thrive and I be cast away,
    The worst was this, my love was my decay.

1 *faint* lose heart **2** *spirit* mind **6** *as* as much as **7** *saucy bark* cheeky little boat **8** *main* ocean; *willfully* recklessly **10** *soundless* unfathomable **11** *wrack'd* shipwrecked **12** *tall building* strong construction; *goodly pride* fine splendor **14** *decay* downfall

Sonnet 80 combines the arguments of Sonnets 78 and 79. The Rival Poet may be a *better spirit* but W.'s love is explicitly pointed to as the important difference between them. This is heightened by the use of contrast throughout the sonnet, which is emphasized by the multiple parentheses. There's also a breathlessness to this sonnet that keeps it moving from beginning to end, with those parenthetical phrases suspending the flow just momentarily, until the point of the argument is revealed at the end.

Sonnet 80 shares with Sonnet 78 the irony of a poem claiming that its author is inferior to the Rival Poet all the while showing off figures of speech that Elizabethans considered the sign of a good poet. Aside from antithesis and parenthesis, there is also alliteration, change in word order, metaphor, and ambiguity. The last two are the most complicated.

Let's deal with the metaphor of the third quatrain first. What is W. saying in these four lines? I think it's best understood by treating lines 9 and 10 independently from 11 and 12 (interpreting *or* to mean "but"). The first two lines then say that W.'s love is so great that he needs very little help from Y.M. to write beautiful poetry, as a small boat needs only shallow water to stay afloat. On the other hand, the Rival Poet needs to "sound the depths" of Y.M.'s virtues to write his verses to him (despite all his talents) since he must rely entirely on him, rather than on his own love, just as a great boat requires a large draft on which to sail. The next two lines make a different point (which we will not fully understand until the final couplet). They say that if the verses aren't good, the poets are like shipwrecked boats, in which case W. has only a worthless boat while the Rival Poet has a good, solidly constructed one. The first line of the couplet is expected: if they are shipwrecked, we expect the Rival Poet to survive and W. to be cast away. Line 14 is the surprise ending: if this were so, the worst one could say was *my love was my decay*.

This last line is the one that's ambiguous. On first reading,

we might understand it to mean, "It was my love for you, which made me willing to take my saucy bark out on the wide ocean, and thus caused me to founder; therefore, the worst I could say is that my downfall was a measure of my (inadequate) love."*
This reading would be in line with the second quatrain and the conventional humility of the sonneteer. But something about that doesn't sound right. Never before has W. questioned the strength of his love for Y.M. It also implicitly gives the Rival Poet more credit than W. has given him so far. The alternative reading would be, "Then if the Rival Poet is successful and I am not, the worst one could say is that *your love for me* was not adequate to aid me." This would be in keeping with line 9: *Your shallowest help will hold me up afloat*. If this is true, and W. is *wrack'd*, it must be because he did *not* receive Y.M.'s *shallowest help*. Have we returned to a note of annoyance at Y.M. for his attention to the Rival Poet at the expense of W.?

81

Or I shall live your Epitaph to make,
Or you survive when I in earth am rotten,
From hence your memory death cannot take,
Although in me each part will be forgotten.
Your name from hence immortal life shall have,
Though I (once gone) to all the world must die,
The earth can yield me but a common grave,
When you entombèd in men's eyes shall lie.
Your monument shall be my gentle verse,
Which eyes not yet created shall o'er-read,
And tongues to be, your being shall rehearse,
When all the breathers of this world are dead.
    You still shall live (such virtue hath my Pen)
    Where breath most breathes, even in the mouths of men.

1-2 *Or...Or* whether...or **4** *in me each part* every characteristic of me **10** *o'er-read* read through **11** *rehearse* recite **12** *this world*, i.e.,

---

* The capital "I" in "If" is in the original. I have kept it to indicate that this word should receive a stress.

today **13** *still* always; *virtue* power **14** *breath* i.e., breath of rumor or fame; *breathes* speaks; *even in the mouths* in the very mouths

There's no mention of the Rival Poet in Sonnet 81 but I feel his presence from the surrounding ones. The theme is familiar and has been hinted at with every mention of the Rival Poet. W.'s poetry has a power that the Rival Poet's lacks: W.'s verse will immortalize Y.M. He makes a good show of it, too, with a virtuoso performance of rhetorical display. He uses the same word or root with different meanings (*from hence* meaning "from the earth" in line 3 and "henceforth" in line 5; *breathers* in line 12 meaning "people" and in line 14 *breath* meaning "rumor" or "fame" and *breathes* meaning "speaks"). There is a play with anatomy, beginning with *in me each part* and proceeding with *eyes, tongues, breath,* and *mouths,* which are all examples of metonymy (using part of something to represent the whole thing). Even more clever is the switching of meanings of metaphors, as in line 6, where *once gone* means "die" and *die* means "gone from memory." Most fascinating is an odd phenomenon noted by William Empson: starting with line 3, any two consecutive lines (except lines 10-11) can make a complete sentence.[*]

I consider this the sixth sonnet in the Rival Poet series. In four, W. has tried arguing about why he should be preferred and in one he presented a gift. Now he is showing his value by comparison. This keeps with W.'s previous methods—he tries one approach for a while and then switches to another. But there's one oddity about this sonnet that I can't get past. Unlike previous sonnets promising to immortalize Y.M., Sonnet 81 promises specifically to immortalize his *name*. This is not only ironic—we haven't been told his name, at least not yet, even if it's fictional, whereas Shakespeare, the real name of the poet, *is* immortal—it's unusual. Most sonnet sequences are either written to a named person (Petrarch had Laura, Samuel Daniel had Delia, Henry Constable had Diana), were written about pairs of lovers (famously Sir Philip Sidney's *Astrophil and Stella*) or mention no

---

[*] Empson, 7 Types of Ambiguity, 53.

names at all. Sonneteers, however, usually promise to immortalize their loved ones, not their *names*. Why does W. do this? Is it just another form of metonymy? Does the name stand for the person? Or is it a request for attention? "Are you paying attention to what I'm saying? I can make your *name* immortal. But in 81 sonnets I've never mentioned your name. Do you want me to? Shall I continue to write sonnets about you? What has the Rival Poet done for you?" Is Sonnet 81 a challenge?

82

I grant thou wert not married to my Muse,
And therefore mayst without attaint o'erlook
The dedicated words which writers use
Of their fair subject, blessing every book.
Thou art as fair in knowledge as in hue,
Finding thy worth a limit past my praise,
And therefore art enforc'd to seek anew
Some fresher stamp of the time bettering days.
And do so love, yet when they have devis'd
What strainèd touches Rhetoric can lend,
Thou truly fair, wert truly sympathiz'd,
In true plain words, by thy true telling friend.
    And their gross painting might be better us'd
    Where cheeks need blood, in thee it is abus'd.

1 *married to my Muse* required to pay attention only to my poetry **2** *attaint* touch of dishonor; *o'er-look* peruse **5** *as fair* as much as you should be; *hue* appearance **6** *a limit past* beyond **8** *stamp* imprint; *time bettering days* days that improve with time **10** *strainèd touches* touches of exaggeration **11** *sympathiz'd* represented **14** *abus'd* i.e., an abuse

Events seem to have taken another turn. If Sonnet 81 was a challenge, it didn't succeed. The Rival Poet (here referred to again in the general as *writers*) appears to have won the favor of Y.M. (lines 6-8). W. stays with his previous argument: "I may not be worthy enough a poet for you, but I speak truly as a friend whereas others only offer exaggerated praises of which you have no need." But the tone of the sonnet is not as ambiguous as the final line of Sonnet 80. There's an increasing irony as the poem proceeds until the final couplet breaks into an obvious complaint.

The first five lines sound innocent enough, *granting* Y.M. that he holds no allegiance to W.'s muse and is free to read the *dedicated words* of others, acknowledging that his knowledge is as *fair* as his beauty. The tone begins to alter with line 6. There's a parallel between the earlier sonnets in which W. protests that his verse is unworthy of the praise Y.M. deserves and the supposed *fairness* of Y.M.'s *knowledge* in Sonnet 82 that his own worth is beyond the limit of W.'s praise. In the former, W. expresses humility, in the latter, Y.M. shows vanity. This doesn't sound very nice. Y.M. is *enforc'd* to seek something fresh in the next line. It sounds more like a forced excuse on the part of W. This makes *And do so love*, in line 9 sound ironic. The *others* are now attacked obliquely. They *devise*, their touches are *strainèd*, they can do nothing but *lend Rhetoric*. W. then makes sure he gets his point across about the value of a poet who is also a friend: the *truly* fair, is *truly* shown, in *true* words, by his *true-telling* friend. The others? *Gross painting*. Overblown praise. You don't need that. It's an *abuse*.

How do we read this sonnet? Do we read it quietly, as if W. is gently demonstrating the obvious? Does the sonnet build an argument in a way that we might expect Y.M. to read it through and find himself agreeing in the end, even feeling complimented by the couplet? Or do we read it with some degree of frustration and annoyance on the part of W.? Do we read it more insistently, hectoring, perhaps even sententiously toward the end? Do we imagine Y.M. reading this and feeling guilty? Annoyed? Betrayed? Or does the vain youth take it all in stride, put the sonnet down and move on to whatever he sees next from the Rival Poet?

83

I never saw that you did painting need,
And therefore to your fair no painting set,
I found (or thought I found) you did exceed,
The barren tender of a poet's debt.
And therefore have I slept in your report,
That you your self being extant well might show,
How far a modern quill doth come too short,
Speaking of worth, what worth in you doth grow.
This silence for my sin you did impute,
Which shall be most my glory being dumb,
For I impair not beauty being mute,
When others would give life, and bring a tomb.
    There lives more life in one of your fair eyes,
    Than both your poets can in praise devise.

1 *painting* cosmetics (figuratively) **2** *fair* beauty; *set* applied **4** *barren tender* worthless offer of payment **5** *slept in your report* refrained from writing about you **7** *modern* trite **8** *Speaking* when speaking; *what worth* by showing what worth **12** *would give* try to give; *tomb* i.e., something which hides your beauty, rather than shows it

The story advances with Sonnet 83. After telling Y.M. to go ahead and let himself be flattered by the verses of others, W. seems to have felt no need to write any more verses himself. After all, Y.M. had found himself *a limit past his praise*. Y.M., failing to read any irony in W.'s tone, has taken him to task (*This silence for my sin you did impute*). I imagine W. waiting for just such a response. He is ready with his answer. He elaborates on the couplet of Sonnet 82. "You need no painting to show your worth; you show the limitations of poetry. It's better that I say nothing than to hide your beauty with imperfect verses." This argument fits the situation well, allowing W. to sound humble and complimentary while, at the same time, taking a swipe at the Rival Poet.

As usual, we have to decide how to read the tone of Sonnet 83. Can we take the argument seriously? Why did W. compose

150

any verses to Y.M. if he *never saw that he did painting need* and he exceeded the *barren tender of a poet's debt?* We could interpret *painting* to mean "gross painting" and understand W. to be saying that his verses would *now* offer only *barren tender*. We might then have a conventional sonnet from a humble poet taking the opportunity of a complaint to compliment the beloved. But the argument sounds phony to me. And what do we make of the parenthetical phrase in line 3: *I found (or thought I found) you did exceed, / The barren tender of a poet's debt.?* I *thought* I found? The implication is that W. has discovered, through Y.M.'s complaint, that he was wrong (or, at least, that Y.M. disagreed). And there's something about the way the complaint in line 9 is stated. W.'s silence is *imputed* to be a sin. This sounds like an accusation. I can't read this without sensing that W. feels not only wrongly accused, but offended by the accusation. Finally, we come to the couplet. We might just read it as a humble compliment to Y.M. But if we get the sense that W. feels hurt, unjustly wronged, unappreciated, angry—any or all of these—the couplet sounds more preachy, even scolding.

84

Who is it that says most, which can say more,
Than this rich praise, that you alone, are you,
In whose confine immurèd is the store,
Which should example where your equal grew.
Lean penury within that Pen doth dwell,
That to his subject lends not some small glory,
But he that writes of you, if he can tell
That you are you, so dignifies his story.
Let him but copy what in you is writ,
Not making worse what nature made so clear,
And such a counterpart shall fame his wit,
Making his style admired everywhere.
    You to your beauteous blessings add a curse,
    Being fond on praise, which makes your praises worse.

1 *Who is it that* it is he who; *which* who **3-4** *immured is the store, Which should example* is hoarded up all that could show **5** *Lean penury* severe poverty; *Pen* i.e., of a poet **6** *his* its **8** *so* thereby **10** *clear* pure **11** *counterpart* copy; *fame* make famous **14** *fond on* fond of

What's going on here? Let's recap. Y.M. has turned his attention to a Rival Poet. W. Tries to divert attention back to himself but fails. He gives up and tells Y.M. he's free to do as he pleases. He stops writing sonnets. Y.M. complains. W. defends himself on grounds of being inadequate to the task of praising Y.M. (we suspect with tongue firmly planted in cheek). Sonnet 84 suggests that Y.M. has continued to complain. He's not buying the excuse.

The language of Sonnet 84 is so elaborate that it's a struggle to decipher. Line 1 uses two different relative pronouns to mean "who," both of which, if not read carefully can be misunderstood as questions. There is a repeated use of nouns as verbs (*example* in line 4, *fame* in line 10) and unusual synonyms (*immurèd* for "confined" and *counterpart* for "copy"). And it's hard not to stop to puzzle out the phrases *you alone, are you* and *you are you.**

At first, it looks like W. is just repeating the argument of Sonnet 83 in more elaborate language. We assume he is trying to impress Y.M. in another attempt to win him over. That is, until we get to the couplet's sour note: "You add a curse to your blessings. You like being praised and it makes it all the worse to praise you." What does W. mean? The previous twelve lines have explained that the highest praise one can give Y.M. is not to praise him but to write about him. Line 13 is confusing because of the antithesis between *blessings* and *curse*, raising the image of Y.M. as a curse. But I don't think it's *that* bad. W. is pointing out how Y.M.'s vanity—he leaves no doubt of its presence—is a curse to those who would praise him. Surely, Y.M. must recognize his vanity and understand that it is not a virtue. So to praise him is to encourage his vice. This, then, is a gentle remonstrance. Does W. hope he can sneak this in under the guise of bolstering his argument for silence? Does he think Y.M. is so vain he won't even notice? Or is this a bit nasty?

---

* Some editors have had problems with *fond on* in line 14 but although Shakespeare more often uses *fond of,* he uses *fond on* twice in the plays to mean *fond of* (*A Midsummer Night's Dream* 2.1.266 and *Twelfth Night* 2.2.35).

85

My tongue-tied Muse in manners holds her still,
While comments of your praise richly compil'd,
Reserve their Character with golden quill,
And precious phrase by all the Muses fil'd.
I think good thoughts, whilst others write good words,
And like unlettered clerk still cry Amen,
To every Hymn that able spirit affords
In polish'd form of well refinèd pen.
Hearing you prais'd, I say "'tis so, 'tis true,"
And to the most of praise add something more,
But that is in my thought, whose love to you
(Though words come hind-most) holds his rank before.
    Then others, for the breath of words respect,
    Me for my dumb thoughts, speaking in effect.

1 *in manners* politely; *holds her still* is silent **3** *Reserve* preserve; *Character* writing **4** *fil'd* polished **6** *unlettered clerk* illiterate parish clerk; *still* always **7** *affords* offers **8** *In...pen* i.e., in the form of a well-written poem **10** *most* utmost **12** *his* its **13** *the breath of words* i.e., words which are mere breath

Nothing has changed. W. still finds himself justifying his poetic silence to Y.M. The argument moves from the empty praises of the Rival Poet to pick up on the theme of Sonnet 23: although I may not say it as well as you might wish, my silent thoughts are always filled with *love to you*. It's instructive to compare Sonnet 85 to Sonnet 23. The themes are so similar: "Respect others for the words they speak, me for the thoughts I have, which speak in effect" (Sonnet 85) and "Learn to read the silent love expressed in my looks, which tells more than the words expressed by others" (Sonnet 23). In the earlier sonnet, W.'s silence is greater than the words of others, in Sonnet 85 they are equal. More noticeable is the difference in tone. Sonnet 23 reads like a love sonnet. Sonnet 85 reads like a discussion. The first quatrain especially reads a bit stiffly, with its *richly compil'd* praises that *Reserve their Character with golden quill*, and the *precious phrase* that *all the Muses* filed (a precious word for polished). There is just a touch of humor, though, with the image of the parish clerk crying "Amen, amen!" parodied by W. echoing Y.M.'s praises with *"'tis so, tis true."*

There's no hint of irony in Sonnet 85. No scolding, condescension, annoyance, bitterness. It sounds humble, resigned.

Has W. given up?

86

Was it the proud full sail of his great verse,
Bound for the prize of (all too precious) you,
That did my ripe thoughts in my brain inhearse,
Making their tomb the womb wherein they grew?
Was it his spirit, by spirits taught to write
Above a mortal pitch, that struck me dead?
No, neither he, nor his compeers by night
Giving him aid, my verse astonishèd.
He nor that affable familiar ghost
Which nightly gulls him with intelligence,
As victors of my silence cannot boast,
I was not sick of any fear from thence.
　　But when your countenance fill'd up his line,
　　Then lack'd I matter, that enfeebled mine.

3 *inhearse* enclose as in a coffin **5** *spirit* intellectual energy; *spirits* divine inspirers **6** *mortal pitch* height obtainable by mortals **7** *compeers by night* collaborators, spirit aids **8** *astonishèd* dumbfounded **10** *gulls him with intelligence* crams him with ideas (with the connotation of false information) **13** *countenance* patronage; *fill'd up* filled up what might be lacking in

I imagine Sonnet 86 to be a response to a taunt from Y.M. "You have such clever excuses for the absence of your poetry. I think you fear you can't match your rival." W. not only denies the accusation, he fights back with a new defense. It's not fear that prevents him from writing, it's disappointment. The gloves are off. He's done arguing. The problem is betrayal. Once Y.M. showed such poor judgment as to patronize the Rival Poet, W.

lost all reason to extol his virtues.

There's not just a change in argument in this sonnet. There's another shift in the relationship that's become irreversible. At first W. tried to dissuade Y.M. of his attachment to the Rival Poet. Then he tried the silent treatment. Now there seems no hope of returning to the same relationship that existed before. One trespass might be forgiven, especially one involving an irresistible temptation but a second trespass, and an intellectual one at that, is not so easily forgotten. This is reflected in the tone of Sonnet 86. There's nothing subtle about it. It's more emotional than the other Rival Poet sonnets. The imagery is vivid, the verse intricate, the pressure of the lines relentless. The rhetorical questions of the first five lines sound smug and condescending. I read nothing complimentary in the parenthetical *all too precious you*. I hear no praise. There is only a glimmer of love beneath the disappointment. Y.M. isn't even discerning enough to notice the *affable familiar ghost* who's cramming the Rival Poet with drivel. W. tells him that something has died. Y.M.'s betrayal has inhearsed his thoughts within his brain, *Making their tomb the womb wherein they grew*. The antithesis of *tomb/womb* heightens the sense of betrayal, which is strengthened by the internal rhyme and the repeated mention of death two lines later, when the *spirits taught to write / Above a mortal pitch* strike him *dead*.

Where do these two go from here?

87

Farewell thou art too dear for my possessing,
And like enough thou know'st thy estimate,
The Charter of thy worth gives thee releasing,
My bonds in thee are all determinate.
For how do I hold thee but by thy granting,
And for that riches where is my deserving?
The cause of this fair gift in me is wanting,
And so my patent back again is swerving.
Thy self thou gav'st, thy own worth then not knowing,
Or me to whom thou gav'st it, else mistaking,
So thy great gift upon misprision growing,

Comes home again, on better judgment making.
Thus have I had thee as a dream doth flatter,
In sleep a King, but waking no such matter.

1 *dear* valuable **2** *estimate* value **3** *Charter* privilege; *releasing* freedom from obligation **4** *bonds* claims; *determinate* ended **7** *cause of* justification for **8** *patent* title, license; *is swerving* returns to you **11** *upon misprision growing* arising from an oversight **12** *on better judgment making* on your forming a better judgment **14** *no such matter* nothing of the kind

Now W. bids Y.M. farewell. He does so humbly, once again in the strains of the conventional sonneteer. W. has nothing deserving of Y.M., making Y.M. free to release himself from their bond of friendship. Y.M.'s great worthiness was beyond his scope from the beginning. He either underestimated his own worth or overestimated that of W. In either case, Y.M., having now made better judgement of the situation, reasonably takes back his gift of love. The metaphors in this sonnet are legal ones: *charter, bonds, granting, patent, misprision, judgment.* Despite this, the sonnet sounds sweet, gentle. And for the first time in a while, W. gives in the couplet a beautiful expression of his love for Y.M., with *King* in the last line reminding us exactly what he felt this relationship was worth back in Sonnet 29. And now it's as if it was all a dream.

Is this sonnet just an addendum to Sonnet 86? After realizing Y.M. had abandoned him emotionally in favor of the Rival Poet, did W. decide he needed to express something more than he had, to make a farewell statement showing forgiveness? Or did he shoot off that dart at the end of Sonnet 86 and wait to see what happened? Did Y.M. reply, saying he could patronize whomever he wished? Did he ask W. why he thought he deserved his patronage? Is Sonnet 87 a reply to the still uncomprehending Y.M.? Is it W.'s statement of his continuing love, or is there an undertone of sarcasm? I can read it either way.

88

When thou shalt be dispos'd to set me light,
And place my merit in the eye of scorn,
Upon thy side, against my self I'll fight,
And prove thee virtuous, though thou art forsworn.
With mine own weakness being best acquainted,
Upon thy part I can set down a story
Of faults conceal'd, wherein I am attainted,
That thou in losing me, shall win much glory.
And I by this will be a gainer too,
For bending all my loving thoughts on thee,
The injuries that to my self I do,
Doing thee vantage, double vantage me.
    Such is my love, to thee I so belong,
    That for thy right, my self will bear all wrong.

1 *set me light* value me little **4** *forsworn* guilty of perjury **7** *attainted* dishonored **8** *losing* forgetting **12** *vantage* advantage

Sonnet 88 is written in the future tense, as if about something that hasn't occurred, but definitely will at a later time. We would *expect* it to be written in the conditional (*if thou shouldst... I would*). Or perhaps the *present* and the future (*since thou art...I shall*). In any event, this tense is unexpected. It makes us aware that it's unusual. Is W. just saying he knows Y.M. will eventually say bad things about him? Or is this a reply to something he has already said? "When you scorn me and even say things about me that are untrue, I will only say worse things about myself to make you look good. What's that you say? Have you already been doing that? Never mind, my love for you is still great enough that I will bear it all."

W. stays with the convention of the humble, self-abnegating sonneteer (as in Sonnet 87). Y.M. is all *right,* he is all *wrong* and yet he gains in the bargain. By giving Y.M. an advantage, he gives himself one at the same time. Where have we heard this before? It was in the sonnets about the liaison between Y.M. and the woman W. cared about, that vague trespass that disrupted their relationship (33-36 and 40-42). Sonnet 35: *Thy adverse party is thy advocate.* Sonnet 36: *I love thee in such sort, / As thou being mine, mine is thy good report.* Sonnet 42: *If I lose thee, my loss is my love's gain.* Same ideas, different feeling. In the liaison sonnets there was a sense of bittersweetness and, in the end, hopefulness, accompanying W.'s love. In Sonnet 88, I hear only resignation and sadness as love's companions. Why the difference? The context is important, but the tense is, too. That predicted future eliminates any sense of hope. There is no room for the relationship to end differently in the scheme of Sonnet 88. No matter what has gone before or what is happening now, what will be is not what has been. W. still loves Y.M., but he is resigned. He is sad.

89

Say that thou didst forsake me for some fault,
And I will comment upon that offense,
Speak of my lameness, and I straight will halt,
Against thy reasons making no defense.
Thou canst not (love) disgrace me half so ill,
To set a form upon desirèd change,
As I'll my self disgrace, knowing thy will,
I will acquaintance strangle and look strange,
Be absent from thy walks and in my tongue,
Thy sweet belovèd name no more shall dwell,
Lest I (too much profane) should do it wrong,
And haply of our old acquaintance tell.
    For thee, against my self I'll vow debate,
    For I must ne'er love him whom thou dost hate.

(Double sonnet to be read with Sonnet 90.)

2 *comment* expound **3** *straight* immediately; *halt* limp **4** *reasons* explanations **6** *To...change* to give a becoming appearance to the change which you desire **8** *strangle* suppress; *strange* unacquainted **11** *profane* common, coarse **12** *haply* perhaps **13** *debate* quarrel

90

Then hate me when thou wilt, if ever, now,
Now while the world is bent my deeds to cross,
Join with the spite of fortune, make me bow,
And do not drop in for an after loss.
Ah do not, when my heart hath scap'd this sorrow,
Come in the rearward of a conquer'd woe,
Give not a windy night a rainy morrow,
To linger out a purpos'd over-throw.
If thou wilt leave me, do not leave me last,
When other petty griefs have done their spite,
But in the onset come, so shall I taste
At first the very worst of fortune's might.
    And other strains of woe, which now seem woe,
    Compar'd with loss of thee, will not seem so.

2 *bent* determined **5** *scap'd* escaped **6** *conquer'd* overcome **8** *purpos'd* predestined

This sonnet pair explains some of what's been going on between W. and Y.M. After reading them, Sonnet 88 looks more complicated than it did before. It may appear that Sonnet 89 is just repeating the theme of Sonnet 88, brought forward into the present. But in Sonnet 88, W. argues that harming himself to benefit Y.M. will also benefit him. In Sonnet 89, he goes further and is willing to forsake Y.M. completely. And the couplet of Sonnet 89 brings in a new word: *hate*. It seems innocent here: "I'll debate against myself because I cannot love anyone you hate." It's one of those surprise couplets that uses a common phrase in an unexpected way. "I can't love anyone you hate—so I can't love myself (since you obviously hate me)." It's funny, but painfully so.

The couplet of Sonnet 89 is *serious*, and it leads directly to the new information we learn in Sonnet 90. It explains why these sonnets are in the present tense. Things are happening to W. *now*. The world is *bent to cross* his deeds. He is suffering under the *spite of fortune*. But this *sorrow*, this *woe*, these *petty griefs* are nothing compared to *loss of thee.* This may explain why W. was so sure Y.M. would speak ill of him in Sonnet 87—things were not going his way. Has he been caught doing something he shouldn't? Or something that merely seems wrong? Are people spreading rumors about him? Has something happened to him that would lower his esteem? We can't tell, but *something* has happened. He appeals to Y.M., but instead of asking him to ignore idle rumors or to disregard talk of his ill fortune, he encourages him to hate him, to leave him—as long as he does it now. "Leave me now," he says, "when everything is going against me. May as well get the worst over with, right from the start. Don't drag out my misery and then make me suffer even worse by leaving me later, after I thought the worst was over."

The language of these sonnets is complex, not because of difficult diction but because of the imagery. So many phrases resist concise explanation, but I love the phrase, *do not drop in for an after loss.* It evokes such a sorrowful image. It doesn't matter that it's quite difficult to say what the words literally mean (they have resisted scholarly explanation), we understand the sense of "hitting a man when he's down." That same sense applies to *come in the rearward of a conquer'd woe. Rearward* and *conquer'd* bring up images of battle and even if it's hard to make the terms apply to the sense we understand, somehow it works. So, too, the *rainy night, windy morrow,* and *purpos'd overthrow* (again bringing up the battle imagery). It's hard to put it together logically, but emotionally it makes sense. We *taste…the very worst of fortune's might.* Perhaps there is even an echo of the request from the bible, "That thou doest, do quickly." *

What can we make of this? Have events been evolving from Sonnets 87 to 89 or were the earlier sonnets all posturing, just a lead up to Sonnet 90's conclusion? Has this been a farewell, or an attempt to preempt Y.M.'s arguments and play on his emotions? How do we imagine Y.M. reacting to this? Does he hear W.'s emotion and respond in kind? Does he feel sorry for W.? Or does he miss the irony and take W.'s request seriously?

---

* John 13:27, cited by T. A. Spalding, "Shakespeare's Sonnets," 315.

Perhaps he's no longer even interested.

91

Some glory in their birth, some in their skill,
Some in their wealth, some in their body's force,
Some in their garments though new-fangled ill,
Some in their Hawks and Hounds, some in their Horse.
And every humor hath his adjunct pleasure,
Wherein it finds a joy above the rest,
But these particulars are not my measure,
All these I better in one general best.
Thy love is better than high birth to me,
Richer than wealth, prouder than garments' cost,
Of more delight than Hawks or Horses be,
And having thee, of all men's pride I boast.
    Wretched in this alone, that thou mayst take
    All this away, and me most wretched make.

(Triple sonnet to be read with Sonnets 92 and 93.)

3 *new-fangled ill* fashionably ugly **5** *humor* disposition; *his* its **7** *measure* standard of happiness **8** *better* surpass **12** *all men's pride* i.e., all the things that men take pride in

92

But do thy worst to steal thy self away,
For term of life thou art assurèd mine,
And life no longer than thy love will stay,
For it depends upon that love of thine.
Then need I not to fear the worst of wrongs,
When in the least of them my life hath end,
I see, a better state to me belongs
Than that, which on thy humor doth depend.
Thou canst not vex me with inconstant mind,
Since that my life on thy revolt doth lie,
Oh what a happy title do I find,
Happy to have thy love, happy to die!
    But what's so blessèd fair that fears no blot?
    Thou mayst be false, and yet I know it not.

2 *term of life* my lifetime **8** *humor* mood **10** *Since that* Since; *on thy revolt doth lie* i.e., ends with your rejection of me **11** *happy title* title to happiness

93

So shall I live, supposing thou art true,
Like a deceivèd husband, so love's face
May still seem love to me, though alter'd new,
Thy looks with me, thy heart in other place.
For there can live no hatred in thine eye,
Therefore in that I cannot know thy change,
In many's looks, the false heart's history
Is writ in moods and frowns and wrinkles strange.
But heaven in thy creation did decree,
That in thy face sweet love should ever dwell,
Whate'er thy thoughts, or thy heart's workings be,
Thy looks should nothing thence, but sweetness tell.
    How like Eve's apple doth thy beauty grow,
    If thy sweet virtue answer not thy show.

2 *face* appearance **3** *though alter'd new* although love has newly changed **8** *strange* new, different **13** *grow* become **14** *answer not* does not agree with; *show* appearance

It seems a double sonnet wasn't strong enough to sway Y.M. Something more was needed to bring him back to his senses. Why not a triple sonnet? The emotional force builds with each of these three sonnets. Sonnet 91 starts out sounding like a sweet sonnet from earlier in the relationship. The diction is simple, with just a couple of phrases requiring any pause for thought (*new-fangled ill*, line 3, *and all men's pride*, line 12). This simplicity is heightened by the sonnet's repetitions: *some* occurring seven times, beginning each of the first four lines, and *better* occurring twice. Reading the first twelve lines, we might think Y.M. has capitulated, forsworn the Rival Poet and all other companions and returned wholly to W. The couplet, though still couched in possibilities (*thou **mayst** take*), tells a different story—its wretchedness echoing the *woe* of Sonnet 90.

The emotion is more complex in Sonnet 92 and so is the diction. There's more displacement of normal word order, more use of metaphor: *face* for "appearance"; *strange* for "new"; *the false heart's history* for "the tale of deception." Sonnet 92 brightens, bringing in a new theme: "I need not fear losing your love because my life depends on that—as soon as I lose your love I die." The sonnet goes on to say that W. will be happy to die, implying that it's because then he won't be *wretched* living without Y.M.'s love. But the couplet, again, won't let the sonnet end on this note. "What if?" W. asks. *Thou mayst be false and yet I know it not.* What if you don't love me but you pretend you do?

Sonnet 93 explores this question. It's an important one for the relationship between W. and Y.M.—and for many relationships. W. is *not* a deceived husband, but he compares himself to one. The question is not one of sexual infidelity but of unfaithfulness in love. What do you do when you love someone who says they love you, but you know they don't mean it anymore? W.'s answer is in keeping with his previous praises of Y.M., always seeing his beauty, his virtue, always admiring. And yet, even before we get to the couplet, it sounds mature, measured, careful, thoughtful—not the excesses of an ecstatic lover or adoring fan. We hear *sweet* twice in the third quatrain, but those lovely sounding lines are not just a compliment, they carry a deeper meaning. This affects how we read the final couplet of this trio. When I read those two lines, I hear calmness. "How like *Eve's* apple doth thy beauty grow, / If thy sweet virtue answer not thy show." And yet, *Eve's apple* does sound sinister. But is it just a statement of what could be—a warning? Or is it a condemnation? What would Y.M. hear?

94

They that have pow'r to hurt, and will do none,
That do not do the thing, they most do show,
Who moving others, are themselves as stone,
Unmovèd, cold, and to temptation slow,
They rightly do inherit heaven's graces,
And husband nature's riches from expense,
They are the Lords and owners of their faces,
Others, but stewards of their excellence.
The summer's flower is to the summer sweet,
Though to it self, it only live and die,
But if that flow'r with base infection meet,
The basest weed out-braves his dignity;
     For sweetest things turn sourest by their deeds,
     Lilies that fester, smell far worse than weeds.

2 *show* i.e., show the ability to do **3-4** *Who moving…as stone* i.e., who are able to affect the actions of others, but who are able to control their own impulses **6** *husband* conserve; *expense* expenditure **7** *faces* appearances **8** *but stewards* mere custodians **12** *his* its

The diction of the first quatrain of Sonnet 94 is not easy. The compressed thought can be hard to understand unless you pay attention to the context. Line 2 may seem unclear, especially the meaning of *show* until you realize that it just repeats line 1. What *they most do show* must be what they show themselves to be able to do. The next two lines are even more difficult. *Who moving others* has to be understood in the context of the beginning of line 1: *They that have power to hurt.* Why do they have power to hurt? Because they are able to move others. They can affect their emotions. If these same people control their own emotions, they *are themselves as stone/Unmovèd, cold and to temptation slow.* They don't harm others. This is the only way to explain the next line: *They rightly do inherit heaven's graces.* They receive God's good will. Now the metaphor of the stewards in line 8 becomes clear if we recognize their role as dispensers of valuable things that belong to others, not themselves. Their value is only borrowed—they have no virtue of themselves. Their appearance of value is false.

After the slow buildup of the previous three sonnets to its final message, Sonnet 94 makes its statement more concisely: "No matter how lovely you look, it's your actions that count." The first two quatrains say this directly; the third quatrain uses the metaphor of flowers spoiled by infection. The couplet ties the quatrains together: "Be careful what you do—you might stink like rotting flowers." W. cautiously takes a step back in Sonnet 94. Instead of addressing his sonnet to Y.M., he speaks in generalities, using the pronouns *they* and *others*. This is understandable. Such strong words require deniability. But this gives Y.M. leeway to ignore Sonnet 94's warning as he seems to have ignored Sonnet 93. Is W. testing Y.M.? Will he be oblivious? Will he be remorseful?

95

How sweet and lovely dost thou make the shame,
Which like a canker in the fragrant Rose,
Doth spot the beauty of thy budding name!
Oh in what sweets dost thou thy sins enclose!
That tongue that tells the story of thy days,
(Making lascivious comments on thy sport)
Cannot dispraise, but in a kind of praise,
Naming thy name, blesses an ill report.
Oh what a mansion have those vices got,
Which for their habitation chose out thee,
Where beauty's veil doth cover every blot,
And all things turns to fair, that eyes can see!
    Take heed (dear heart) of this large privilege,
    The hardest knife ill us'd doth lose his edge.

2 *canker* worm **3** *name* reputation **6** *sport* amorous play **12** *all things turns to fair* turns all things to fair **14** *his* its

The stern, remote tone of Sonnet 94 is replaced by acid wittiness in Sonnet 95. Something has happened between the two sonnets. Before Sonnet 95, Y.M. *might* have done something wrong. Now, he's done it. He's been sinful, promiscuous, *lascivious.* W. can afford to be blatantly truthful. Whatever his own faults were (as mentioned in Sonnets 89 and 90), they're forgotten. It's Y.M.'s reputation that's now at stake.

Although Sonnet 95 reverts to convention in lavishing praise on Y.M., it takes away each praise with equal *dispraise*. Almost every line that has a good word in it also has a bad one: *sweet and lovely/shame, fragrant rose/canker, beauty/blot, sweets/sins, sport/lascivious, praise/dispraise, blesses/ill report, mansion/vices, beauty/blot*. The only exception is *fair*, unchallenged in line 12. And in contrast to Sonnet 94, the couplet is directed to Y.M., not to *others*. W. warns: "You may brush all this aside now, but don't count on it working for too long."

The diction is clear in this sonnet. Line 12 might cause some problem with "And all things turns to fair," but this is a typical change in word order, where the meaning is: "beauty's veil doth cover every blot and turns all things to fair." On the whole, the argument of this sonnet is made in plain language: "You get away with many things because of your beauty—be careful of this privilege." How does Y.M. read this sonnet? Does he think W. is being cheeky or doesn't he even care what he thinks anymore? Is he callous enough to ignore his own faults and enjoy the compliments, or does he take the warning seriously?

96

Some say thy fault is youth, some wantonness,
Some say thy grace is youth and gentle sport,
Both grace and faults are lov'd of more and less,
Thou mak'st faults graces, that to thee resort.
As on the finger of a thronèd Queen,
The basest Jewel will be well esteem'd,
So are the errors that in thee are seen,
To truths translated, and for true things deem'd.
How many Lambs might the stern Wolf betray,
If like a Lamb he could his looks translate?
How many gazers migh'st thou lead away,
If thou wouldst use the strength of all thy state?
    But do not so, I love thee in such sort,

As thou being mine, mine is thy good report.

2 *gentle* gentlemanly; *sport* amorous play **3** *of more and less* by great and small **8** *truths* virtues; *translated* transformed; *true* virtuous

The basic ideas in Sonnet 96 are easy to understand even if some of the language is ambiguous. "Youth and wantonness are faults to some, graces to others, but everyone loves both faults and graces when it comes to you—you turn faults into graces. Just like the lowliest jewel will be thought a fine gem when worn by a queen, your errors seem like virtues. And just as a wolf in lamb's clothing could fool many a lamb, how many people could you lead astray if you were false to them?" The only difficulties in the sonnet are *of more or less*, which makes sense if we read it as "by great and small" (meaning "everyone") and line 10, with its change it word order. The sense is "If he could translate his looks [to make him look] like a lamb." I don't think it's useful to go further into these allusions, especially in light of the concluding couplet. This reads to me as a summary. It combines the arguments of Sonnets 94 and 95 and the conclusion of Sonnet 88. I remarked how Sonnet 88 reminded me of the liaison sonnets, including the couplet of Sonnet 36. Many editors have pondered over the fact that the couplet of Sonnet 96 is identical to the couplet of Sonnet 36. Is this an error, or is there a reason for the identical sentiment? The context is different, the relationship is different, but some things just don't change. I'm also reminded of the first seventeen sonnets on the theme of procreation. There's something similarly insistent about the repeated theme here. W. has to tell Y.M. over and over to watch himself, he's abusing his privilege. By the end of those first seventeen sonnets I was starting to feel Y.M. was a blockhead. I get the same sense with these sonnets. I hear W. saying to himself, "Are you listening? Do you hear what I'm saying? This is important!" I imagine Y.M. smiling charmingly—and I want to wipe the smile off his face.

It's amusing. These sonnets, presumably written to show the virtues of Y.M., instead make his faults show more. Just as Sonnets 93 to 95 predicted. Not too surprising, maybe—just a matter of self-fulfilling prophecy. But it proves the point that "The evil that men do lives after them; / The good is oft interred with their bones."[*] I heard hope after the couplet of Sonnet 36. I hear a sigh of resignation after the same couplet in Sonnet 96. "I will always say good things about you (whether you deserve it or not, my dear)."

97

How like a Winter hath my absence been
From thee, the pleasure of the fleeting year!
What freezings have I felt, what dark days seen!
What old December's bareness everywhere!
And yet this time remov'd was summer's time,
The teeming Autumn big with rich increase,
Bearing the wanton burthen of the prime,
Like widowed wombs after their Lords' decease.
Yet this abundant issue seem'd to me,
But hope of Orphans, and unfathered fruit,
For Summer and his pleasures wait on thee,
And thou away, the very birds are mute.
   Or if they sing, 'tis with so dull a cheer,
   That leaves look pale, dreading the Winter's near.

5 *time remov'd* time of absence **6** *Autumn* harvest; *increase* progeny (i.e., fruits) **7** *wanton burthen* i.e., fruit of wantonness; *prime* spring **8** *widowed wombs* wombs of widows **9** *issue* progeny **10** *But hope of Orphans* mere hope of orphans, i.e., life without a father **11** *his* its **14** *near* nearness

Our story now begins a new chapter. An absence is announced but we don't know much about it. Was it a physical or emotional separation? How long has it been? What was the cause? Was it amicable or acrimonious? Why has it ended? We have many questions but only two facts: there was an absence and it has ended. Our natural assumption is that it had to do with the differences that arose in the previous sonnets.

---

[*] *Julius Caesar* 3.2.80-81.

Something drove W. and Y.M. apart—but what has brought them back together again? Has absence made the heart grow fonder?

Sonnet 97 is a curious blend of a simple statement and some difficult language. We have no problem understanding the sentiment. "Without you, everything seemed like winter—even though it was summer. There is no pleasure without you." This is clear from the first five lines. And it gives us a clue about how long the separation was—line 5 wouldn't make sense if it had lasted much more than one summer. (We can't tell how short it might have been, but it could not have been long enough to have included a winter, so it must have been less than a year.) The rest of the sonnet elaborates on the theme, finding different ways to say the same thing. Shakespeare is freer with his language, playing with word order, transferring modifiers from one word to another, using adjectives as adverbs—all typical Elizabethan showmanship.

If you don't get lost in the grammar, the meaning is obvious from the context. *Autumn*, then, means "harvest," not the season (otherwise, we'd be totally lost from line 6 on). Note how describing the harvest as *big with rich increase* makes us think of a description of a pregnant woman. The simile then follows: it bears *the wanton burthen of the prime, / Like widowed wombs, after their Lords' decease*. The pregnant harvest is like a pregnant widow. We have to twist everything around to get at this meaning—the wantonness of the prime (the spring) created the burden (the fruit of the harvest) just as the deceased Lords made their ladies have pregnant wombs, and those wombs are now in the bodies of widows. (Why does he use that word *wanton*? How can we not think of that line, *Some say thy fault is youth, some wantonness?*) The sonnet goes on to elaborate why the harvest is like a widow's womb: the *father* is not there. The fruit is like a fatherless child—an *orphan* (a common Elizabethan use of the word). The fruit of the harvest represents all the pleasures of summer and *Summer and his pleasures wait on thee*. To understand this, the context suggests we read *Yet* loosely and interpret the two parts of line 10 as saying the same thing in different ways (*But hope of Orphans* and

171

unfather'd fruit).

An unusual feature of Sonnet 97 is its organization not as three quatrains and a couplet, but as octet-sestet. The first eight lines make up one thought and the next six another. Most obvious is the continuation of thought from line 12 through lines 13 and 14. The last two lines don't work well on their own. But there's something hauntingly beautiful about those last four lines. This is a very different beauty from anything expressed by W. before.

98

From you have I been absent in the spring,
When proud pied April (dress'd in all his trim)
Hath put a spirit of youth in every thing,
That heavy *Saturn* laugh'd and leapt with him.
Yet nor the lays of birds, nor the sweet smell
Of different flowers in odor and in hue,
Could make me any summer's story tell,
Or from their proud lap pluck them where they grew.
Nor did I wonder at the Lily's white,
Nor praise the deep vermilion in the Rose,
They were but sweet, but figures of delight,
Drawn after you, you pattern of all those.
    Yet seem'd it Winter still, and you away,
    As with your shadow I with these did play.

2 *proud pied* beautifully varied; *trim* fine attire **4** *That* so that; *heavy Saturn* (the melancholy planet) **5** *nor...nor* neither...nor; *lays* songs **6** *different flowers* flowers different **7** *summer's* summery, happy **8** *their proud lap* i.e., the earth (referring to the flowers); *where* from where **11** *figures* emblems **12** *you pattern* you who is the pattern **14** *shadow* image

Sonnet 98 tells the same story as Sonnet 97. W. is repeating his argument to Y.M. As I read *The Sonnets*, I've come to expect this, as if W. knows Y.M. needs to hear things more than once. Aside from the theme ("in your absence I could find no pleasure") there are other similarities between the two sonnets: the mention of *spring* (*prime*), *birds, summer, winter.* In Sonnet 97, Y.M. was the *father* of all the fruit of the harvest; in Sonnet 98, he is the *pattern* of all the beauties of summer. It's essential to allow for poetic license when reading this sonnet. This is a poem, not a dissertation, so it's ok that in Sonnet 97 W. was absent in *summer's time* and here he has been absent *in the spring.* The concept is the same, especially since the time of absence in Sonnet 97 alluded to the spring and its fruits, the harvest. He could even have been absent in both spring and summer. The point of both sonnets is the exclusion of the dreary winter. (Springtime is so lovely in Sonnet 98, even the melancholy Saturn has a great time.) We can also ignore the grammar of the second quatrain that says that neither the songs of birds nor the different smells and colors of flowers could make W. think of summer *or pluck them from where they grew,* where the last clause could only apply to flowers, not birds. And we have to use our imagination to understand what that last line means. It may not even dawn on us until we read the couplet. Of course, he's saying, despite the beauty of the flowers, he's not even moved to pluck them, smell them, play with them joyfully as he normally would during *proud pied April.*

The emotion of Sonnet 97 is summed up in its last four lines with the imagery of birds struck dumb, or nearly so, with melancholy. Sonnet 98 saves the emotion for the couplet, using the imagery of the flowers of the preceding quatrain, unplucked, consigned to mere lackluster play, as if they were but a shadow of beauty—of the absent Y.M.

99

The forward violet thus did I chide:
Sweet thief whence didst thou steal thy sweet that smells
If not from my love's breath? The purple pride,
Which on thy soft cheek for complexion dwells,
In my love's veins thou hast too grossly dyed.
The Lily I condemnèd for thy hand,
And buds of marjoram had stol'n thy hair,
The Roses fearfully on thorns did stand,
One blushing shame, another white despair,
A third nor red, nor white, had stol'n of both,
And to his robb'ry had annex'd thy breath,
But for his theft in pride of all his growth
A vengeful canker eat him up to death.
    More flowers I noted, yet I none could see,
    But sweet, or color it had stol'n from thee.

2 *thy sweet* your perfume **3** *pride* splendor **5** *grossly* evidently **6** *for* on account of; *thy hand* (i.e., for the theft of its whiteness) **7** *buds of marjoram* (known for their sweet scent) **11** *annex'd* i.e., also stolen **12** *in pride of* at the height of **13** *canker* worm; *eat* ate **15** *sweet* perfume

Sonnet 99 takes its time cataloging the different flowers and their attributes that were *stolen* from Y.M. It's the only sonnet in the series with 15 lines.* The comparisons are conventional— purple veins, blushing cheeks, pale skin, perfumed breath. The charming part is the extended rose metaphor. The red rose is *blushing shame* personified, the white rose is *despair,* the multicolored rose is the worst thief of all, stealing Y.M.'s rosy cheeks, pale complexion, and perfumed breath. That villain gets his comeuppance—he's eaten by a canker worm. The sonnet ends with a summary couplet that reiterates the theme with a quick fillip.

This sonnet takes its idea from the third quatrain of Sonnet

---

* This is not unique among Elizabethan sonnet sequences. See, for example, Spenser's *Amoretti*, Sonnet 58. M. Evans, M., *Elizabethan Sonnets,* 129.

98: all the beauty of the flowers of spring are just a pattern of Y.M.'s beauty. What's most surprising is the sonnet's charm. It sounds like it belongs to an earlier chapter of the relationship. Unlike the previous two sonnets, it's happy, gleeful. It's not clear whether it discusses the same period of absence or if it has nothing to do with it. However, it is stubbornly written in the past tense. All the complaints against the flowers are past complaints. They sound like an elaboration of the charge made against them in Sonnet 98: they're just images of Y.M. The change in tone could be due to a change in perspective. The previous sonnets were told from the point of view of being absent. Sonnet 99 is told from the point of view of *having been absent, but not being absent anymore*. Still, it seems as if the absence must have made the past grow dim. Has all been forgiven? Is the feeling reciprocated?

100

Where art thou, Muse, that thou forget'st so long,
To speak of that which gives thee all thy might?
Spend'st thou thy fury on some worthless song,
Dark'ning thy pow'r to lend base subjects light?
Return, forgetful Muse, and straight redeem,
In gentle numbers time so idly spent,
Sing to the ear that doth thy lays esteem,
And gives thy pen both skill and argument.
Rise resty Muse, my love's sweet face survey,
If time have any wrinkle graven there,
If any, be a *Satire* to decay,
And make time's spoils despisèd everywhere.
    Give my love fame faster than time wastes life,
    So thou prevent'st his scythe, and crooked knife.

3 *fury* poetic energy **4** *Dark'ning* diminishing **6** *gentle numbers* noble verses **7** *lays* songs **9** *resty* sluggish **11** *be a Satire to* satirize **14** *prevent'st* forestall

Here we go again. We find W. defending himself for his lapse in writing poetry in praise of Y.M. We had three sonnets after an absence and now this. Let's look at the sonnet to see

175

what it tells us.

W. complains to his muse, blaming it for forgetting to *speak of that which gives thee all thy might,* obviously Y.M. He goes further, asking if he's been wasting his time writing *worthless* poems to *base subjects.* This is a twist. Just a few sonnets ago, W. was accusing Y.M. of *receiving* poems from worthless poets. Now he's accusing himself of *sending* poems to worthless subjects. He had asked Y.M. to listen to the poems of the poet who appreciates him. Now he asks his muse to write poems to the subject who appreciates *him.* His next plea to his muse is interesting—see if time has made Y.M.'s face wrinkled with age. If so, make the spoils of time hated, write verses that will enshrine Y.M.'s beauty and prevent the ravages of time. So, we're back to the immortality of verse, but now with the specific mention of an aging youth.

Sonnet 100 gives me the impression that something has happened. It's not as clear as with earlier sonnets that Y.M. has complained about a lapse of poetic output. It sounds more like W. is trying to get his attention and knows he's going to be questioned about his poetic absence. Maybe W. has been writing sonnets to someone else and knows Y.M. has found out. He now wants to make sure he can save whatever is left of their relationship. Whatever the reason, there's something unengaging about Sonnet 100. Is it because it's addressed to a Muse and not Y.M.? Is it the rather stodgy verse (like line 9's *Rise resty Muse*)? Is it the return to the conventional theme we've heard before? The clichés? (The Muse, the song, the wrinkles, death personified as Time's scythe—repeated as a crooked knife.) Or is it that the argument just doesn't sound very convincing? It's not even really an argument, is it? "Oh, sorry. Busy writing poems to some worthless lout—forgot all about you. Have to rouse my Muse from slumber—be with you again in a jiff!" What's up next, I wonder?

101

Oh truant Muse, what shall be thy amends
For thy neglect of truth in beauty dy'd?
Both truth and beauty on my love depends,
So dost thou too, and therein dignifi'd.
Make answer Muse, wilt thou not haply say,
Truth needs no color with his color fix'd,
Beauty no pencil, beauty's truth to lay,
But best is best, if never intermix'd?
Because he needs no praise, wilt thou be dumb?
Excuse not silence so, for't lies in thee,
To make him much outlive a gilded tomb
And to be prais'd of ages yet to be.
    Then do thy office Muse, I teach thee how,
    To make him seem long hence, as he shows now.

2 *truth* virtue **4** *dignifi'd* (art thou) dignified **5** *haply* perchance **6** *no color* i.e., no added color; *his color fix'd* its unchangeable color **7** *pencil* paintbrush; *lay* apply **8** *intermix'd* adulterated **9** *dumb* silent **13** *office* duty

So maybe the argument of Sonnet 100 wasn't very convincing. Sonnet 101 stays with the same theme, the same approach—a stylized appeal to the poet's muse—with a slightly different argument. W. takes it in steps. The muse has been a truant, neglecting the only thing that gives it dignity—Y.M.'s truth and beauty. "What does the muse intend to do to make up for it," W. wonders? He asks if he might excuse himself on grounds that beauty doesn't need any painting to make it more beautiful. "Because he needs no praise, wilt thou be dumb?" Where have we heard this before? It was Sonnet 83: *I never saw that you did painting need, / And therefore to your fair no painting set.../ For I impair not beauty being mute.* Then, compared to the Rival Poet, W.'s silence was golden. Now, he chides his muse for failing to immortalize Y.M. in verse. It's as if W. has changed places with the Rival Poet. Sonnet 101 sounds just like a poem I imagine the Rival Poet would write. *My love* occurs once, replaced by the pronouns *he* or *him* three times. *Muse* occurs three times and the abstractions, *truth* and *beauty*, together occur seven times. The diction is simple, the metaphors direct, the verse as stolid as the previous sonnet's. There is none of the passion of earlier sonnets. This is very different from Sonnet 15's *all in war with Time for love of you.* Does Y.M. notice?

102

My love is strengthened though more weak in seeming,
I love not less, though less the show appear:
That love is merchandiz'd, whose rich esteeming,
The owner's tongue doth publish everywhere.
Our love was new, and then but in the spring,
When I was wont to greet it with my lays,
As *Philomel* in summer's front doth sing,
And stops her pipe in growth of riper days.
Not that the summer is less pleasant now
Than when her mournful hymns did hush the night,
But that wild music burthens every bough,
And sweets grown common lose their dear delight.
    Therefore like her, I sometime hold my tongue
    Because I would not dull you with my song.

1 *seeming* appearance **3** *esteeming* valuation **6** *lays* songs **7** *Philomel* the nightingale; *front* beginning **8** *riper* later **11** *burthens* burdens **14** *dull you* i.e., the edge of your appetite

It might seem that Sonnet 102 has the same theme as the two previous sonnets. It could be read as just another excuse for W.'s lack of poetic attention to Y.M. But it comes to a different conclusion. Rather than promising to do better, he congratulates himself for his good sense. "The summer night's too noisy—I don't want to sound common and dull you with yet another song."

There's something more important being said in Sonnet 102. This is a more personal sonnet. It sounds like Y.M. was unhappy with W.'s flimsy arguments and has complained that he doesn't love him like he used to. W. drops his phony dialog with his muse and addresses Y.M. directly. He gives a variation of his argument from Sonnet 21: *Let them say more that like of hearsay well, / I will not praise that purpose not to sell.* The turning point of the sonnet is the second quatrain. Here, W. points out the difference between a love that is new (in the spring) and a mature love (in the summer). He compares it to the nightingale, a bird thought (by English poets, anyway) to sing beautifully but to stop singing toward the end of summer. His reason for not singing praises now sounds different. He was young before and eager to show his love. He's more mature and wiser now. He knows there's such a thing as too much of a good thing. He said as much in Sonnet 52 when he compared himself to a miser who wouldn't look at his treasure every hour so as not to blunt *the fine point of seldom pleasure.* His love is no less now than it was before, but now he understands the value of silence. He sounds sincere in this poem in speaking of *when her mournful hymns did hush the night.* And he speaks as well as he did in Sonnet 52 when he notes that *sweets grown common lose their dear delight.* Whether or not we believe W.'s sincerity, we understand the truth of the underlying argument. New love and mature love are different. W. understands this. We understand this. Does Y.M.?

103

Alack what poverty my Muse brings forth,
That having such a scope to show her pride,
The argument all bare is of more worth
Than when it hath my added praise beside.
Oh blame me not if I no more can write!
Look in your glass and there appears a face,
That over-goes my blunt invention quite,
Dulling my lines, and doing me disgrace.
Were it not sinful then, striving to mend,
To mar the subject that before was well,
For to no other pass my verses tend,
Than of your graces and your gifts to tell.
    And more, much more than in my verse can sit,
    Your own glass shows you, when you look in it.

2 *pride* splendor **3** *argument* theme **6, 14** *glass* mirror **11** *pass* purpose **13** *sit* dwell

After a more sincere approach in Sonnet 102, W. retreats to his muse in this sonnet. His theme is similar, no longer apologetic, excusing himself on the basis of good sense. In the past seven sonnets I've pointed out echoes of five earlier sonnets. (I could add a sixth: I find *pluck* in line 8 of Sonnet 98 an unusual enough word that it reminds me of Sonnet 19: *Pluck the keen teeth from the fierce Tiger's jaws*). Sonnet 103 adds five more to the list. Line 2 recalls *the **scope** and tenor of thy jealousy* (Sonnet 61); line 6 the request from Sonnet 3 to **Look** *in thy glass*; line 8 *be it not said the edge should **duller** be than appetite* (Sonnet 56) and the theme repeats that of Sonnets 23 (O *learn to read what silent love hath writ*) and 85 (*respect / Me for my dumb thoughts, speaking in effect*). It sounds like he has nothing new to say. No passion. No mention of love. On initial reading, the couplet reinforces this feeling for me. It's unique among the 103 sonnets we've read so far in saying nothing that hasn't been said in the body of the sonnet. It's hardly more than a restatement of lines 6 and 7. And it uses more words than it needs, without adding any beauty to the lines. "Your own glass shows you more than my verse can" is more economical and *sounds better.* Poetry is supposed to be more beautiful than prose. It sounds like W. isn't trying. Unless we read it almost like prose.

Because the meter of this sonnet may be the key to understanding it, I'm going to discuss it here instead of just in a footnote. There are a few irregular lines, but that's not so important.* The rhythm of Sonnet 103 is driven by the flow of thought, not the lines. Sometimes the pauses at the ends of lines are brief; they are virtually absent at the ends of lines 3, 6, and 11—the thought flows through to the next lines. The rhymes lose importance, they become secondary. This is crucial for the couplet. Normally, we would need a strong emphasis on *it* to keep the rhyme with *can sit* (which sounds awful to my ear). But if the rhymes are weak, and the flow of thought dominates, it's easier to read the sonnet as one long rant with the emphasis in the last line on *look.* W. sounds annoyed to me now. All those allusions to previous sonnets make sense. "How many times do I have to tell you the *same thing?*"

---

* They do emphasize key phrases, so I'll just mention the initial trochees in lines 6 and 8 and the midline trochee in line 9 at *striving.*

104

To me fair friend you never can be old,
For as you were when first your eye I eyed,
Such seems your beauty still: Three Winters cold,
Have from the forests shook three summers' pride,
Three beauteous springs to yellow Autumn turn'd,
In process of the seasons have I seen,
Three April perfumes in three hot Junes burn'd,
Since first I saw you fresh which yet are green.
Ah yet doth beauty like a Dial hand,
Steal from his figure, and no pace perceiv'd,
So your sweet hue, which me thinks still doth stand
Hath motion, and my eye may be deceiv'd.
    For fear of which, hear this thou age unbred,
    Ere you were born was beauty's summer dead.

4 *pride* splendor **6** *process* progress **9** *Dial* watch **10** *his figure* its (the dial's) numeral; *and no pace perceiv'd* i.e., with imperceptible movement **11** *hue* appearance; *still doth stand* doth stand still **13** *unbred* unborn **14** *beauty's summer* the time when Beauty was at her best

I find myself kept continuously off balance by Sonnet 104. The first line is so unexpected after the preceding sonnets. It sounds like a breath of fresh air. So calm and gentle—like a compliment at first. But we read on and the passage of time is mentioned. Now it sounds like a response to fear of getting old. And there's the unusual image for the first meeting between W. and Y.M.: *when first your eye I eyed.* We have to decide how to read that. Is it awkward? Strained? Clever? Or does it have a touch of sincere reminiscence, when first they looked into each other's eyes? I've read it each of these ways. The imagery continues: *three cold winters shaking summer's pride from the forests, three springs turning to yellow autumn,* the *perfumes* of *three Aprils burning in three hot Junes* (like throwing incense on a fire).* And after all this talk of winter, autumn, burning June, passing time, we return to the

---

* The image of throwing incense on a fire is from Beeching, *Sonnets,* 111.

comparison in line 8: when you were first *fresh;* yet you are (still) *green.* But the very next moment, line 9 begins with *Ah yet.* Another image appears: the imperceptible motion of the hand of the watch dial. Grammatically, beauty is said to steal from itself, but we understand through the metaphor of the watch that it's Time that is stealing from beauty (as in Sonnets 5 and 12). The metaphor is extended further: the motion of the watch hand is transferred to the *sweet hue* (another metaphor, color for appearance) of Y.M., which figuratively *moves* with time instead of just *changing.* But most unexpected is the last word of Sonnet 104: *dead.*

That final word ends the sonnet on a dull note. The argument of the sonnet is conventional. You're beautiful, you'll always be beautiful, but Time will eventually have his way so I will proclaim your beauty for all time to come. Nothing unusual there, except the way it's said. "Don't worry, you can never be old. But you may be getting old. I better tell the future—long before they were born, you, the most beautiful of all, *died.*" Well, that's a nice cheerful way to end a compliment. And that's what fascinates me. This sonnet is told upside down. If it were a conventional sonnet, it would be written the other way around. "Let me tell you, you future generations, before you were born, the greatest beauty of the world had already died. To me, my love seems as beautiful as ever. But beauty slips away imperceptibly, so I may not notice what will come in the future. My love, you could never seem old to me. You are as fresh and green as when we first met. Your beauty will always seem so." That says the same thing, but it's a different sonnet. It's a sonnet of youth, when age and death are far away. Sonnet 104 is a sonnet of maturity, when age and death must be reckoned with. In the first line there is *old,* in the last line, *dead.* That *dead* summer heightens the previous mention of *winter, autumn, burn'd, deceiv'd. Beauty* has been stolen from the *forests, summer, spring, April's perfumes,* and *sweet hues.*

Why this sonnet now? Perhaps W. is just continuing his references to previous themes. Or perhaps Y.M. has asked if W.'s neglect is because he's getting old. Whatever has gone on since

Sonnet 103 to prompt it, this sonnet is at best only a superficial compliment. Sonnet 104 sounds like a warning to me.

105

Let not my love be call'd Idolatry,
Nor my belovèd as an Idol show,
Since all alike my songs and praises be
To one, of one, still such, and ever so.
Kind is my love today, tomorrow kind,
Still constant in a wondrous excellence,
Therefore my verse to constancy confin'd,
One thing expressing, leaves out difference.
Fair, kind, and true, is all my argument,
Fair, kind and true, varying to other words,
And in this change is my invention spent,
Three themes in one, which wondrous scope affords.
    Fair, kind, and true, have often liv'd alone.
    Which three till now, never kept seat in one.

3 *Since* just because **4, 6** *still* always **8** *difference* variety **9** *argument* theme **11** *change* variety of expression; *invention* poetic creativity **14** *kept seat* was lodged

Sonnet 105 reads as a response to a complaint that W. is merely idolizing Y.M., not truly complimenting him. He seems to have been accused of narrowness of invention, of repeating the same praises. Has Y.M. been told this with the implication that his poet lacks talent? Has he repeated this to W.? If so, this reply refutes the claim and compliments Y.M. with no sense of hurt. It's all restraint.

The word *Since* in line 3 must be understood to mean "just because" to make sense of the argument. We have to follow this train of thought throughout to keep from reading the sonnet sarcastically. We must take it all seriously to have it make sense and keep the poem from sounding like drivel. The question is, can we take this seriously? Has Y.M. been *fair, kind and true*? We may accept *fair* to mean "beautiful" but it's hard not to think of Y.M.'s unfairness in the past (Sonnet 41: *Aye me, but yet thou migh'st my seat forbear.*) We know at some level he has been untrue (emotionally and poetically) and at times he does not seem to have been kind. Is this another poem of conventional self-abnegation? Y.M. is *known* to be fair, kind and true. *Everyone* knows this. Who is the lowly W. to say different? How petty would any complaints of his seem in comparison to the great worth of Y.M.? And so he is *kind, kind, wondrous excellent.* W.'s verses are *constant* because Y.M. is *constant. Fair, kind and true.* Three things in one Y.M. And to emphasize his point, he repeats it three times. How does Y.M. take it? Is he complimented? Does he appreciate W.'s selflessness? Does he feel guilty? Or is he oblivious?

106

When in the Chronicle of wasted time,
I see descriptions of the fairest wights,
And beauty making beautiful old rhyme,
In praise of Ladies dead, and lovely Knights,
Then in the blazon of sweet beauty's best,
Of hand, of foot, of lip, of eye, of brow,
I see their antique Pen would have express'd
Even such a beauty as you master now.
So all their praises are but prophesies
Of this our time, all you prefiguring,
And for they look'd but with divining eyes,
They had not still enough your worth to sing:
    For we which now behold these present days,
    Have eyes to wonder, but lack tongues to praise.

1 *wasted* past **2** *wights* persons **5** *blazon* proclamation **8** *master* possess **10** *prefiguring* depicting in advance **11** *for* because; *but* only **12** *still enough* great enough (praises) **11-12** *And...sing* i.e., because they were only making prophesies, they could not praise you adequately **14** *lack tongues to praise* i.e., are dumbstruck

Sonnet 106 is a complement to Sonnet 104, comparing the beauty of Y.M. to those of the long past instead of the far future. Like Sonnet 104, it uses imagery to enhance its argument. The imagery is more complicated than might seem at first. The archaic word *wights* brings up times of chivalry. And the unexpected *Ladies dead, and lovely Knights* (where would expect "lovely ladies and dead knights") makes us think of the ladies *and* the knights as being both dead and lovely. The *blazon* of beauty (a heraldic term) reminds us of a coat of arms, keeping us in the chivalric frame of reference. All this makes the conventional line 6, the literal enactment of line 2, seem purposeful: "See, this is how they would have said it then." And what's the point of the sonnet? The third quatrain explains that poets of the past, describing the beauties of their time were describing no more than the beauty that Y.M. possesses (since he is the model of all beauty). And since they were only making prophesies, they lacked ability to show his true worth. The couplet comes to the point: we in the present can see you, but we are so awed with *wonder,* we *lack tongues to praise.* W. has found another excuse for his lack of poetic output. This one is clothed in nothing but praise. Does Y.M. buy it?

107

Not mine own fears, nor the prophetic soul
Of the wide world, dreaming on things to come,
Can yet the lease of my true love control,
Suppos'd as forfeit to a cónfin'd doom.
The mortal Moon hath her eclipse endur'd,
And the sad Augurs mock their own presage,
Incertainties now crown them-selves assur'd,
And peace proclaims Olives of endless age.
Now with the drops of this most balmy time,
My love looks fresh, and death to me subscribes,
Since spite of him I'll live in this poor rhyme,
While he insults o'er dull and speechless tribes.
    And thou in this shalt find thy monument,
    When tyrants crests and tombs of brass are spent.

4 *cónfin'd doom* limited duration **6** *sad Augurs* prophets of disaster; *presage* predictions **7** *Incertainties* i.e., things thought to be uncertain **10** *subscribes* submits **12** *insults* triumphs; *tribes* multitudes

Sonnet 107 does what W. promises to do in Sonnet 101 (and before)—immortalize Y.M. in verse. The key argument is explained by the first quatrain. Lines 3-4 compare W.'s love to a lease that comes due at a fixed date. The whole quatrain then says, "nothing can make my love come to an end, it's been a mistake to think it subject to fate that limits other things."* It's easy to get lost trying to find specific meanings for some of the allusions in this sonnet.† I think it's better to view it as a vague presentment of future prophesies that don't come true. It seems like we should be able to understand the metaphors, but they feel just out of reach, the way some prophesies do.‡ The whole sense of unattainability is heightened by the unusual rhythms of the sonnet.§ In the same way, we understand the word reversal of line 8 (we know the olive branch is a symbol of peace so despite the confusing syntax the line must mean that peace is proclaimed for all time by the olive branch). And do we notice that even before W. announces that his verse will be a monument for Y.M., he claims it as his own source of immortality? **

I feel like Sonnet 107 is W.'s best answer to all Y.M.'s complaints. "You want a sonnet? I'll show you a sonnet! Let's see what you do with this one!"

---

* I am paraphrasing Beeching, *Sonnets*, 113, and Reed, *Sonnets*, 86.

† Many editors have.

‡ This was pointed out by Booth, *Sonnets*, 346.

§ The meter of Sonnet 107 is like nothing we've seen before. The beginning octet is highly irregular while the ensuing sestet is mostly regular. The octet is so irregular the meter gives us the same sense of unattainability as the sonnet as a whole. The iambic pentameter is as hard to find as the meaning of the metaphors—but we feel it there in the background, inescapable. The change from the octave to the sestet underscores the change from the incorrect prophesies of a love that has an end (all vagueness and confusion) to the steadfast love immortalized in verse (clear and straightforward). The whole is a masterpiece of tone.

** This is commonplace among poets as far back as ancient Rome. See Rollins, *New Variorum*, 51.

108

What's in the brain that Ink may character,
Which hath not figur'd to thee my true spirit,
What's new to speak, what now to register,
That may express my love, or thy dear merit?
Nothing sweet boy, but yet like prayers divine,
I must each day say o'er the very same,
Counting no old thing old, thou mine, I thine,
Even as when first I hallow'd thy fair name.
So that eternal love in love's fresh case,
Weighs not the dust and injury of age,
Nor gives to necessary wrinkles place,
But makes antiquity for aye his page,
    Finding the first conceit of love there bred,
    Where time and outward form would show it dead.

1 *character* write **2** *figur'd to* portrayed **9** *So that* So; *fresh case* youthful exterior **10** *Weighs not* does not carry **12** *for aye* forever; *his page* i.e., his servant **13** *conceit* conception

Sonnet 107 was mysteriously vague. Sonnet 108 is ambiguously confusing. Sonnet 107 promised immortality in verse. Sonnet 108 promises eternal youth through love, but the theme of Sonnet 108 is familiar. Like Sonnet 76, it sounds like a response to a complaint, "Why do all your sonnets sound the same?" In Sonnet 76, the answer was simple, "Because I always write of you." In Sonnet 108, the answer is more complicated, and it sounds more annoyed. Instead of the *sweet love* of Sonnet 76, we have the *sweet boy* of Sonnet 108. We've heard that condescending tone before. And in this sonnet, W. is saying that he *must* repeat himself. I hear an unwillingness behind that phrase. He seems to be lecturing Y.M. "Am I boring you? Does my repetition bother you? When we pray, don't we repeat our prayers just the same, over and over? Does that make our love of God any less? Do you demand more than that?" And in case Y.M. didn't get the point, line 8 echoes the line from the Lord's

Prayer, "hallowed be thy name."*

But it's the last six lines that are confusing. So many words are unclear, hard to pin down. What exactly is meant by *so that, fresh, case, antiquity*, and *page*? Editors have gotten lost in flights of fancies over some of these. But if we look at the lines overall and ignore some of the ambiguities, we can make out a fair sense of them: "Eternal love does not carry around the dust and injury of age, nor gives place to (otherwise) necessary wrinkles, finding the first thought of love where Time and outward form would show it dead." There's that word again. Just like Sonnet 104, this is a mature sonnet, telling Y.M. that W.'s love will always keep him young, but reminding him that he will get old and one day he will be *dead*. Nothing's simple anymore.

---

* The reference, probably obvious to many editors before him, was first pointed out by Alden, *Sonnets*, 253.

109

O never say that I was false of heart,
Though absence seem'd my flame to qualify,
As easy might I from my self depart,
As from my soul which in thy breast doth lie.
That is my home of love; if I have rang'd,
Like him that travels I return again,
Just to the time, not with the time exchang'd,
So that my self bring water for my stain.
Never believe though in my nature reign'd,
All frailties that besiege all kinds of blood,
That it could so preposterously be stain'd,
To leave for nothing all thy sum of good.
    For nothing this wide Universe I call,
    Save thou, my Rose, in it thou art my all.

2 *qualify* moderate, temper **5** *my home of love* the home of my love; *rang'd* wandered **7** *Just...exchang'd* loyal to one's society, not a different one **8** *water* i.e., tears of repentance **10** *blood* i.e., the seat of animal appetite **12** *for* in exchange for **13** *nothing...call* I call everything in the world "nothing" **14** *Save* except

Something new has happened. Y.M. now accuses W. of being *false of heart*. The offense appears to be W.'s absence. There's a suggestion of a physical absence, not the poetical absence Y.M. complained about before. The terminology is persistent: *depart, home, rang'd, travels, return, bring, leave*. But is this a new offense or just a metaphor for the same one? It's hard to know, but the complaint is definitely different. W. is not just inattentive, he's false, he's betrayed Y.M. W., not denying his absence, proclaims his constancy.

The language of Sonnet 109 is not easy. The order of words in some phrases is so unusual that the meaning is strained. *My home of love* in line 5 must mean "the home of my love" and line 12 must mean "For I call this wide Universe 'nothing.'" We can tell this only from the context and Shakespeare's usual liberty with word order. The meaning of lines 7 and 10 (see glosses) also must be inferred from the context (and contemporary usage). I find most interesting the use of the word *Rose* in the last line, a word used often in earlier sonnets. Here, it's used for the first time as a term of address.

It seems Sonnet 109 is a response to an aggressive attack by Y.M.—W. defends himself no less aggressively. With all that's gone before, we might have difficulty taking either of them very seriously. Whom do we favor when we read Sonnet 109? Is Y.M. justified? Is W. just hunting for excuses? Is Y.M. just complaining again, unable to appreciate true love? Is W. appropriately offended, especially after how Y.M. has treated him? I don't know about you, but I'm feeling jaded about both of them by now.

110

Alas, 'tis true, I have gone here and there,
And made my self a motley to the view,
Gor'd mine own thoughts, sold cheap what is most dear,
Made old offenses of affections new.
Most true it is, that I have look'd on truth
Askance and strangely: But by all above,
These blenches gave my heart another youth,
And worse assays prov'd thee my best of love.
Now all is done, have what shall have no end,
Mine appetite I never more will grind
On newer proof, to try an older friend,
A God in love, to whom I am confin'd.
    Then give me welcome, next my heav'n the best,
    Even to thy pure and most, most loving breast.

2 *motley* jester; *to the view* i.e, to the world's view **3** *Gor'd* wounded **4** *Made…new* hurt old relationships by making new ones **5** *truth* honesty, loyalty **6** *Askance and strangely* disdainfully and as if never known **7** *blenches* side glances **8** *worse assays* trials of worse friendships **9** *have what…end* i.e., no matter what **10** *grind* whet **11** *proof* test **13** *next my heaven the best* my next-best-thing-to-heaven

Sonnet 110 continues the theme of W.'s offense. Like

Sonnet 109, line 1 suggests a physical absence: *I have gone here and there.* But as before, it's not clear whether this is just a metaphor. The remainder of the sonnet is all about self-reproach for what W. has done, but he never says what that is. Everything is couched in imagery. He has made himself *a motley to the view, gor'd* his *thought, sold cheap what is most dear, made old offenses of affections new, look'd on truth askance and strangely.* Has he done this while physically absent? Or has he done this poetically? Are these personal actions or literary ones? Even his promise is ambiguous: *Mine appetite I never more will grind / On newer proof, to try an older friend.* Is this a poetic appetite (for recognition) or an emotional appetite (for love)?

We are again in the position of wondering about W.'s sincerity. How convincing is the excuse he gives in lines 6 to 8? "Yes, I've done all that, but those tests of other friendships proved to me that you are the best I could ever have." And after promising never to do it again, he asks to be welcomed back in the couplet. Awkwardly. "Then give me welcome to thy loving breast," is the couplet's simple request. *Next my heaven the best* (my next best thing to heaven) is a lovely interpolation to fill the first line. Adding either *Even* or *most* to fill the next line would not be remarkable, but adding both, duplicating *most* and adding *pure* makes the line sound forced to me. It feels like he's stumbling for words.

111

O for my sake do you wish fortune chide,
The guilty goddess of my harmful deeds,
That did not better for my life provide,
Than public means which public manners breeds.
Thence comes it that my name receives a brand,
And almost thence my nature is subdu'd
To what it works in, like the Dyer's hand.
Pity me then, and wish I were renew'd,
Whilst like a willing patient I will drink
Potions of Eisell 'gainst my strong infection,
No bitterness that I will bitter think,

Nor double penance to correct correction.
 Pity me then dear friend, and I assure ye,
 Even that your pity is enough to cure me.

1 *fortune chide* Fortune to chide **2** *guilty goddess of* goddess who is guilty of **4** *public means* public resources for livelihood **6-7** *subdued To* reduced to **10** *Eisell* vinegar (thought to prevent contagion) **11** *No bitterness* There is no bitterness **12** *to correct correction* to be punished (with a bitter remedy) for an ailment that is itself a punishment

The focus of Sonnet 111 shifts from what W. has done to the company he keeps. The language is difficult if you try to make out the meaning of all the words and phrases. But this is one of those sonnets whose meaning we understand not through the clarity of its statement but through its general sense. There are key words that guide us: *chide, guilty, harmful deeds, public means, public manners, brand, subdu'd, pity, renew'd, potions, eisell, infection, bitterness, penance, pity, cure.* The format is similar to the one we saw in Sonnet 110: confession, excuse, promise, request. "Do you chide me" W. asks? "Yes, I write for the public and that shows a lack of grace. But if you have pity on me, I will be penitent and all will be well."

But that's not what this sonnet is about. That's just what it *says.* If you read the sonnet for its meaning, it's a struggle—the phrases are difficult to interpret, the flow of thought obscure. Why *For my sake?* What does *do you wish fortune chide* mean? What *public means?* (Editors have had a field day with this one, imagining all sorts of confessions by Shakespeare related to his feelings about writing for the stage, or being an actor, or being poor. I think this is just a poem.) Why *almost thence?* Then we have to work through the imagery of the *Dyer's hand*, the *willing patient*, the *potions* of vinegar, *infection, penance* and *correction.* But if you allow the sonnet's language to take hold and let it go, reading the sonnet through without stopping to think about it, the *sense* is clear, and so is the emotion. The sonnet starts with *chide* and ends with *cure.* In the middle is *guilt, public manners, brand*, and a *subdu'd nature, like the Dyer's hand.* I read a powerful version of a conventional conceit. The conventional sonneteer says to his beloved, "I am worthless, you are wonderful. Have pity on me. I will do anything for you. *I will drink vinegar and not think it bitter.* Just have pity on me and I will be cured." In the conventional sonnet, "having pity" would mean to return the sonneteer's love and "cure" would mean release from love sickness. In Sonnet 111, the terms are being used differently, but it's not clear exactly what they mean. The ambiguities are strong. Is W. guilty or is Fortune? Is Y.M. the only one chiding or is Fortune also chiding? Are others as well? Who is giving W.'s name a brand? If Fortune *did not better for my life provide / Than public means*, how will Y.M.'s pity *cure* him? Is W. implicitly chiding Y.M. for making him rely on public means instead of providing him patronage?

Those questions rely on our taking the meaning of the words at face value. But there's a flow that helps us find another way of understanding the sonnet. It's the imagery that builds successively from one thought to another. We start with chiding fortune, guilt, harmful deeds, and move to public means and public manners branding W.'s name. This moves to a nature subdued and the image of a dyer's hand indelibly steeped in ink. Next comes pity and renewal and the image of a willing patient drinking a noxious potion to effect his cure. This leads to penance and forgiveness, the penitent's cure. I don't think W. is asking to be cured of his public manners bred of his need for public means. He's just asking for forgiveness, to be welcomed back. To be loved again. This is the same request he made in Sonnet 110. What stands out is the deliberate twisting of conventional sonnet terminology to turn an unconventional situation into a conventional sonnet form.

112

Your love and pity doth th' impression fill,
Which vulgar scandal stamp'd upon my brow,
For what care I who calls me well or ill,
So you o'er-green my bad, my good allow?
You are my All the world, and I must strive
To know my shames and praises from your tongue,

None else to me, nor I to none alive,
That my steel'd sense or changes right or wrong.
In so profound *Abysm* I throw all care
Of others' voices, that my Adder's sense
To critic and to flatterer stoppèd are.
Mark how with my neglect I do dispense:
    You are so strongly in my purpose bred,
    That all the world besides me thinks y'are dead.

4 *o'er-green my bad* conceal my sins; *allow* approve **7-8** *None...wrong* i.e., there is no one else who affects my firm ideas about what is right or wrong; *or...or* either...or **9** *Abysm* abyss **10** *Adder's sense* deaf ears **12** *how...dispense* how I excuse my neglect (of others) **13** *so...bred* so rooted in my thought **14** *besides me thinks y'are* besides you methinks are (i.e., everyone is dead to me except you)

In Sonnet 112, the *brand* of Sonnet 111 has become an *impression* that's been *stamp'd* on W.'s forehead by *vulgar scandal* and is now filled by Y.M.'s love and pity. Like a conventional sonnet, W.'s request for pity was indeed a request for love. Unlike a conventional sonnet, the request has been granted. Also like a conventional sonnet is the cataloging of the parts of the body. W. says, "You are my All the world" and in the course of the sonnet mentions the *brow* (forehead), *tongue* (or mouth), *voices* (throat), *Adder's sense* (ears), and *sense* (mind, or heart). Like Sonnet 111, the language is not easy, but the sentiment is not hard to understand. The diction is typically Shakespearean, with omitted words that can be understood from the context ("[There is] None else to me, nor I to none else alive") and change in word order (*That my steel'd sense or changes right or wrong* for "That changes my steel'd sense [of] either right or wrong."). The most difficult line is probably the simplest, line 14, where *all the world besides me thinks y'are dead* is likely a word order change for "all the world besides ye, me thinks are dead," (everyone but you, to me is dead) the obvious meaning in the context. Shakespeare doesn't often resort to such awkward phrases to make his lines work out right. But I think he was ok with it when the context made the meaning obvious, as here. As with Sonnet 111, if you just read the Sonnet and trust your impressions, you're likely to get the meaning if you don't fuss at it too much.*

How do we read this sonnet? To me, the key is line 3: *For what care I who calls me well or ill.* Once I read this line, it sets up a contented tone that persists through the rest of the sonnet. Everything else is affected by it, uplifted. I find a *joy* that has been absent for a long time. But there's one exception. Sonnet 112 ends with the same word that Sonnet 108 did: *dead.* In Sonnet 108, I found it a reminder of Y.M.'s mortality. Here, it announces the "allness" of Y.M. to W.—the rest of the world is dead to him. But what an image! The two of them alone and the rest of the world—*dead.* An interesting choice. I have to wonder what that means.

113

Since I left you, mine eye is in my mind,
And that which governs me to go about,
Doth part his function, and is partly blind,
Seems seeing, but effectually is out;
For it no form delivers to the heart
Of bird, of flow'r, or shape which it doth latch,
Of his quick objects hath the mind no part,
Nor his own vision holds what it doth catch;
For if it see the rud'st or gentlest sight,
The most sweet-favor or deformèd'st creature,
The mountain, or the sea, the day, or night,
The Crow, or Dove, it shapes them to your feature.
    Incapable of more, replete with you,
    My most true mind thus maketh mine untrue.

3 *part* depart from **3, 7, 8** *his* its **4** *effectually* in fact **6** *latch* catch sight of **7** *quick* swift **10** *sweet-favor* lovely face **12** *feature* likeness **13** *replete* filled **14** *true mind* i.e., faithful to you; *untrue* untruth

---

* Too many editors have fallen into the trap of fussing over the meaning of every word and phrase in Shakespeare's sonnets. I confess to having fallen victim to this illness in the past myself.

Sonnet 113 discusses an absence again. There is no question that this is a physical absence. The sonnet's inventiveness involves using so many words to say so little. "Everything I see reminds me of you." That's all it says, but it expresses much more. This sonnet is written in the same light tone of Sonnet 112 but differs in its clarity of speech. That clarity allows it to carry its image of W.—partly blinded by his inward seeing eyes, groping around, mistaking everything he sees, as fast as the images come to him, for images of Y.M.—all the way through to the couplet. The beautiful phrasing of the last two lines overshadows any difficulty we might have deciphering the last two words (or pausing over the failure to repeat *the most* before *deformèds't creature* in line 10). Does it matter what *mine untrue* means when W. is *Incapable of more, replete with you*? If he were writing about me, I wouldn't care. I doubt Y.M. would either.

The joyful tone of Sonnet 112 is continued in Sonnet 113, this time without any reservation. This makes this absence sonnet different from previous ones. There is no talk of sleepless nights (Sonnets 27, 28, 61), *torment* (39), *injurious distance* (44), *melancholy* (45), sad interims *full of care* (56), waiting in *hell* (58), or *winter* (97, 98). W. is away from him, but since everything he sees reminds him of Y.M., he is happy. There is no sadness is Sonnet 113, only the humor of even the ugliest things being turned beautiful by W.'s *true mind* creating untruths. The conventional compliment of the absence sonnet is preserved, but the demeanor seems more mature to me.

114

Or whether doth my mind being crown'd with you
Drink up this monarch's plague this flattery?
Or whether shall I say mine eye saith true,
And that your love taught it this Alchemy?
To make of monsters, and things indigest,
Such cherubins as your sweet self resemble,
Creating every bad a perfect best
As fast as objects to his beams assemble.
O 'tis the first, 'tis flatt'ry in my seeing,
And my great mind most kingly drinks it up,
Mine eye well knows what with his gust is greeing,
And to his palate doth prepare the cup.
    If it be poison'd, 'tis the lesser sin,
    That mine eye loves it and doth first begin.

1, 3 *Or whether doth*...*Or whether* Doth...or (in modern English we would omit the first "Or whether") **4** *Alchemy* power of trans-mutation **5** *indigest* shapeless **8** *to his beams assemble* i.e., are presented to the eye's gaze **11** *with his gust is greeing* is agreeable to the mind's taste **14** *first begin* is the first victim

This sonnet explains why W's eye is false, as the couplet of Sonnet 113 made it out to be. The answer is a sonnet about flat-tery, with the same light tone of the previous two sonnets. The first two quatrains of Sonnet 114 ask, "Does my mind accept the flattering presentations of my eye because it feels like a king, be-ing loved by you (as truth is improved for a monarch's ear)? Or has your love taught me to see the goodness in all things?" The third quatrain answers the former. That's surprising. I expect "love" to be the answer. Sure, it's flattering for W. to tell Y.M. he makes him feel like a king, but wouldn't it be better to say his love transforms all the world's ills to good? Is there an underly-ing cynicism here?

The imagery is complex, even tortured (Elizabethans loved that). The mind is a king who gets to see and hear only what is agreeable to him. (Line 8 is based on the Elizabethan idea that eyes threw beams of light to make objects visible.) In the last four lines, the eye is a servant (a butler in lines 11 and 12, a taster in lines 13 and 14) to the mind (the king). The couplet says that the eye's guilt in offering poisoned wine (untruth) to the mind is lessened by the fact that the eye (as taster) thinks it good (*loves it*) and is the first victim (*doth first begin*). Never mind that a taster that offers poison to his king is a failure as a taster. Why does W. bother excusing the eyes fooled by flattery? Presumably because everyone's having such a great time hearing, seeing and tasting what they want. The *poison* that the mind is *drinking* is nothing more than the image of Y.M. that isn't really there. How bad is that? (Bad, I suppose if it's supposed to be seeing a *monster indigest*, but c'mon, how likely is that?)*

---

* In deciphering the metaphors of Sonnet 114, I had the help of a couple of editors: Wyndham, *Poems*, 317, and Booth, *Sonnets*, 378.

115

Those lines that I before have writ do lie,
Even those that said I could not love you dearer,
But then my judgment knew no reason why,
My most full flame should afterwards burn clearer.
But reckoning time, whose million'd accidents
Creep in twixt vows, and change decrees of Kings,
Tan sacred beauty, blunt the sharp'st intents,
Diverts strong minds to th' course of alt'ring things.
Alas, why fearing of time's tyranny
Might I not then say "now I love you best,"
When I was certain o'er incertainty,
Crowning the present, doubting of the rest.
    Love is a babe, then might I not say so,
    To give full growth to that which still doth grow.

7 *Tan* darken (and thus make less beautiful); *intents* intentions **8** *th' course of alt'ring things* the way things change **11** *o'er incertainty* beyond all possibility of doubt **12** *Crowning* giving precedence to **13** *then may I not say so* therefore may I not say "now I love you best" **14** *still* always

Continuing the light-hearted mood of the previous three sonnets, Sonnet 115 is a joke. The punchline comes right at the beginning, in the first quatrain. (Maybe W. didn't want Y.M. to worry that he was being serious.) The rest of the sonnet is an extended explanation of the uncertainty of the times and ends with the happy note of ever-growing love. As with Sonnet 114, a lot of words are used to make a simple statement: "I love you more than I ever thought possible." The expression of that statement is anything but simple.

The diction of the second quatrain can be tricky to follow, but you just have to keep track of the parenthetical thoughts. The main idea is that "reckoning time...diverts strong minds to the course of altering things."* (Even the strongest minds recall

---

* Critical to understanding this quatrain is Edmund Capell's (1766) emendation of *Divert* in line 8 to *Diverts*. See Atkins, *Sonnets*, 284-85.

how the reckoning of time changes everything.) *Whose million'd accidents* refers to *time* (the millions of accidents of time) and everything else describes the effects of those accidents: they *creep in twixt vows, change decrees of Kings, tan sacred beauty,* and *blunt the sharp'st intents.* Because those millions of accidents do all those things, we are *diverted* to the changes of *reckoning time.*

There's something so evocative about the lover *fearing time's tyranny,* being *certain* of *the present, doubting* the future. And there's a calmness about the couplet's image of *love* as a *babe* which must be allowed *full growth.*

Where are we in the story? Y.M. has accepted W. back. W. seems comfortable in their renewed relationship. Everything is cozy again.

116

Let me not to the marriage of true minds
Admit impediments, love is not love
Which alters when it alteration finds,
Or bends with the remover to remove.
O no, it is an ever fixèd mark
That looks on tempests and is never shaken;
It is the star to every wand'ring bark,
Whose worth's unknown, although his height be taken.
Love's not Time's fool, though rosy lips and cheeks
Within his bending sickle's compass come,
Love alters not with his brief hours and weeks,
But bears it out even to the edge of doom.
    If this be error and upon me prov'd,
    I never writ, nor no man ever lov'd.

4 *bends...remove* yields by going away in face of change (or death?) **5** *mark* sea-mark **8** *unknown* incalculably great; *his height* the star's position above the horizon **10** *Within...compass* i.e., within the range of Time's curving sickle **12** *bears it out* survives; *doom* last judgment **13** *upon me proved* proved against me

Having just talked about how wrong he was in the past to wonder what the alterations of time might bring and doubt that his love might grow, W. now claims that love cannot be altered by time. This sounds like a response to Y.M. "What? Do you truly believe that love can only grow with time? Isn't it possible for people to fall *out* of love?" It's in this sense that W. is saying love cannot alter—it can't change for the worse, be *removed, shaken,* fall within *Time's bending sickle's compass* (whether this refers to aging or to death).

Sonnet 116 restates the same idea three times. The first quatrain says that *love is not love* that allows itself to change or be removed. Despite the awkwardness of the phrase *bends with the remover to remove* the context allows us to understand the meaning: if you stop loving someone because he stops loving you, you never loved him in the first place. This is standard sonnet fare, reminiscent of Petrarch (see discussion of Sonnet 23). The second quatrain uses the metaphor of the unmoving North Star that guides sailors, regardless of the weather, to re-emphasize the steadfastness of love. Finally, the third quatrain calls upon the entire extent of time—from *brief hours to the edge of doom* to show the extent of love's immutability. The couplet dares anyone (especially, we presume, Y.M.) to prove the point false. The tone I get is mock defiance. (He's not really expecting an argument, is he?)

117

Accuse me thus, that I have scanted all,
Wherein I should your great deserts repay,
Forgot upon your dearest love to call,
Whereto all bonds do tie me day by day,
That I have frequent been with unknown minds,
And giv'n to time your own dear purchas'd right,
That I have hoisted sail to all the winds
Which should transport me farthest from your sight.
Book both my willfulness and errors down,
And on just proof, surmise accumulate,
Bring me within the level of your frown,
But shoot not at me in your waken'd hate,
    Since my appeal says I did strive to prove

The constancy and virtue of your love.

1 *scanted* neglected **4** *bonds* obligations **5** *frequent* often; *unknown minds* strangers **6** *giv'n to time* wasted away **9** *Book* record **10** *on…accumulate* add to what you can prove, all that you may suspect **11** *level* line of fire **13** *appeal* plea; *prove* test

In this sonnet, W. is being accused of neglect, betrayal even, and by his own account, rightfully so. He doesn't mind, he says, if Y.M. even adds his own suspicions to what he may justly charge him with. Let him be angry with him (*bring me within the level of your frown*). He can tolerate all this as long as Y.M. does not *hate* him. There is a sweeping beauty to many of the lines that I find ties me to feeling compassion for W. as he says *all bonds* tie him *day by day* to Y.M.'s *dearest love*. He's given away his *own dear purchas'd right* and *hoisted sail to all the winds*. This compassion makes me think of Sonnet 90: *Then hate me when thou wilt, if ever now….* He asked him then if he were going to leave him to do it right away and not to *linger out a purposed over-throw*. As I re-read Sonnet 90, I take pity on W., I feel his pain, I can't imagine how Y.M. could do anything but forgive him now. But what is W.'s excuse? He was only trying to prove the *constancy and virtue* of Y.M.'s love. Uh-oh. This is exactly what he promised never to do again in Sonnet 110: *Mine appetite I never more will grind, / On newer proof to try an older friend*. There seems to be a reciprocal problem with commitments in this relationship. And amnesia.

Maybe W. hoped his honest confession might be disarming. Or he might get credit for his willingness to accept all blame. But this is still bold. How does Y.M. react to this? How would you? There's a lot of history between these two that makes the answer complicated.

118

Like as to make our appetites more keen
With eager compounds we our palate urge,
As to prevent our maladies unseen,
We sicken to shun sickness when we purge.
Even so being full of your ne'er cloying sweetness,
To bitter sauces did I frame my feeding,
And sick of welfare found a kind of meetness,
To be diseas'd ere that there was true needing.
Thus policy in love t'anticipate
The ills that were not, grew to faults assured,
And brought to medicine a healthful state
Which rank of goodness would by ill be cured.
    But thence I learn and find the lesson true,
    Drugs poison him that so fell sick of you.

1 *Like as* just as **2** *eager* pungent; *urge* stimulate **6** *frame* direct **7** *meetness* appropriateness **9** *policy* prudent conduct; *t'anticipate* in anticipating **11** *medicine* medical treatment **12** *rank of* filled to excess with **14** *so* thus

Sonnet 118 puts together some crafty metaphors to expand on the excuse of Sonnet 117. The metaphors blend into one another. It starts with the use of pungent foods to stimulate the appetite to more pleasant dishes to come. This then is likened to the use of unpleasant purgatives to prevent more unpleasant illnesses. The second quatrain draws the direct analogy: Y.M. is like a sweet dish; W. attempted to clear his palate with a bitter sauce. The sweetness of Y.M. (that he is described as never-cloying only makes us more likely to think of him as cloying) is then compared to being *sick of welfare* (having too much of a good thing) which he thought it *meet* to correct by becoming unnecessarily *sick* (having a bad thing).* The third quatrain twists all the

---

* This is one of those instances where modernization causes difficulties. The original text has *nere cloying*. Although this is the usual spelling of *ne'er* in *The Sonnets* (three other instances) and *neere* is the usual spelling of *near* (five

contradictions into place: by anticipating ills that didn't exist (in order to prevent worse ones, as we do by purging), W. committed the faults he is accused of (and admits to). This was a good thing because it brought just what was needed—faults—to cure an excess of goodness. Q.E.D. All this, however, is tongue-in-cheek, because the couplet is a surprise punchline. It was no cure at all—his own medicine (*drugs*) poisoned him. That's what happens to someone who *falls sick* of Y.M.

What's this about? I imagine Y.M. saying to W. after the previous sonnet, "What! Is that all you have to say for yourself?" His answer is Sonnet 118: "No, of course not. I wasn't really testing *you*. I was—um—protecting myself. Yeah! That's it! *Sicken to shun sickness.* Making ourselves throw up to get rid of poison. That's what I was trying to do." And then he tries to butter him up with the punchline in the couplet: *Drugs poison him that fell so sick of you.* It's an excuse *and* a pun. "I tried to cure myself of you and only hurt myself." There's also the sense (meant as a compliment, of course) that being in love with Y.M. is an incurable illness.[*] Charming? Coy? Too soon? Let's see.

---

instances) it's hard to say for sure whether one or the other or both may have been intended (consistency in spelling not being a feature the 1609 Quarto can claim).

[*] This is pointed out by Kerrigan, who calls it a "black joke." Kerrigan, *Sonnets,* 337.

119

What potions have I drunk of Siren tears
Distill'd from Limbecks foul as hell within,
Applying fears to hopes, and hopes to fears,
Still losing when I saw my self to win!
What wretched errors hath my heart committed,
Whilst it hath thought it self so blessèd never!
How have mine eyes out of their Spheres been fitted
In the distraction of this madding fever!
O benefit of ill, now I find true
That better is, by evil still made better.
And ruin'd love when it is built anew
Grows fairer than at first, more strong, far greater.
    So I return, rebuk'd to my content,
    And gain by ill thrice more than I have spent.

1 *Siren tears* tears such as sirens weep **2** *Limbecks* alembics, vessels for stills **4** *Still* always; *saw my self* expected **6** *thought it self so blessèd never* never thought it self so blessed **7** *out of their Spheres been fitted* been shaken out of their proper spheres by a fit **8** *madding* maddening **10** *still* always **13** *So...content* So I, rebuked, return to what contents me

The diction is not easy, but the imagery of this sonnet is rich. The phrase *Siren tears* makes us think of the irresistible enticement of sirens' songs. How much harder would it be for W. to fight the spell induced by a potion distilled from the *tears* of sirens! And if those tears were distilled in a vessel *foul as hell?* One shudders to think. The vague struggle between fear and hope is evident in line 3, but the language makes it hard to figure out what W. is saying. I think this catches the sense nicely: "checking the sanguine hopes with drafts of fear, and cheering with drafts of hope too desperate fears."[*] This makes clear why he is always losing when he *sees himself* (expects) to win. Line 6 is as tortured as W.—the word *never* is moved from before *thought*, where it

---

[*]This is from Ingram and Redpath, *Sonnets*, 174. (I have Americanized the spelling. I hope they forgive me.)

belongs, to the end of the line, five words later. The change in word order in the next line is almost as severe, but easier to decipher. We just have to understand the unusual use of the verb *fitted*, meaning "shaken by a fit" (the context is the key to the meaning). The diction of the rest of the sonnet offers no problems. (I'll just note the typically Elizabethan use of the comma in line 12. It puts a slight pause after *is*, indicating how the line should be phrased. It has nothing to do with the grammar. In modern English, we would leave the comma out.) [*]

W. has apparently gotten nowhere with his previous two sonnets, so he tries a third approach in Sonnet 119. We've seen this tactic before—one argument doesn't work, so let's keep trying another. Here he says that *better is made even better by evil.* This contradicts his previous argument that he got worse, not better, by wandering off, but this is standard fare for *The Sonnets.* New arguments are just as likely to contradict as to support previous ones. We have come to expect no more consistency in arguments than in the love between the protagonists.

There *is* a consistency running through these sonnets, though. First, we have the *potions,* brought forward from the *eager compounds* of Sonnet 118. They remind us, even further back, of the *potions of Eisell* of Sonnet 111. But most of all, these sonnets are tied together by antithesis. Sonnet 117 has *scant/great, tie/hoist sail, proof/surmise, love/hate.* Sonnet 118: *bitter/sweet, sick/welfare, good/ill, drugs/poison.* And Sonnet 119: *fears/hopes, lose/win, hell/blessed, benefit/evil, gain/spent.*

Where is all this going? How do we expect Y.M. to respond? Where do we expect the relationship to go from here? How will this all end?

---

[*] As long as I'm discussing punctuation, I might as well mention that all three exclamation points are printed as question marks in the original. This is a common usage and, in this case, perfectly shows the intermediate situation of an exclamation with a questioning tone.

120

That you were once unkind befriends me now,
And for that sorrow, which I then did feel,
Needs must I under my transgression bow,
Unless my Nerves were brass or hammered steel.
For if you were by my unkindness shaken
As I by yours, y' have passed a hell of Time,
And I a tyrant have no leisure taken
To weigh how once I suffered in your crime.
O that our night of woe might have rememb'red
My deepest sense, how hard true sorrow hits,
And soon to you, as you to me then tend'red
The humble salve, which wounded bosoms fits!
    But that your trespass now becomes a fee,
    Mine ransoms yours, and yours must ransom me.

2 *for* because of **4** *Nerves* sinews **9** *rememb'red* reminded **10** *sense* feeling **11** *soon* as soon **12** *fits* suits **13** *But that your trespass* But that trespass of yours

W. now turns from excuses to apology. The diction is almost as difficult as in the previous sonnet, but the rich imagery is lacking. We have only the image of *nerves* of *steel, hammered* under unseen blows and the *salve* of humility (*humble salve*) that suits *wounded bosoms*. But everything is mixed up in this sonnet. Phrases are turned around, words transposed, ideas in unexpected places. It's hard to get through this sonnet without doubling back to think about something that made you scratch your head. It starts right away with line 1. We're *expected* to be confused as to how W. can consider a past unkindness something that *befriends him now*. This is the point of the sonnet, the key to its wordplay. Everything *is* what it seems like it shouldn't be. Line 2 then discusses W.'s sorrow during that time. We expect to hear next something about what Y.M. should do. Instead, we hear about what W. should do about his *transgression* (now). He takes a circuitous route, saying: 1) I must bow (be weighed down) under my transgression 2) unless I have nerves of steel 3) if you were as affected by my unkindness as I was by yours 4) you've had a *time of hell* (we would expect "a hell of a time") 5) I've been a tyrant by not taking the time to consider how I had suffered when you hurt me. Oddly, if you read 1-5 backwards, it makes sense.

Line 9 is one of the most interesting in *The Sonnets.* It describes an incident from the past in more detail than we've heard. This must be about the time when W. learned that Y.M. was having an affair with the woman he was also seeing. Now we learn it happened at night. Did he discover them in bed? He calls it *our night of woe*—a time of shared misery, not just something that bothered W.—Y.M. was upset, too! This is a side of things we haven't known about. But wait. That *humble salve* of Sonnet 34 no longer sounds like a lover making excuses for his callow friend. Those were real tears he cried!

We've had to wait for the couplet to understand the meaning of line 1. We might have thought the past unkindness was being good to W. by reminding him of his own past hurt and consequently making him understand the need to offer the same *salve* to Y.M. (tears of humility) that were offered to him. But he admits he's been too slow. Instead, he has another solution in mind: tit for tat. You hurt me, I hurt you. My bad deed ransoms yours, yours ransoms mine. There's a slight difference. It may just be for the sake of rhyme, but W. says to Y.M., *yours must ransom **me***. Does he want more, or does he feel like he's been *that* bad? Or does he just need the rhyme?

121

'Tis better to be vile than vile esteem'd,
When not to be, receives reproach of being,
And the just pleasure lost, which is so deem'd,
Not by our feeling, but by others' seeing.
For why should others' false adulterate eyes
Give salutation to my sportive blood?
Or on my frailties why are frailer spies,
Which in their wills count bad what I think good?
No, I am that I am, and they that level
At my abuses, reckon up their own,
I may be straight though they them-selves be bevel;
By their rank thoughts, my deeds must not be shown,
    Unless this general evil they maintain:
    "All men are bad and in their badness reign."

1 *esteem'd* considered **2** *When not...being* when not to be vile receives the reproach of being vile **3** *so* i.e., vile **4** *Not...seeing* i.e., not in our own mind, but in the view of others **5** *adulterate* adulterous **6** *Give salutation to* take notice of; *sportive blood* wantonness **7** *frailer spies* onlookers with greater frailties **8** *in their wills* willfully; *think good* look at innocently **9** *level* take aim **10** *abuses* wrongs **11** *bevel* crooked **12** *rank* foul, lustful

Someone's said something nasty and W. doesn't like it at all. He's mad, offended, defensive. He's been accused of something he says he didn't do. This sounds like a schoolyard argument. Oh, he has *frailties*, but *others' false adulterate eyes* have said something about him that he didn't have the *pleasure* of doing. He would rather have been *vile* enough to have done that than to be *reproached* for being vile and not even have done whatever it was. It's those *frailer spies* than he who look at him and *count bad what he thinks good.* They're just pots calling a kettle black! When they take aim at his faults, *they reckon up their own.* Whatever they say bounces off him and sticks to them. If you believe he's bad because of what they say, then everyone is bad.

    I'm intrigued. What could this be? W. has already admitted

he's been *sportive*, he's committed *wretched errors* under the influence of a *madding fever* (Sonnet 119). He's *hoisted sail to all the winds* (Sonnet 117). We can only imagine that these were hyperbole, just like his previous praises of Y.M. His attentions were spent where they shouldn't have been. But that's not the same as saying he was an adulterer! Could it even be Y.M. is the accuser? Did he take W. seriously and *on surmise, accumulate?* (Sonnet 117) If so, he most likely couched the accusation in general terms: "I've heard that…" W. responds in kind, with a general reproach that, nevertheless, includes Y.M. He becomes a *frailer spy*, he *reckons up his own abuses*, his thoughts are *rank*. And if W. is bad so, too, is Y.M. Most important is the strong statement of individuality in line 9: *I am that I am*. So very different from earlier statements (Sonnet 22: *all the beauty that doth cover thee, / Is but the seemly raiment of my heart.*) This line is so audacious, reminiscent as it is of Exodus 3:14.* The relationship continues to deteriorate.

---

* "And God said unto Moses, I AM THAT I AM: and he said, Thus shalt thou say unto the children of Israel, I AM hath sent me unto you." (King James Bible) Even recognizing that is just the equivalent in Elizabethan English of "I am what I am," the echo seems hard to ignore.

122

Thy gift, thy tables, are within my brain
Full character'd with lasting memory,
Which shall above that idle rank remain
Beyond all date even to eternity.
Or at the least, so long as brain and heart
Have faculty by nature to subsist,
Till each to raz'd oblivion yield his part
Of thee, thy record never can be miss'd:
That poor retention could not so much hold,
Nor need I tallies thy dear love to score,
Therefore to give them from me was I bold,
To trust those tables that receive thee more.
    To keep an adjunct to remember thee,
    Were to import forgetfulness in me.

1 *tables* writing tablet **2** *Full character'd* written in full **3** *that idle rank* that useless series of leaves (of the tablet) **6** *faculty…subsist* natural power to survive **7** *raz'd oblivion* oblivion that razes all; *his* its **9** *retention* retainer (the writing tablet) **10** *tallies* that on which scores are kept **12** *those…more* i.e., my memory **13** *adjunct* aid **14** *import* imply

Now he's done it. Y.M. has given W. a gift of a writing tablet. And what's he done? He's given it away! Let's suppose he already had his own favorite writing tablet and didn't want a new one. Or maybe it was ugly as sin. But *everyone* knows you *have to* keep gifts from close friends and relatives so you can trot them out when they ask you about them. This is Relationships 101! And he doesn't just discard it, he gives it away! Ouch. And what a cheesy excuse: "I don't need to write anything down to remember you, I could never forget your love." He even contradicts his own argument. His memory can last only as long as he lives. If he had kept the writing tablet, what he wrote in it could have lasted forever (you know, *like his verses*). And what about the book W. gave to Y.M. (Sonnet 77)? Did that mean as little to W. as this discarded gift from Y.M.?

What's this about? Was the gift given a long time ago and W. thought Y.M. might not even remember about it? Or did he give it away a long time ago and Y.M. just found out about it? Or has he just given it away in a fit of pique over their recent disagreement? Is the excuse so cheesy because he doesn't really mean it? Maybe he doesn't care what Y.M. thinks any more. How bad has the relationship gotten?

123

No! Time, thou shalt not boast that I do change,
Thy pyramids built up with newer might
To me are nothing novel, nothing strange,
They are but dressings of a former sight.
Our dates are brief, and therefore we admire
What thou dost foist upon us that is old,
And rather make them born to our desire,
Than think that we before have heard them told.
Thy registers and thee I both defy,
Not wond'ring at the present, nor the past,
For thy records, and what we see doth lie,
Made more or less by thy continual haste.
   This I do vow and this shall ever be,
   I will be true despite thy scythe and thee.

4 *dressings* i.e., superficially changed versions **5** *dates* life spans **7** *make them born to our desire* think them the novelties we wish to see **8** *told* reckoned **9** *Thy registers* your (Time's) records **11** *thy records, and what we see* i.e., both past and present; *lie* misrepresent

Sonnet 123 can be confusing until you recognize that what it has to say is stated in the first and last lines. Everything in between is an elaboration of W.'s denial that he could ever be subject to the changes brought by time. The implication is that Y.M. has accused him of just that. Can we blame him? After giving away his personal gift and offering a flimsy excuse for doing so, he might very well be entitled to say, "You've changed. You're not the same person I used to know. You never would have done or said these things before. Do you even love me anymore?" The word *love* is conspicuously absent from Sonnet 123. W., instead, promises to be forever *true*. In a different context, the word *desire* makes an appearance in line 7. It sounds cold and distant, like the pyramids of line 2, a reminder of what's missing from the relationship now, 122 sonnets after we first heard of it. (The last time *desire* was used was in Sonnet 57—there it had the meaning of loving desire).

The intervening lines between the first and last have the same effect as those in Sonnet 107. They give a vague sense of importance. We feel like they should be explaining something, building an argument that will prove the truth of W.'s point. They sound logical, cogent, proverbial. But the diction is difficult and, once deciphered, the meaning is hard to piece together into a coherent whole. The first quatrain says that the pyramids are nothing new—they're just re-embodiments of older wonders. This is the same Ovidian argument we heard in Sonnet 59 (*If there be nothing new, but that which is, / Hath been before*). The second quatrain says that because our days are brief (axiomatic) we (presumably, the unenlightened public) admire things that are old (*not* axiomatic, but plausible) and prefer to think them *born to our desire*. This is a difficult phrase. The context suggests it means "first appreciated by us." This is contrasted with rather than *think that we before have heard them told*, which seems to mean "instead of thinking they were admired by others before" (the rationale for this escapes me). These three ideas, our days are short, we admire old things, and we prefer to think we are the first to admire them, are presented as logically connected, but the connection is at best tenuous, if not absent. Moving on to the third quatrain, we expect a connection to what's gone before, but the only thing in common is Time. W. defies both Time and his records, presumably meaning the past and the future, although he confusingly refers to the past and present.

So between the first line and the last we have a confusing jumble of statements about time, the past, the present and the future. In line 12, W. mentions time's *haste*. An interesting contrast to Sonnet 77 in which time moved with *thievish progress to eternity*. He is now feeling the press of time. Is the relationship pressing on him as well?

124

If my dear love were but the child of state,
It might for fortune's bastard be unfather'd,
As subject to times love, or to times hate,
Weeds among weeds, or flowers with flowers gather'd.
No it was builded far from accident,
It suffers not in smiling pomp, nor falls
Under the blow of thrallèd discontent,
Whereto th' inviting time our fashion calls;
It fears not policy that *Heretic*,
Which works on leases of short numb'red hours,
But all alone stands hugely politic,
That it nor grows with heat, nor drowns with showers.
    To this I witness call the fools of time,
      Which die for goodness, who have liv'd for crime.

1 *If my…child of state* If my love was merely born of political advantage **2** *for…unfathered* be branded as the fatherless son of Fortune **4** *Weeds…gather'd* as we call something a weed or a flower depending on circumstances **5** *accident* chance occurrence **6** *suffers not in* is not affected by **7** *thrallèd discontent* the enslavement of discontent **8** *Whereto…calls* to which the changing times bring us **9** *policy that Heretic* self-interest, which has no true faith **11** *hugely politic* infinitely prudent **12** *That it nor* so that it neither **13** *witness call* call as witness; *fools of time* those who foolishly trust time **14** *Which…crime* who suffer if they are righteous, and flourish if they do wrong

    Sonnet 124 seems to repeat the statement of the previous sonnet that W.'s love will never change. The language is even harder to work out (as can be seen by the extensive glosses). Looking closer, this sounds to me like a response to Y.M. I hear him saying, after Sonnet 123, "You're not constant, you're a fairweather friend. You abandon me whenever you like and you come running back when it suits your needs." Sonnet 124 is his indignant denial. It comes in the form of detailing what his love *would be* if he were a fair-weather friend and says it isn't. And what proof does he offer for this? That the good suffer and the bad flourish—they are not subject to Time as we would expect, and neither is his love. In very complicated language. As if we might not notice how weak the argument is if we have to struggle to understand every line.

What will Y.M. think of this latest response? Will he finally think W. is sincere? Will he welcome him to his *most, most loving breast*? How is W. holding up? Can he continue to counter Y.M.'s doubts?

125

Were't aught to me I bore the canopy,
With my extern the outward honoring,
Or laid great bases for eternity,
Which proves more short than waste or ruining?
Have I not seen dwellers on form and favor
Lose all, or more by paying too much rent
For compound sweet; Forgoing simple savor,
Pitiful thrivers in their gazing spent.
No, let me be obsequious in thy heart,
And take thou my oblation, poor but free,
Which is not mix'd with seconds, knows no art,
But mutual render only me for thee.
  Hence, thou suborn'd *Informer*, a true soul
  When most impeach'd, stands least in thy control.

1 *Were't aught* would it be anything; *canopy* cloth covering carried over a dignitary in a procession **2** *With…honoring* outwardly honoring the external **3** *bases* foundations (of monuments) **5** *dwellers on* admirers of **6** *compound sweet* sweet concoction; *simple savor* wholesome flavor **8** *Pitiful thrivers* those who thrive pitifully because their gains are empty; *in their gazing spent* exhausted while gazing **9** *obsequious* dutiful **10** *oblation* offering **11** *seconds* inferior matter; *art* artifice **12** *mutual render* fair exchange **13** *suborn'd Informer* false witness **14** *impeach'd* accused

Another mysterious sonnet, with complicated language,

difficult to navigate. The thoughts are condensed, the imagery rich, the metaphors paradoxical. Let's look at the first quatrain. It asks the rhetorical question, "Would I honor only the external? Would I lay foundations for monuments to your beauty, which last for eternity, an eternity which is shorter than the time it takes to waste or ruin them?" The point, I guess, is what seems eternal isn't, and that beauty is not what's important. That's a paradox (eternity that's not eternal) and a contradiction of much of what's been said before.

Let's move on to the second quatrain. "Haven't I seen those who admire only form (beauty, once again) for the sake of favor, lose everything because they've paid attention to nothing else? Like someone who chooses to pay too much rent for a house that looks pretty instead of paying less for a simple one that has good inner qualities." The idea here is that flatterers are worthless fools. And W. is not one of those. That's the point of the third quatrain. He will be *poor but free* (free of *seconds*, without artifice). He is not looking for favors, but merely *mutual render, me for thee*. The couplet says, "I am untouched by anyone who would falsely say otherwise."

I don't know about you, but with all these complicated sonnets, I'm exhausted! I'm ready for W. to come out and say what he means in plain language. But the story of *The Sonnets* is vague enough that I'm not sure what I want him to say. Is it, "Don't you understand that I've loved you since we first met? Yes, I have strayed, and so have you. But that has not changed our mutual love. We are soulmates. We will always be. Is that so hard for you to understand?" Or is it, "We love each other, we always will. I know I haven't always paid as much attention to you as you would like, and you haven't always behaved as I would like. But that doesn't change the love we have for each other and always will. Don't you understand that?" Not this time. Instead, we have an intricate message that says, "I'm not one of those who just showers you with obsequious compliments of your beauty to gain some pitiful favor from you. No, my praises come from my heart, they are pure, unmixed with artifice." (There's a lot of denying going on—this is the third sonnet in a row with a line that starts with *no.*) Does the couplet suggest that W. is responding to an accusation reported to Y.M. by someone else? Does *surmise accumulate*? Does Y.M. trust everyone except W., or does he insist on testing W.'s integrity every time his suspicion is aroused? I imagine W. getting tired of this game. *I'm* getting tired of it. These complicated arguments hardly seem worth it. Y.M. hardly seems worth it. The *relationship* doesn't seem worth it. Maybe that's the point.

126

O thou my lovely Boy who in thy power,
Dost hold time's fickle glass, his sickle, hour:
Who hast by waning grown, and therein show'st,
Thy lover's withering, as thy sweet self grow'st.
If Nature (sovereign mistress over wrack)
As thou goest onwards still will pluck thee back,
She keeps thee to this purpose, that her skill
May time disgrace, and wretched minute kill.
Yet fear her, O thou minion of her pleasure,
She may detain, but not still keep her treasure!
Her *Audit* (though delay'd) answer'd must be,
And her *Quietus* is to render thee.

2 *glass* mirror; *his sickle, hour* i.e., that with which he kills, the hour **3** *by waning grown* become more beautiful by growing older **5** *wrack* ruin **6, 10** *still* always **9** *minion* darling (favorite) **11** *Audit* final account; *answer'd* paid **12** *Quietus* final settlement; *render* surrender

In contrast with the preceding three sonnets, Sonnet 126 is brilliantly clear, its imagery dense. It's a warning to Y.M. (ominously referred to as *my lovely Boy*). "Nature has made you grow more beautiful as you age, which makes me appear to be *withering* all the more in comparison," W. admits. But he asks him to consider that Nature does this to show her power over Time, and his *fickle sickle*, which is only temporary. In the end, she will have to *render* him up and her *Audit* (and his) will have to be answered (she has the power to *kill minute*, to stop time, but not forever.) There's nothing pleasant or hopeful about this sonnet. Y.M. is a *minion* at the beck and call of Nature. He must *fear* her and her *Quietus*. Y.M. is left alone with his melancholy thoughts. (Whether this was written before or after Hamlet's famous soliloquy, I can't help but think of the only other use of the word *quietus* by Shakespeare [*Hamlet* 3.1.70-76]: "For who would bear the whips and scorns of time, /...When he himself might his quietus make / With a bare bodkin?")

We must imagine what could have prompted this warning. There have been so many ups and downs between these two. Especially since the Rival Poet, W. and Y.M. have had an on-again, off-again relationship. W. has been mostly on the defensive, constantly having to justify himself. Meanwhile, Y.M.'s questionable behavior has faded further into the past. I imagine Y.M. feeling more and more self-satisfied, surrounded by a circle of admirers—younger, handsomer, shinier than W. He feels empowered and tells W. he's growing old, physically and emotionally. He's grown tired of him. He's outlived his usefulness. This is goodbye. W. is done arguing. He, too, is now tired of it all. No more excuses. Instead, he delivers a warning. I'll take my goodbye, but you'll get yours.

127

In the old age black was not counted fair,
Or if it were it bore not beauty's name,
But now is black beauty's successive heir,
And Beauty slander'd with a bastard shame.
For since each hand hath put on Nature's power,
Fairing the foul with Art's false borrow'd face,
Sweet beauty hath no name no holy bower,
But is profan'd, if not lives in disgrace.
Therefore my Mistress' eyes are Raven black,
Her eyes so suited, and they mourners seem,
At such who not born fair no beauty lack,
Sland'ring Creation with a false esteem.
    Yet so they mourn becoming of their woe,
    That every tongue says beauty should look so.

1 *old* former; *black* dark; *fair* beautiful **3** *successive heir* heir by succession **4** *with a bastard shame* a shame such as bastards endure **6** *Fairing* making beautiful; *Art's...face* i.e., cosmetics **7** *holy bower* i.e., shrine **8** *But...disgrace* but is either profaned or disgraced (by imitators) **11** *At such* to those **11-12** *who...esteem* who, not born beautiful, appear so artificially, misrepresenting Nature, and gaining false esteem **13** *so they mourn* they mourn so; *becoming of* gracing

This sonnet is based on the notion that light hair and complexion were considered the height of beauty. It introduces us to a new character, commonly referred to as the Dark Lady, who makes her appearance in line 9. Y.M. is nowhere to be found. Instead, we have a sonnet to a mistress. Sonnet 127 sounds like a new beginning, as much of a first sonnet as Sonnet 1. But we have already read 126 sonnets. And we can't help wondering if this Dark Lady is the same person we heard about in the liaison sonnets (33-35 and 40-42). We can't tell at this point. We didn't learn anything about her back then, even whether she was a mistress (we just guessed that). Now we only know this woman is *dark*. That seems fitting, but not enough to go on. We also don't know where Sonnet 127 fits in W.'s life. Are we hearing about his relationship with his mistress *before* he meets Y.M.? Or does this series begin at the same time as Sonnet 1? This light-hearted sonnet doesn't seem appropriate during the whole liaison disaster. Could this be an epilogue? Could W. be done with Y.M. and Y.M. be done with his mistress? Is it all past? Of course, we can't tell. This is a sonnet sequence, after all. We're not supposed to understand too much.

The form of Sonnet 127 is an explanation. Why would W. have a *dark* mistress? Why not a conventional *fair* mistress. As usual, he has an explanation. Traditional beauty has been disgraced by cosmetics (we heard this same favorite Elizabethan topic—the railing against the use of cosmetics to create the false appearance of beauty—in Sonnet 68). The Dark Lady's *raven black* eyes mourn the *slander* and their beauty in so doing is enough to convince everyone that black should now be considered the reigning beauty of the day—the heir in succession to the fair. This sets the tone for our new series.

The sense of Sonnet 127 is obvious even if the language is twisted in places. Shakespeare minces words when he plays with *fair* and *beauty*. He usually uses them to mean the same thing, but in lines 1 and 2, he makes a distinction. We understand *fair*, in line 1 to mean "good looking," not as elevated a rank as the *beauty* of line 2. That doesn't keep him from using it to mean "beautiful" in line 11 or, in the verb form, to mean "beautifying" in line 6. There are the typical Shakespearean condensed adjectives: *successive heir* for "heir of succession," and *bastard shame* for "shame of bastards." We understand the unusual verb form "fairing" in the condensed phrase *fairing the foul*: "making beautiful what is ugly." This is easier than lines 7 and 8, which are more condensed—although the thought is plain enough, I find I have to pause to work the missing grammar out in my head. The rest flows more easily, with just a few word transpositions that are not too difficult to work out.

This is one of those sonnets whose first and last lines tell it all. In between, there's a story condensed into 12 lines that makes it fun to get from one to the other. I hear a wry slyness that leaves me smiling.

This sonnet is not addressed to anyone in particular. Do we imagine the Dark Lady reading it? If so, how do we imagine her reacting to it? Does she smile wryly? Does she care what others think of her?

128

How oft when thou, my music, music play'st,
Upon that blessèd wood whose motion sounds
With thy sweet fingers when thou gently sway'st,
The wiry concord that mine ear confounds,
Do I envy those Jacks that nimble leap,
To kiss the tender inward of thy hand,
Whilst my poor lips which should that harvest reap,
At the wood's boldness by thee blushing stand.
To be so tickled they would change their state
And situation with those dancing chips,
O'er whom thy fingers walk with gentle gait,
Making dead wood more blest than living lips.
    Since saucy jacks so happy are in this,
    Give them thy fingers, me thy lips to kiss.

2 *wood* keys of the virginal 3 *sway'st* move 4 *wiry concord* harmony of strings; *confounds* drinks up 5 *Jacks* strictly speaking, the levers, but referring here to the keys 9 *state* position 13 *saucy jacks* the keys (with pun on ill-bred fellows)

In the last line of this second sonnet of the Dark Lady series we find something that was absent from the 126 sonnets about the loving relationship between W. and Y.M.—a kiss. This tells us right away how different this series is going to be and reminds us that there's more than one kind of love. This one has an eroticism that the relationship that occupied our attention for 126 sonnets did not. (I don't want to belabor this point, nor do I want to argue with those who insist that the relationship between W. and Y.M. must have a homosexual component. I just want to point out that it's different. There's no mention of kissing in the Y.M. sonnets.) There's a charm and playfulness to Sonnet

128 that we haven't heard in a long time. It sounds so innocent.

The diction in Sonnet 128 is playfully difficult. To follow it, you have to realize that the first eight lines are one long sentence with an elaborate series of parenthetical thoughts. It also helps to know that the popular keyboard instrument in sixteenth and seventeenth century England was the virginal, similar to a small piano of today, whose keys were made usually of wood (not ivory). Let's untangle the sentence making up the first two quatrains. The simple phrase would be: "How oft when thou playest music do I envy those jacks that nimbl(y) leap to kiss thy hand, whilst my poor, blushing, lips stand by thee." To make this last eight lines, seven modifying phrases are added: 1. *my music* (modifying *thou*; line 1) 2. *Upon that blessed wood* (modifying *playst*; line 1) 3. *whose motion sounds the wiry concord* (modifying *wood*; line 2) 4. *that mine ear confounds* (modifying *concord*; line 4) 5. *With thy sweet fingers* (modifying *sounds*; line 2) 6. *when thou gently swayst* (also modifying *sounds*; line 2) 7. *which should that harvest reap* (modifying *lips*; line 7). Put those modifiers in and reorder some words and there you have the first two quatrains. Now that's a sentence!

Not content with the elaborate sentence, the third quatrain literally tickles us with a setup for the joke in the couplet. Let those saucy *jacks* have your fingers, W. declares, and give me your lips to kiss!* That's as much fun as we've had in a long time. What about the Dark Lady? Is she having fun, too?

---

* Technically, the jacks are levers connected to the backs of the keys that pluck the strings. But anyone who is concerned about technicalities when a little poetic license allows for the delicious pun on *saucy jacks* is just too dry for me.

129

Th' expense of Spirit in a waste of shame
Is lust in action, and till action, lust
Is perjur'd, murd'rous, bloody full of blame,
Savage, extreme, rude, cruel, not to trust,
Enjoy'd no sooner but despisèd straight,
Past reason hunted, and no sooner had
Past reason hated as a swallowed bait,
On purpose laid to make the taker mad.
Mad In pursuit and in possession so,
Had, having, and in quest to have, extreme,
A bliss in proof and prov'd a very woe,
Before a joy propos'd behind a dream.
　　All this the world well knows yet none knows well,
　　To shun the heav'n that leads men to this hell.

1 *waste of shame* shameful waste **4** *rude* uncivil, brutal; *not to trust* not to be trusted **10** *quest* pursuit **11** *in proof* when being experienced; *prov'd* tried, having been experienced

We knew this series was going to be different. But this is very different. The emotional pace is much faster—it took 126 sonnets for us to ride the emotional roller coaster of the first series. Here with just three sonnets, we have travelled just as far. But the territory is not the same. We had a group of sonnets in the first series reminiscent of Ovid's *Metamorphoses*. This sonnet reminds me of Ovid's *Amores*, deeply erotic, misogynistic and disturbing (see Appendix for Christopher Marlowe's English translation of Book 1).* It's written in a sonnet form, with 14

---

* Although misogyny in the Dark Lady sonnets has been discussed, editors usually focus instead on how they differ from the love sonnets to a mistress typified by Petrarch's and imitated by most Elizabethan sonneteers. Kathryn Schwarz deals with misogyny in extraordinary detail (Schwarz, "Will in Overplus"). M. L. Stapleton shows the correspondence of the Dark Lady sonnets to Christopher Marlowe's translation of *Amores* (Stapleton, *Harmful Eloquence*, Chapter 6, 133-57.) Horace Gregory gives a modern translation of selected poems from the *Amores* that is particularly erotic and emotionally

lines of iambic pentameter, 12 lines in alternate rhymes and ending in a rhyming couplet. We can hear that form as we read it, but it doesn't sound close to any other sonnet we've read. It explodes from the very first line. Normally, a series of lists, like lines 3 and 4 would sound boring. Not in this sonnet! We tear through them. We can hardly take a breath from the beginning of the poem to the end. I feel as wasted as the shame the sonnet describes when I read this poem.

Sonnet 129 reads as a soliloquy. The diction is direct, brutal. There's hardly any barrier between the words and the meaning. A couple of direct metaphors: hunting, pursuit, swallowed bait; heaven, hell. A play on joy/dream. A pun on proof and prove. Mostly, it's a stream of invective: *perjur'd, murd'rous, bloody, blame, savage, extreme, rude, cruel, not to trust, despised, past reason, hated, mad, woe.* Not pulling any punches!

How did we get from a charming kiss next to a virginal to a tirade about lust? We don't know anything about this relationship—or about any other relationships W. might have (we don't know if he's met Y.M. yet). Is he married? Was he just flirting with the Dark Lady and things got further out of hand than he planned? Or was he planning to have sex from the start but feels guilty about having an affair with a mistress, married or not? Or is she married? We can't tell. We just know that he feels really bad about what's going on. This is not a happy relationship for him. What is it like for the Dark Lady, I wonder?

---

charged (Gregory, *Love Poems of Ovid,* 27-95). Shakespeare's familiarity with *Amores* is evident from his first publication, *Venus and Adonis,* which opens with a quotation, in Latin, from Elegy XV of Book I of that work.

130

My Mistress' eyes are nothing like the Sun,
Coral is far more red, than her lips red,
If snow be white, why then her breasts are dun,
If hairs be wires, black wires grow on her head.
I have seen Roses damask'd, red and white,
But no such Roses see I in her cheeks,
And in some perfumes is there more delight,
Than in the breath that from my Mistress reeks.
I love to hear her speak, yet well I know,
That Music hath a far more pleasing sound;
I grant I never saw a goddess go,
My Mistress when she walks treads on the ground.
    And yet by heav'n I think my love as rare,
    As any she belied with false compare.

3 *dun* dull, dingy brown 5 *damask'd* mingled red and white 8 *reeks* is emitted 11 *go* walk 14 *she* woman; *compare* comparison

W. has gotten past his self-disgust. He's calmed down enough to make a joke. Sonnet 130 is a parody of English sonneteers. It makes fun of the comparisons they make of their beloveds, claiming none of them for the Dark Lady. The couplet makes the point: W. counts the Dark Lady as beautiful as any of those ridiculously compared to what they could never be. (Does W. include his sonnets about Y.M. in the ridicule? It's hard not to think especially of the damasked rose of Sonnet 99.) This is similar to the argument of Sonnet 21 (*So is it not with me as with that Muse*). What's different is the point of view. In Sonnet 130 W. says, *I **think** my love as rare / As any she* whereas in Sonnet 21 he says, *believe me, my love **is** as fair / As any mother's child.* In the one, he expresses his personal opinion, in the other he insists on a fact that all must agree to.

To whom is this sonnet addressed? It doesn't read as a reply to the Dark Lady—it's about her but not *to* her. There's nothing to suggest that another character has been introduced yet, someone who might have asked about the Dark Lady. It sounds more like another soliloquy. Like W. is justifying himself, as in Sonnet 127. This sonnet doesn't sound much different to me.

Sonnet 130 returns to the playful spirit of Sonnet 128. We are teased through 12 lines of what sounds like disparagement of the Dark Lady. Her eyes don't shine like the sun, her lips aren't red, her breasts aren't snow white, her hair is black (instead of golden). The reference to wires, by the way, is a slap at the sonneteering convention of describing their beloveds as having hair like gold wires.* There are no roses in her cheeks and her breath doesn't smell like perfume (*reek* did not always have the negative connotation in Elizabethan English it does now). Her voice doesn't sound like music and she walks on the ground like a mortal, not some goddess who walks on air. After all this, comes the reversing couplet. She's as rare as any of those others *belied with false compare.*

Sonnet 130 is the counterpart in the Dark Lady series to Sonnet 21 in the sonnets to Y.M. In Sonnet 21, W. similarly refused to make comparisons that other poets do (to *seas rich gems* and *all things rare*). That sonnet ended with the declaration that *I will not praise that purpose not to sell.* The striking difference in Sonnet 130 is the tone. In Sonnet 21, it's clear from the start that W. is mocking other poets. In Sonnet 130, W. teasingly mocks the Dark Lady for 12 lines before the reversing couplet turns the mockery against other poets. And instead of calling the poets hucksters, as he did in Sonnet 21, he now calls them liars.

There's something that seems unfriendly about this sonnet that sends a chill down my spine. I always wonder when I read it how the Dark Lady would react to it.

---

* See Tucker, *Sonnets,* 211.

227

131

Thou art as tyrannous, so as thou art,
As those whose beauties proudly make them cruel;
For well thou know'st to my dear doting heart
Thou art the fairest and most precious Jewel.
Yet in good faith some say that thee behold,
Thy face hath not the power to make love groan;
To say they err, I dare not be so bold,
Although I swear it to my self alone.
And to be sure that is not false I swear:
A thousand groans but thinking on thy face,
One on another's neck do witness bear
Thy black is fairest in my judgment's place.
    In nothing art thou black save in thy deeds,
    And thence this slander as I think proceeds.

1 *so as thou art* even as you are **3** *dear* fond **9** *to be sure* i.e., for proof **10** *but thinking on* when I but think of **12** *in my judgment's place* where my judgment is **13** *black* not fair, foul

The emotions alternate swiftly. Contradictions pile up. The Dark Lady was said to be so beautiful in Sonnet 127 that, even though she is black instead of fair, all should think her so. In Sonnet 131, W. admits that others say she's not beautiful. More importantly, he resorts to the age-old complaint of sonneteers—he calls his mistress cruel. This is not your usual sonnet complaint, though. Most sonnet mistresses are cruel because they are chaste. They may be *tyrannous* in their chastity. They may cause the sonneteer to *groan*. They may be *proud*. But their deeds are not *black*. That one phrase, *In nothing art thou black save in thy deeds*, has a terrible sound to it. It has the same chilling tone as Sonnet 129 did. There's no way to interpret it as a compliment. But what are those *black deeds*? This seems a harsh description for refusing his advances (and Sonnet 129 sounded more like *lust in action* than *a joy propos'd*). Is W. complaining about being led *to this hell*? Or has he reason to suspect the Dark Lady guilty of some other offense?

The diction is more complex in Sonnet 131, the wordplay more evident. Repetition is prominent. *Thou art as* is reversed in the first line to *as thou art*, echoed in *As those whose*, returned at the end of the quatrain to *Thou art*, and reversed again in the final couplet to *art thou*. Also repeated are *groan(s), I swear,* and *black.* The repetition of *black* is heightened by the antithesis in line 12: *Thy black is fairest.* The rapidity with which this wordplay is presented is mirrored by the imagery of line 11's description of W.'s groans: *One on another's neck do witness bear.* The vicious pun on *black/foul* is saved for the couplet.

For the first time in this series, the sonnet is addressed to the Dark Lady. Everything about the sonnet is negative. It reads like a negative of a sonnet to Y.M. To Y.M. he might have said, "Nobody says enough good things about you. Only I truly love you and think you the most precious." Instead, to the Dark Lady he says, "Everybody says foul things about you. Only I disagree and think you the most precious." And the final blow is in the couplet: "The only truly foul thing about you is your deeds."

The blackness of the tyrannous, cruel, and groan-inducing mistress is emphasized twice toward the end of Sonnet 131. The antithesis suggests the problem. Sonnet 130 ended in lies and falseness. Sonnet 131 ends in *slander*. But who is doing the slandering? Echoes of Ovid's misogynistic strains from *Amores* are strong.

132

Thine eyes I love, and they as pitying me,
Knowing thy heart torment me with disdain,
Have put on black, and loving mourners be,
Looking with pretty ruth upon my pain.
And truly not the morning Sun of Heaven
Better becomes the gray cheeks of the East,
Nor that full Star that ushers in the Even
Doth half the glory to the sober West
As those two mourning eyes become thy face.
O let it then as well beseem thy heart
To mourn for me since mourning doth thee grace,
And suit thy pity like in every part.
    Then will I swear beauty her self is black,
    And all they foul that thy complexion lack.

2 *torment* to torment **4** *ruth* pity **7** *Even* evening **10** *beseem* become **12** *suit thy pity like in every part* i.e., dress your heart as well as your eyes alike in pity

Sonnet 132 is another bizarre twist on the sonnet convention. The typical words of complaint are there: *pity, torment, disdain, mourning, pain.* The first twelve lines could be written by any sonneteer to his reluctant beloved. But this is not addressed to a typical sonnet beloved, but to the Dark Lady. The difference is made obvious by the anomalous couplet. Beauty is *black* and anyone who is not is *foul.*

The diction of Sonnet 132 is complicated. There are multiple parenthetical thoughts in the first quatrain, but instead of digressing from the main idea, they amplify it. It makes it more difficult to follow the train of thought, but the richness grows with each line. "I love thine eyes, and they...have put on black...looking with pretty ruth upon my pain." Each parenthetical thought is an explanation. Why have thine eyes put on black? Because they pity me. Why do they pity me? Because they know thy heart torments me with disdain.* Why do they put on black when they pity me? Because they are then mourners. This could not be so elegantly stated in prose.

Sonnet 132 then breaks all conventional rules, dividing the remainder of the poem into a structure of five lines, three lines and the two-line couplet. The rhymes don't go with the sense of the lines, but they maintain a coherence within the sonnet. The five lines following the first quatrain combine two images about the Dark Lady. These are standard sonnet comparisons with non-standard variations. The images are of the dawn and the evening star. But instead of a rosy dawn, we find the Sun complementing the *gray cheeks of the East.* And instead of a bright star shining in the night, we are given a *full* star in the *sober West.* Both of these are said to pale in comparison to the way *those two mourning eyes become thy face.* The tone of these lines is somber. This isn't unusual for conventional sonnets. The sonneteer is heartbroken, the beloved chaste, cold, unmoved. The next three lines continue in the same vein, asking the Dark Lady to have her heart follow the same path as her eyes. This is typical sonneteer's ploy—to ask for pity is to ask for love to be requited. The couplet, however, takes the undercurrent of what is different in this sonnet and shoves it right in our faces. We hadn't seen the word "black," but *gray* and *somber* were reminders that it was simmering beneath the surface. And there it is—love me and I will declare beauty black and everyone who is not black *foul.* This is a disturbing way of saying, "The only thing I care about is you—I don't care about the rest of the world."

The couplet continues to play on the ambivalence of the meaning of the word *black* that's been running through the Dark Lady series (and was most prominent in Sonnet 131). We see the same ambivalence in the relationship W. has with the Dark Lady. Is she dark and beautiful or black and foul? We still don't know what the relationship means to her. What does she think when

---

* Elizabethans (especially poets) were loose about grammar. If we understand *torment* to be the infinitive, *to torment,* the sense is equivalent to *torments.* See Abbott, *A Shakespearean Grammar,* 249.

she reads this sonnet? Is she indifferent? Is she haughty? Is she moved?

133

Beshrew that heart that makes my heart to groan
For that deep wound it gives my friend and me;
Is't not enough to torture me alone,
But slave to slavery my sweet'st friend must be?
Me from my self thy cruel eye hath taken,
And my next self thou harder hast engrossed.
Of him, my self, and thee I am forsaken,
A torment thrice three-fold thus to be crossed.
Prison my heart in thy steel bosom's ward,
But then my friend's heart let my poor heart bale,
Whoe'er keeps me, let my heart be his guard,
Thou canst not then use rigor in my Jail.
    And yet thou wilt, for I being pent in thee,
    Perforce am thine and all that is in me.

(Double sonnet to be read with Sonnet 134.)

1 *Beshrew* woe to **2** *For* because of **4** *slave to slavery* i.e., also a slave **6** *my...engrossed* i.e., you have placed my friend under even greater bondage **8** *crossed* thwarted **9** *ward* dungeon **10** *bale* confiné **11** *keeps* guards; *his guard* my friend's guardhouse **12** *rigor* harshness **13** *pent* confined

134

So now I have confess'd that he is thine,
And I my self am mortgag'd to thy will,
My self I'll forfeit, so that other mine,
Thou wilt restore to be my comfort still.
But thou wilt not, nor he will not be free,
For thou art covetous, and he is kind,
He learn'd but surety-like to write for me,
Under that bond that him as fast doth bind.
The statute of thy beauty thou wilt take,

Thou usurer that put'st forth all to use,
And sue a friend, came debtor for my sake.
So him I lose through my unkind abuse,
 Him have I lost, thou hast both him and me,
 He pays the whole, and yet I am not free.

3 *other mine* my alter ego **4** *still* always **6** *kind* gracious **7-8** *He...bind* he came to you because of me, as he would if he were securing a loan, and was bound under the same terms **9** *take* invoke **10** *use* profit **11** *came* who became **12** *my unkind abuse* this unkind ill-treatment of me

Another piece of the puzzle is revealed. Until now, we couldn't tell whether the Dark Lady was the same person as the mistress who was involved in the liaison with Y.M. We expected as much, but now we know she was. We also know more about the chronology. Sonnet 127 started before the liaison. Sonnets 133 and 134 are contemporaneous with the liaison sonnets of the Young Man series (33-36 and 40-42). The style of the sonnets is similar to ones we've seen in the earlier series: a sonnet with an argument that changes with the couplet and, in the case of a double sonnet like this, with the succeeding sonnet.

Sonnet 133 starts with a slavery metaphor. W. complains that it's unfair that not only should he be enslaved by the Dark Lady but that she should also enslave his friend. He then moves to a prison metaphor and asks for a favor: "take my heart as a prisoner but let me hold my friend's heart as my prisoner." He hopes that then she won't be able to be severe with him since Y.M. will be in his jail, not hers. On reflection, in the couplet, he recognizes his error: he is her prisoner, therefore he is hers and all that he has, including Y.M., belongs to her.

The tone of Sonnet 133 is lighter than we might expect from its content. The couplet, in another context, could be a joke. There are plenty of negative words: *groan, wound, torture, slave, cruel, cross, prison, rigor.* But these are conventional sonnet words. Noticeably absent are *black, foul, dark.* Those were also missing from Sonnet 129, but that sonnet sounded angry, this one does not. It's hard to define tone sometimes. Is it the word *beshrew* that sounds not quite so serious? Or is it the alliteration of *slave to slavery*? Or perhaps it's *thrice threefold* that doesn't sound nasty. Anyway, it has a very different feel from Sonnet 129.

The couplet of Sonnet 133 leads directly to the beginning of Sonnet 134. W. has concluded that Y.M. and he both belong entirely to the Dark Lady. Then he has another idea. Using a real estate metaphor, he declares he is *mortgag'd to her will* so he suggests that he will *forfeit* himself. This doesn't survive past the first quatrain. She is too *covetous* and he is too *kind*. We heard this argument directed to Y.M.—he was *fair, kind and true*. W. now embarks on a contorted argument, staying with the real estate metaphor, to explain how Y.M., in consorting with his mistress was doing him a kindness. (This has to be a good one, right?) He says that the only reason he entangled himself with the Dark Lady was on account of W. (as if he were securing a loan for him). She insisted on making good on the loan, enforcing the *statue* (law) of her beauty (she being the sort who always insists on making her profit), and he (being *fair, kind and true*) was forced to oblige. He ends the two sonnets submissively, putting all the blame on the Dark Lady: I have lost him through your unkind abuse of me, Y.M. pays the entire sum (on my behalf), and I am still enslaved. That's the metaphor.

What's really gone on? W. has sent Y.M. to see the Dark Lady for some reason (as a go-between?). Things didn't go as planned. Y.M. was seduced by the Dark Lady, or vice versa. In this sonnet pair, W. blames only the Dark Lady. He considers Y.M. to have paid a price for the encounter, having himself been enslaved by this woman whom W. feels so ambivalent about.

And what does the Dark Lady think of this? Is she bothered that W. has discovered her seduction or is she reveling in her accomplishment? Does she not care what either of her lovers think? Or is she the one who has been seduced by Y.M., or by both of them? Has she lost more than either of them? Would either of them care about her loss?

135

Who ever hath her wish, thou hast thy *Will,*
And *Will* to boot, and *Will* in over-plus,
More than enough am I that vex thee still,
To thy sweet will making addition thus.
Wilt thou whose will is large and spacious,
Not once vouchsafe to hide my will in thine?
Shall will in others seem right gracious,
And in my will no fair acceptance shine?
The sea all water, yet receives rain still,
And in abundance addeth to his store,
So thou being rich in *Will* add to thy *Will,*
One will of mine to make thy large *Will* more.
    Let no unkind, no fair beseechers kill,
    Think all but one, and me in that one *Will.*

1 *Will* (1) William (2) wish (3) power of choice (4) sexual desire or capacity (5) sexual organ **2** *to boot* in addition **3, 9** *still* always **4** *making addition thus* i.e., by adding myself **6** *vouchsafe* deign; *hide* shelter **8** *acceptance* acceptability **10** *his* its **13** *no unkind* no unkindness; *no fair beseechers* none who entreat you (the double negative is normal in Elizabethan English) **14** *and me* and accept me

This is another misogynistic sonnet in the style of Ovid's erotic poems. W. is now explicit about the Dark Lady's foul deeds. He calls her a loose woman. He doesn't say it, but he makes her sound like a whore: *thou whose will is large and spacious.* In context, *will* in this line means "sexual desire" or "sexual capacity." Not very complimentary. Unlike Sonnet 129, the tone of this sonnet is gentle and sweet, but the meaning is just as vicious.

The language of Sonnet 135 is deceptive. The words are simple enough, but they don't say what they normally should. It starts with the first line. We have to think about it before we realize that *Who ever* must mean "whoever else." This begins the play on wish/will. "They may get their wish, but you get your will." We're not quite sure how she has *Will* twice more, *to boot,* and, *over-plus* until we get to lines 3 and 4. At first, we might be puzzled why W. is *more than enough* until he points out that he's *making addition* to the Dark Lady's *sweet will*. But which *will* is it? Is it just her sexual capacity? Or is he a second *Will*? Is Y.M. also named Will? This would fit best with line 2. It also fits with the use of the adjective *sweet*.* This punning on the word *will* with its deliberate confusion that makes it hard for us to know which of its many meanings is intended at any particular time is familiar. We saw the same technique in Sonnet 40. In that sonnet the pun was on *love* and we were left just as confused about the multiple meanings of that word in the earlier sonnet. There are other throwbacks, too. The word *gracious* was used four times in the Young Man series. Its use here in line 8 is a mockery of its usual meaning. So many words in this sonnet are oddly reminiscent of sonnets from the earlier series: *sweet, vouchsafe, gracious, fair, sea, store, rich*. They carry a different connotation in the Dark Lady series. Deeper, slyer, more sinister.

Sonnet 135 is funny in a way. The image of a rejected suitor using his name as a pun to plead for acceptance back into his mistress's good graces is so pathetic we might imagine it working. But to do so, he has to treat her with disdain. The only way this can be funny is if W. assumes she agrees with his assessment of her and doesn't care. Her reputation means nothing to her. She *loves* the fact that he doesn't ask her to reject her other lover(s) in favor of him—he just wants to be one of the gang. This sonnet only makes sense if we imagine W. thinks the Dark Lady will enjoy it. Does she have a sense of humor about the situation? Is she laughing out loud? Or does she find W. cluelessly insulting?

---

* Martin Seymour-Smith says: "This sonnet strongly suggests that the 'friend' of 133 and 134…was known as 'Will'. It would read very flatly otherwise." Seymour-Smith, *Sonnets*, 181. Some have seen evidence for this elsewhere in Y.M. series and the dedication to *The Sonnets*, signed by "T.T." (assumed to be the publisher, Thomas Thorpe) and mysteriously referring to "Mr. W. H." Oscar Wilde was convinced *The Sonnets* were autobiographical and Y.M. was an actor named Willie Hughes (Wilde, "The Portrait of Mr. W. H.").

136

If thy soul check thee that I come so near,
Swear to thy blind soul that I was thy Will,
And will, thy soul knows, is admitted there,
Thus far for love, my love-suit sweet fulfill.
Will, will fulfill the treasure of thy love,
Ay fill it full with wills, and my will one,
In things of great receipt with ease we prove,
Among a number one is reckon'd none.
Then in the number let me pass untold,
Though in thy store's account I one must be,
For nothing hold me so it please thee hold,
That nothing me, a something sweet to thee.
    Make but my name thy love, and love that still,
    And then thou lov'st me for my name is *Will*.

1 *check* rebuke **2** *Will* (1) William (2) wish (3) power of choice (4) sexual desire or capacity (5) sexual organ **5** *fulfill the treasure* fill the treasury **6** *one* among them **7** *receipt* capacity **8** *reckon'd none* not counted (an adage of the time was "one is no number") **9** *untold* uncounted **10** *thy store's account* the inventory of your property **13** *still* always

Sonnet 136 is a variation on the theme of Sonnet 135. It stays with the pun on W.'s name, but instead of arguing that more *will* is better, W. now argues that "the will" is a worthy companion for the soul and since his name is Will, if the Dark Lady loves *will* she loves him. The jump from the argument of the first quatrain, that the Dark Lady's soul should not reject W. for coming *so near* because will *is admitted there* is based on the Elizabethan idea that intellect and will were the two rational faculties of the soul (the soul, being within the body did not have the benefit of the eyes and so was "blind"). The link to the conclusion of the couplet is tenuous. The best W. can do is argue that *will* will fulfill the Dark Lady's love. I like the way John Kerrigan explains the wordplay on *fulfill:* "lecherously unfolding the word as though undressing it, exposing with seductive tardiness its sexual potential."* After this argument, the rest of the second and third quatrains are a rationale for ignoring W. This sounds like a backup argument—if you're really worried about adding me to your store of treasures (alluding back to Sonnet 135), I'm only one, and one is *no number*, it doesn't count. But it's all adds up to an old complaint: "I just want to have sex with you!"

Taken on its own, Sonnet 136 sounds playful. It revels in wordplay, as in lines 11-12, where *for nothing hold me* (count me as nothing) is reversed literally and figuratively into *hold that nothing me* (as long as you hold in your arms that nothing that is me—or, if we take it more sexually, hold in your hands)—a *nothing* that is a *something sweet to thee*. It may be bawdy, but it lacks the nastiness of Sonnet 135 or 131. (Is he something sweet to her, or is his thing sweet to her?) However, the links to Sonnet 135 deprive it of innocence. We can't separate *fulfill* from *make thy large Will more*. Sonnet 136 sounds sweeter than Sonnet 135, but the nasty undertone of the series is simmering under its surface. Is the Dark Lady laughing now?

137

Thou blind fool love, what dost thou to mine eyes,
That they behold and see not what they see?
They know what beauty is, see where it lies,
Yet what the best is, take the worst to be.
If eyes corrupt by over-partial looks
Be anchor'd in the bay where all men ride,
Why of eyes' falsehood hast thou forgèd hooks,
Whereto the judgment of my heart is tied?
Why should my heart think that a several plot,
Which my heart knows the wide world's common place?
Or mine eyes seeing this, say "this is not"
To put fair truth upon so foul a face.
    In things right true my heart and eyes have erred,
    And to this false plague are they now transferred.

---

* Kerrigan, *Sonnets*, 367.

5 *corrupt* corrupted **6** *the bay where all men ride* the harbor where all men find a place (with sexual innuendo) **9** *that a several plot* that plot a private one **10** *knows* knows to be **14** *false plague* plague of falseness, i.e., the Dark Lady; *transferred* given over to

W. has stopped joking. He's not amused anymore. The Dark Lady has done something that has made him doubt his own judgment. Ten sonnets ago, W. said everyone should think the Dark Lady was beautiful. Now he questions what could make him think her so. What has caused this reversal? He's been *over-partial*. He has lost faith in his judgment—of his heart and his eyes. He thought she was all his (*a several plot*) when she was really *the bay where all men ride*. In Sonnet 135 W. implied that the Dark Lady was a whore. It's impossible to interpret Sonnet 137 as saying anything else. Everything about her is wrong. She's not just Dark and foul. She's no longer beautiful, she's not his. She's a whore. And as line 12 implies, she's a liar.

Sonnet 137 is constructed as a complaint to Love. It's in the form of a series of rhetorical questions. Why have you done this to me? Why do you make me see and judge things wrong? No answer is expected and none is given. The couplet reads as a sigh of resignation after a long complaint. The argument of the sonnet has been that love, being blind, has made W. see the truth falsely and his heart to make the same error. The couplet concludes that as a result, they have been *transferred* to this plague of falseness. *Transferred* is an unusual word in this context (and its only use by Shakespeare). In what way are the heart and eye transferred to the plague of falseness? This phrase would have no meaning if we take the sense to be that they are *converted to falseness* because they've already been false from the start. The only way I can understand this is to assume the *false plague* is the Dark Lady. The heart and eye have erred and are therefore given over to her and are under her control, the Mistress of Falseness.

As usual, we have to decide how to read this sonnet. Is it sad and plaintive, or teasingly provocative? Do we read it quietly or angrily?

The contrast to the series about Y.M. is striking. W.'s love for Y.M. also made his eyes see falsely (Sonnets 113 and 114), but then it was a blessing, not a plague. Y.M. made *the most deformed'st creature* seem beautiful; the Dark Lady makes W. take *what the best is* to be the worst. Sonnet 137 makes clear that for W., these two loves of his are polar opposites.

138

When my love swears that she is made of truth,
I do believe her though I know she lies,
That she might think me some untutor'd youth,
Unlearnèd in the world's false subtleties.
Thus vainly thinking that she thinks me young,
Although she knows my days are past the best,
Simply I credit her false speaking tongue,
On both sides thus is simple truth suppress'd.
But wherefore says she not she is unjust?
And wherefore say not I that I am old?
O love's best habit is in seeming trust,
And age in love, loves not to have years told.
   Therefore I lie with her, and she with me,
   And in our faults by lies we flattered be.

1 *truth* fidelity **5** *vainly* falsely **9** *unjust* untruthful **11** *habit* appearance; *seeming* apparent **12** *told* counted

W. is in the mood for joking again. (Maybe he *was* teasing in Sonnet 138.) This is another sonnet whose wordplay is deliberately tricky, daring the reader to keep up with it. It's similar to the play on the word *love* in Sonnet 40 and on *will* in Sonnets 135 and 136. In Sonnet 138 we have an extended setup for a pun on the word *lie* in the couplet. In the quatrains, it's used to mean prevaricate, to say something untrue. But we have to be careful to watch out for who is doing the lying and who is being fooled by the lies. The Dark Lady may not be taken in by lies so easily. Although W. says she lies to him, W. doesn't lie to her. He chooses to believe her lies so he can believe she thinks him an *untutor'd youth,* not so that she will believe his lies. Truth is suppressed *on both sides* only because they both lie, not because they both *believe* lies. When W. says he's not old he's lying to *himself*, not to the Dark Lady. He knows she doesn't think him young—he says so in lines 5 and 6.

In the couplet, W. lies *with* the mistress, not to her. (The pun on the sexual sense of *lie with* is unmistakable.) They lie together, but not in the same way. We expect W. to say, "She accepts my lies to her, I accept her lies to me, and so we flatter each other." Instead he says, "I accept *my* lies to her and she also accepts *my* lies to her: we are both flattered." (He is flattered that she is willing to believe him, she is flattered that he wishes to be believed.) And somehow, I imagine her not caring about being flattered. She seems above all that.

There are several types of wordplay in this sonnet, but only *lie with* in line 13 is a pun (a word used with more than one meaning at the same time). Other variations include ambiguity, and change in the word's meaning, form, or function in different places. Sometimes words are also just repeated, as *wherefore,* in lines 9 and 10. Words based on *simple* are used twice, *lie* three times, and *love* four times. *Truth* (line 1) and *unjust* (line 9) are ambiguous: they may mean either "honesty" and "dishonest," or "faithfulness" and "unfaithful." Regardless, the Dark Lady is being accused of being false. The ambiguity makes little difference to the sense. The meaning of *love* varies subtly: in line 1, it means "beloved," in line 11, it's Love personified, and in line 12 the repetition without an intervening word gives the noun, meaning "love in the abstract," and the verb, meaning "likes." Similarly, *lie* is used as a verb in lines 2 and 13 (the latter with two meanings, as noted) and as a noun in line 14. *Simply,* in line 7, may mean "in my simplicity," or "foolishly," but in the next line, the meaning of *simple* shifts to "without addition." All of these variations in meaning are delicate. Their subtlety contrasts with unsubtle pun in line 13.

Another element of Sonnet 138 is the paradox. This is the basis of line 2 where W. claims he believes what he knows to be untrue. This is not possible, but we understand what he means: part of him believes the Dark Lady and part of him does not. The contradiction is another way of expressing ambiguity. It's meant to be clever. I think it is. Do you? Would the Dark Lady?

139

O call me not to justify the wrong
That thy unkindness lays upon my heart,
Wound me not with thine eye but with thy tongue,
Use power with power, and slay me not by Art.
Tell me thou lov'st elsewhere, but in my sight,
Dear heart, forbear to glance thine eye aside;
What need'st thou wound with cunning when thy might
Is more than my o'er-press'd defense can bide?
Let me excuse thee: ah my love well knows,
Her pretty looks have been mine enemies,
And therefore from my face she turns my foes,
That they elsewhere might dart their injuries.
    Yet do not so, but since I am near slain,
    Kill me outright with looks, and rid my pain.

3 *not…tongue* i.e., not with roving looks but with actual words **4** *Use power with power* i.e., use your power directly; *Art* artifice **8** *bide* tolerate **11** *foes* i.e., the pretty looks **14** *rid* remove

This is a reply sonnet. The Dark Lady has asked W. to forgive her for something she's done. In lines 5 and 6 we find out what that was. She has snubbed him—deliberately looked away from him when she saw him. He was deeply hurt. In typical form, he says in the first two lines that he doesn't want to *justify* her wrong, but then does just that in lines 9 to 12. He reverses course again in the couplet and asks her to ignore the elaborate excuse he's made up for her.

The excuse isn't meant to be taken seriously. The Dark Lady is imagined to say that since the beauty of her eyes have been the cause of pain to W. (his *enemies*) she thought it best to turn away from him and direct their *injuries* toward someone else. He knows this is not true, but argues instead that if it were her intention, she's got it wrong—he's on his deathbed from her injuries anyway, she may as well look straight at him, kill him off and put him out of his misery. This is a dark version (no pun intended) of the typical sonnet convention of the cruel-because-she-is-chaste beloved being chastised by the love-sick poet, who asks to be put out of his misery with a mere glance from the mistress, a sign of requited love.

Sonnet 139 is strongly reminiscent of two sonnets from the Young Man series. Sonnets 36 and 96 end with the same couplet, which begins, *But do not so...* They both discuss Y.M.'s faults. Comparing those sonnets to Sonnet 139 shows the difference in the relationships between W. and his two beloveds and the dramatic difference in character between those two individuals. Y.M. may have been wanton, callous, unkind, even cruel, but we would not call him *vicious*. W. asked Y.M. to forget him, leave him sooner rather than later *so I shall taste / At first the very worst of fortune's might.* He asks the Dark Lady, on the other hand, to say whatever she wants, but not to glance aside, to *Kill me outright with looks and rid my pain.* His self-abnegation is as vicious as the adjectives he heaps on the Dark Lady. Of course, this is playful. He knows her looks will not kill him—death is a metaphor for curing his love-sickness. He's still asking for sex. But I heard hope in the couplet of Sonnet 36 and resignation in the couplet of Sonnet 96. In Sonnet 139 I hear the bitterness of Ovid's stalking lover from the *Amores*—never satisfied with no. Does the Dark Lady give in, or does laughter turn into mockery?

140

Be wise as thou are cruel, do not press
My tongue-tied patience with too much disdain,
Lest sorrow lend me words and words express
The manner of my pity wanting pain.
If I might teach thee wit better it were,
Though not to love, yet love to tell me so,
As testy sick-men when their deaths be near,
No news but health from their Physicians know.
For if I should despair I should grow mad,
And in my madness might speak ill of thee,
Now this ill wresting world is grown so bad,
Mad slanderers by mad ears believèd be.
    That I may not be so, nor thou belied,
    Bear thine eyes straight, though thy proud heart go wide.

1 *press* strain **4** *pity wanting* unpitied **5** *wit* wisdom **6** *so* i.e., that you do love me **11** *ill wresting* i.e., that wrests things to an evil sense **13** *so* i.e., a "mad slanderer"; *belied* slandered **14** *wide* astray

Sonnet 140 takes off from the previous sonnet. W. has just told the Dark Lady it's okay to say she doesn't love him as long as she doesn't ignore him completely by looking away from him. Now he changes his mind. He complains that her verbal disdain might overtax his patience, leading him to break his silence and *speak ill* of her. Not content to stop there, he returns to the theme of Sonnet 139 and tells her again: *bear thine eyes straight, though thy proud heart go wide.*

The tone of Sonnet 140 is set out in the first two lines. W. wants to teach the Dark Lady to be as wise as she is cruel. Cruelty underlies the entire sonnet. The wisdom he teaches her is how to lie to him so he won't say cruel things about her. This sonnet is even more pressured than Sonnet 139. The verse flows through lines without stopping at the ends with breathless rapidity. And there's a word repetition that runs through the sonnet that keeps us moving relentlessly to the end. *Sorrow* lends words and *words express.* He teaches that it's better *not to love,* yet *love to tell* him so. If he grows *mad*, in his *madness* he will *speak ill*. *Mad slanderers* by *mad ears* will be believed. In the middle of all this is the image of the *testy* sick man hearing nothing but good news from his physician. W. is testy and wishes for nothing but good news from the Dark Lady, whom he would teach to be as *wise* as a physician.

The anger in Sonnet 139 seemed sudden. It was a response to a single act. The Dark Lady had done something and the sonnet was a response. The anger in Sonnet 140 seems more settled to me. It feels seething, like it's not just a reaction of the moment but an emotion that's been building up. W.'s *tongue-tied patience* has reached its limits. I wonder what we're going to hear next?

141

In faith I do not love thee with mine eyes,
For they in thee a thousand errors note,
But 'tis my heart that loves what they despise,
Who in despite of view is pleas'd to dote.
Nor are mine ears with thy tongue's tune delighted,
Nor tender feeling to base touches prone,
Nor taste, nor smell, desire to be invited
To any sensual feast with thee alone.
But my five wits, nor my five senses can
Dissuade one foolish heart from serving thee,
Who leaves unsway'd the likeness of a man,
Thy proud heart's slave and vassal wretch to be.
    Only my plague thus far I count my gain,
    That she that makes me sin, awards me pain.

4 *Who in despite of view* despite what it sees **6** *Nor...prone* nor is my sense of touch eager for your caresses **8** *sensual feast* feast of senses **9** *But my* but neither my; *five wits* mental faculties **11** *Who leaves unsway'd* i.e., the heart is unswayed and leaves behind **13** *Only...my gain* i.e., I count my plague to be my gain only thus far **14** *pain* punishment

The relationship continues to deteriorate. In Sonnet 137 W. wondered how his eyes could have deceived him. He blamed

Love for blinding them. In Sonnet 141, he finds fault with all of his senses and his wits as well. His heart alone is foolish enough to love the Dark Lady.

Is this just another angry outburst, born out of despair and anger? Or is this a reply to the Dark Lady? It's not written impersonally; it's directed to her. What could have happened to elicit this response? Perhaps they were making love and W. turned away. The Dark Lady reaches over to touch him, but he pulls back. "Am I so distasteful to you that you can't even stand my touch? Can't you even look at me," she asks? "I thought you loved me?" Sonnet 141 is W.'s unvarnished reply. He doesn't love her with his eyes. He doesn't care for her touches. None of his senses nor his wits are charmed by her. (According to contemporary thought, the five wits of line 9 refers to 1) common wit, 2) imagination, 3) fantasy, 4) estimation, and 5) memory.) *
His heart is simply her slave and *vassal wretch*. The only good he gets out of her, the woman he counts as his *plague*, is that she who is responsible for his sin is also responsible for his punishment.

There's a lot of conventional sonneteering here. The suffering poet, the lover as slave, the wretchedness, the pain, the foolish heart. The acceptance of unrequited love. The conventional sonneteer must be rebuffed because his lady is chaste. But everything is twisted. W.'s heart loves what the eyes, ears and touch despise. Even smell and taste are repulsed. He is out of his wits in love—obsessed. He is the mad lover of Sonnet 140, speaking ill of his mistress. And we see that same, sick, misogynistic strain of Ovid's erotic poetry—the compulsion of sinful loving that puts all the blame on the woman and demands punishment for absolution. An odd similarity between all conventional sonnet poetry and Shakespeare's twisted take on it is that nowhere do we find any sense of caring for the woman so ardently adored. In stark contrast to the Young Man series, where caring was a prominent aspect of the relationship, sexual attraction seems to be the only component of the love depicted

---

* See Boswell, *Plays and Poems,* 20:347.

between the man and his woman. The aching heart is nothing more than testosterone-powered libido. The woman's love is non-existent. In conventional sonnets, the mistress is cold, chaste, unwilling to return the poet's love. In the Dark Lady series, she is haughty, promiscuous, unloving, unmoved by W.'s torment. They both reject the poet, but for different reasons: the one because he is too presumptuous, the other because he is too—shallow? I imagine the Dark Lady responding to this sonnet by saying, "Oh, get over yourself!"

142

Love is my sin, and thy dear virtue hate,
Hate of my sin, grounded on sinful loving,
O but with mine, compare thou thine own state,
And thou shalt find it merits not reproving.
Or if it do, not from those lips of thine,
That have profan'd their scarlet ornaments,
And seal'd false bonds of love as oft as mine,
Robb'd others' beds' revenues of their rents.
Be it lawful I love thee as thou lov'st those,
Whom thine eyes woo as mine importune thee,
Root pity in thy heart that when it grows,
Thy pity may deserve to pitied be.
    If thou dost seek to have what thou dost hide,
    By self example may'st thou be denied.

2 *on sinful loving* on the fact that my love is sinful **4** *it* i.e., my state **8** *Robb'd…rents* i.e., stolen from spouses the due of the marriage bed **9** *Be it* let it be **12** *Thy…be* i.e., your pity will make you deserving of pity **13** *hide* withhold

The downward spiral of the relationship continues. In Sonnet 141 W. told the Dark Lady the only good thing about her was that she punished him for his sin of loving her. Sonnet 142 takes off from there. Like Sonnet 141, it's also addressed to the Dark Lady. I read it as another reply sonnet. I hear the Dark Lady saying, "You're right, you are a sinner, and I hate you." W. answers using typically elaborate Elizabethan wordplay. There is antithesis (*love/hate, sin/virtue, seek/hide*), paradox (love is my sin, hate is your virtue), and mirror image (love/sin:virtue/hate; hate/sin:sin/loving). Word repetition (in different forms) is also prominent: *love* occurs five times, *sin* three, *pity* three, *thou/thee/thine/thy* fourteen. *Love, sin, virtue, hate, thou, thee, thine, thy.* W. cannot resolve the ambivalence of this relationship. It's *profaned* by her *lips, seal'd* by *false bonds of love* by both of them. He moves from religious language to legal metaphors. (The appropriation of religious language is a sonnet tradition not to be confused with blasphemy.) * From profanity to broken contracts, stolen rents, the lawfulness (or unlawfulness) of love. He's tortured by the way her eyes *woo* others as his *importune* her. He asks for her *pity* so he may pity her in exchange. He warns in the couplet that her refusal may invoke a reciprocal refusal on his part. This is *not* the usual repartee of sonneteer. The threats of a conventional sonneteer are limited to his own demise. He will despair, he will pine away, he will die. But he will not threaten the beloved herself. Of course, the word *pity* is ambivalent. Is W. asking to be forgiven for his sin and saying he will forgive the Dark Lady's sin? This sounds like a cover story. Is W.'s greatest concern about sin and forgiveness? Or is he just asking to have his wooing accepted? Is he complaining that he gets what he wants only when the Dark Lady allows it, while she gets what she wants whenever she likes? Maybe he's saying if she doesn't accept his advances, he won't accept hers. Do we believe him? Do we think the Dark Lady would believe him—even for a minute?

---

* Some editors see similarities to the Songs of Solomon in lines 6 and 7, presumably, "Thy lips are like a thread of scarlet..." (4:4) and "Set me as a seal upon thy heart, as a seal upon thine arm..." (8:6). At any rate, the word *profaned* is a religious word, but it's in keeping with sonnet tradition.

143

Lo, as a careful huswife runs to catch
One of her feathered creatures broke away,
Sets down her babe and makes all swift dispatch
In pursuit of the thing she would have stay,
Whilst her neglected child holds her in chase,
Cries to catch her whose busy care is bent
To follow that which flies before her face,
Not prizing her poor infant's discontent;
So runst thou after that which flies from thee,
Whilst I, thy babe, chase thee afar behind,
But if thou catch thy hope, turn back to me,
And play the mother's part, kiss me, be kind.
    So will I pray that thou mayst have thy Will,
    If thou turn back and my loud crying still.

1 *huswife* housewife (pronounced *hussif*) **3** *dispatch* haste **5** *holds her in chase* chases her **11** *hope* hoped-for object **13** *Will* (1) William (2) wish (3) sexual desire

W. has tried everything he can think of to win the Dark Lady back to him in this series of sonnets: contrition (133-134), joking (135, 136, 138), calumny (137), self-abnegation (139, 141), and threats (140, 142). Nothing seems to have worked. Now he tries a simile. (Compare this with the simile used in Sonnet 33, also dealing with the liaison, or the one in Sonnet 7, which also begins with the word *Lo*. These are all examples of an ancient form, the epic simile, in which as much or more space is given to the simile as the action it's compared to. In Sonnet 143, the simile is almost silly, not intended to be taken too seriously. I think Shakespeare is having a good laugh at poets, including himself.) In a reversal from the seriousness of the more recent sonnets, the scene Sonnet 143 calls up is a comic one. A house-wife is caring at the same time for her baby and her chickens. One of the chickens runs away and she chases after it. The baby chases after its mother, crying all the while. The mother is so intent on catching the chicken who *flies before her face* (we get the image of the bird both flying away from the woman and flying in her face to taunt her) she ignores her inconsolable child. We learn something about what's going on with our three characters as W. explains how the simile relates to them. The Dark Lady runs after the one *which flies from* her, while W. *chases her* from behind. He returns to the pun on *Will*, telling her he hopes she gets her *Will*, as long as she plays *the mother's part* by turning back, kissing him and being *kind* (we may suspect he has something more than kissing in mind when he says *be kind*).

This puts a fresh look on things. It appears Y.M. (the other *Will*), had his fling with the Dark Lady and then had enough. She made further advances and he rejected her. Perhaps she just wasn't the sort he wanted to run around with on a regular basis. Or perhaps he hadn't known she was W.'s mistress and didn't want to continue his relationship with her on that account. Maybe the reason the Dark Lady didn't acknowledge W., making him so angry (Sonnet 139), was because she didn't want Y.M. to know they knew each other. We also know W. to be prone to hyperbole (like any good sonneteer). He has made the Dark Lady out to be promiscuous, a loose woman having sex with many men. But maybe her having sex with *one* other man is the same to W. as having sex with many. That difference may be meaningless to him. She is an unfaithful seductress—one or one thousand, it doesn't matter. And that's why in this sonnet all he asks is that once she is done with her *Will*, she come back to him, and *my loud crying still.*

This is a completely different approach. The tone of the sonnet is light, but do we hear some tenderness toward the Dark Lady? Is there some allowance for her to have what she wants, because she wants it? Would she come back to W. on these terms?

144

Two loves I have of comfort and despair,
Which like two spirits do suggest me still,
The better angel is a man right fair,
The worser spirit a woman color'd ill.

To win me soon to hell my female evil
Tempteth my better angel from my side,
And would corrupt my saint to be a devil,
Wooing his purity with her foul pride.
And whether that my angel be turn'd fiend,
Suspect I may, yet not directly tell,
But being both from me both to each friend,
I guess one angel in another's hell.
    Yet this shall I ne'er know but live in doubt,
    Till my bad angel fire my good one out.

2 *suggest me still* always prompt me **4** *color'd ill* i.e., dark **11** *from away* from; *each* each other **12** *another's* the other's **14** *fire...out* drive my good one away

W. resorts again to allegory, this time speaking to himself, not to the Dark Lady. The story is an old one about two angels, one good, one evil, each urging W. in one direction or the other, representing his moral choices. Unlike the usual story, the bad angel, wanting to get an advantage, instead of tempting W., tempts his good angel and off they go together. W. is left uncertain of the outcome until *my bad angel fire my good one out.*

There are some interesting points about this allegory. Most importantly, all the blame is placed on the Dark Lady. The sportive, wanton Y.M. of the earlier sonnets, whom others said all sorts of bad things about, is all *purity* in Sonnet 144, a *better angel,* a *saint.* If he is *turn'd fiend,* it's because he's been corrupted by the Dark Lady's *foul pride.* She's a *bad angel,* the embodiment of *hell.* No doubt there's a lighter, humorous side to this sonnet. Sexual innuendos are likely intended. The story from Bocaccio's *Decameron* illustrates the probable pun on *hell.* In the tenth tale of the third day, a monk deceives a pious and beautiful but simple girl into standing naked with him. When "the resurrection of the flesh came to pass," she asks, "What is it thou hast that thrusts itself out in front and that I have not?" He explains that it is the Devil and that "he gives me such sore trouble that I can hardly bear it." When she expresses her relief that she has no devil, he explains that she instead has "Hell" and that it is her Christian duty to "put the Devil in Hell." He proceeds to "set about show-ing her how to shut the accursed one in his prison."[*] The term to "fire out" in line 14 is difficult to understand without assum-ing a reference to the Elizabethan meaning "to give a venereal disease" in addition to the sense "chase him away."[†] But this only strengthens the misogynistic strain we have seen before. And unlike the usual morality story about good and bad angels, W. is completely absolved of any moral responsibility. He wonders only whether he is left with *any* good angels or whether he now has two evil ones. *His* only role is to listen to his angels. Even with one good angel, he seemed to say, "No wonder I act the way I do. I have one angel telling me to do one thing and another telling me to do another!" And if they both turn out to be bad, well—what's a fella to do?

The couplet is also surprising. Why is W. in doubt until Y.M. is chased out by the Dark Lady? We just heard that she had to go running after him. We would assume Y.M. was rejecting *her*. We would expect W. to say he would be in doubt until Y.M. chased away the Dark Lady. After all, that's what he said he was waiting for in Sonnet 143. But the allegory tells us something has changed. Line 6 says that the Dark Lady has tempted Y.M. from W.'s side. She has succeeded, she is no longer rejected. Now W. must wait until *she* rejects Y.M. He has no doubt this will happen. He suggests she will either get tired of him (the blandest read-ing), she will be too much for him (the heat of her desire will be too intense), or she will become undesirable (she will give him a venereal disease).

Where does this sonnet fit into the relationship between W. and Y.M.? What is likely to come next between W. and the Dark Lady?

---

[*] The allusion to this story was first suggested by R. Shindler, "The Sto-len Key."

[†] See Rollins, *New Variorum*, I, 371.

145

Those lips that Love's own hand did make,
Breath'd forth the sound that said "I hate,"
To me that languish'd for her sake.
But when she saw my woeful state,
Straight in her heart did mercy come,
Chiding that tongue that ever sweet,
Was us'd in giving gentle doom,
And thought it thus anew to greet:
"I hate" she alter'd with an end,
That follow'd it as gentle day
Doth follow night who like a fiend
From heav'n to hell is flown away.
    "I hate," from hate away she threw,
    And sav'd my life saying "not you."

7 *doom* sentence, judgment

We immediately notice something different about Sonnet 145. It's written in tetramers (lines with four feet of two syllables each) instead of pentameter. This not only sets it apart from all the other sonnets, it also makes it sound less serious. This is fitting for a sonnet that is one long set up for the joke in the couplet. But more than just a joke, Sonnet 145 adds to our story. Since the first liaison sonnet of the Dark Lady series, Sonnet 133, W. has been vying for attention and hate has been a prominent theme. He's been asking to have her back, for her pity, and now he seems to have gotten what he wants.

I think the simplicity of Sonnet 145 is deceptive. The joke—changing the meaning of a phrase in mid-sentence—is saved for the couplet. Shakespeare makes it more fun by repeating *I hate* three times and stretching out the set up for twelve lines. The organization of the sonnet is also complicated. There are four sentences arranged in a structure of three lines, five lines, four lines, and two lines. The imagery is rich as well. The sonnet starts out with the image of the Dark Lady's lips *breathing forth* the word *hate*. The image is softened by the image of Love, whose own hands made those lips. We then see the woeful W., languishing, the sight of which brings *mercy* to her heart, which then chides the *sweet* tongue that had pronounced the *gentle doom*. The result is a new greeting and new images. *Gentle day* follows *night*, which is compared to a *fiend* flying away from *heav'n to hell* (remember Sonnet 144?). *Hate* is thrown away from "hate" when the Dark Lady says, "not you." Like she's *firing it out*.

The tone of Sonnet 145 makes it function as comic relief. The dramatic distinction from the previous sonnets makes us expect that something very different is coming next.

146

Poor soul, the center of my sinful earth,
My sinful earth these rebel powers array,
Why dost thou pine within and suffer dearth
Painting thy outward walls so costly gay?
Why so large cost having so short a lease,
Dost thou upon thy fading mansion spend?
Shall worms, inheritors of this excess,
Eat up thy charge? is this thy body's end?
Then soul live thou upon thy servant's loss,
And let that pine to aggravate thy store;
Buy terms divine in selling hours of dross,
Within be fed, without be rich no more.
    So shalt thou feed on death, that feeds on men,
    And death, once dead, there's no more dying then.

1 *earth* i.e., the body **2** *array* dress, enclose **4** *costly gay* expensively showy **8** *charge* i.e., the body **9** *servant's* body's **10** *aggravate* increase **11** *terms* long periods of time; *hours of dross* wasteful hours

We go from the most comical to the most serious of sonnets. Here is another allegory written as a soliloquy. W. looks into his soul and questions his actions. Why has he allowed *these rebel powers* to dress his sinful body in costly, showy garments when his time on earth is so short?* His body is fading, it is the due of worms. Is it worth the expense? No, he says. He should let the body starve to feed the soul. *Without be rich no more*—the rich do not get into heaven.

Why this sonnet now? W. has been guilty of *sinful loving*. We're not sure what that means (is it premarital sex or adultery— his or hers?). But it's the analogy in this poem for riches. Those *rebel powers* are his sexual urges. His *sinful earth* is his sinful body. He is painting his *outward walls so costly gay* by having *sinful loving*. He exhorts himself to let the body *pine*, to be celibate, and in doing so to *buy terms divine*. He is only *selling hours of dross*, giving up what is worthless, to be *fed* within, to nourish his soul, giving up being *rich* in sexual favors.

Let's look at what's happened. W. was having an affair with the Dark Lady and she had an affair with Y.M. W. tried to woo her back to him. At first, he wanted her to give his friend up. Then he wanted her under any terms. Then he was content to let her have Y.M. as long as she came back to him. In Sonnet 144 W. tells us that she tempted Y.M. away. He didn't even seem to care if she turned him into a devil. In Sonnet 145, he got his wish—the Dark Lady had come back to W. Sonnet 146 reads as a sonnet written by someone who has gotten everything he wanted and now realizes it's all worthless.

Most important is the imagery of the couplet. The words of St. Paul are not far away: "O death, where is they sting?"† But

---

* In the original, line 2 has *that thee* inserted before the last word, *array*, giving the line at least 12 syllables, an obvious misprint. Most editors assume the repetition of "My sinful earth" at the beginning of the line is the culprit, delete it, and either leave it blank or replace it with some two-syllable phrase to regularize the line. I have adopted Massey's emendation, assuming with him that the compositor was confused by the grammar, thinking that the *sinful earth* was the subject and the *rebel powers* the object of the verb *array*, instead of the other way around. The compositor thought he was helping by providing the extra words but instead just muddied things up. Reading the line as the powers arraying the earth (i.e., dressing them) makes sense when we read line 4. *That thee* looks like the error. See discussion in Atkins, *Sonnets*, 358.

† I Corinthians 15:55. The comparison was first made by Wilson, *Sonnets*, 263.

the religious allegory and the reality coincide. We hear them both at the same time. *Death that feeds on men, death, dead, dying.* A chilling end to a chilling sonnet. How will W. deal with his relationship with the Dark Lady now? Will he starve his body to feed his soul?

147

My love is as a fever longing still
For that which longer nurseth the disease,
Feeding on that which doth preserve the ill,
Th' uncertain sickly appetite to please.
My reason, the Physician to my love,
Angry that his prescriptions are not kept,
Hath left me, and I desperate now approve,
Desire is death, which Physic did except.
Past cure I am, now Reason is past care,
And frantic mad with evermore unrest,
My thoughts and my discourse as mad men's are,
At random from the truth vainly express'd.
    For I have sworn thee fair, and thought thee bright,
    Who art as black as hell, as dark as night.

1 *still* always **3** *preserve the ill* maintain the illness **4** *uncertain* fickle **6** *kept* followed **7** *approve* prove **8** *Desire...except* i.e., desire, which objected to reason's medicine, is fatal **9** *Past cure...past care* i.e., now that reason is past caring about me, I am past cure **12** *At random* randomly varying; *vainly* without effect

Sonnet 147 returns to simile for its argument. The contemporary theory of illness was based on the four humors (black bile, yellow bile, phlegm, and blood). These would become abnormal during illness, causing patients to do things that would make their illness worse. Physicians would prescribe measures that would make their humors return to normal and cure them. Reason is compared to the physician, who is angered that his prescriptions are ignored and leaves in a huff. The patient, having lost his reason, is now *frantic mad* and is unable to say anything close to the truth. This explains why he has *sworn thee fair, and thought thee bright, / Who art as black as hell, and dark as night.*

We've heard this complaint about the Dark Lady from W. before. This is more than an explanation of how he should be so deranged as to think she is what she is not. He had her. He lost her. He desperately sought her back. He won her again. He looked at what he had and at himself and didn't like what he saw. He asked his soul to redeem himself. He has failed. As we begin reading Sonnet 147, it looks as if W. may finally have assigned himself some moral responsibility. He is sick. He has ignored Reason, his physician. Desire is death. Until we read the couplet. The Dark Lady remains the culprit, *as black as hell, as dark as night*. He can't let that go. He's a sinner, he's sick, he has turned his back on reason. But it's her fault. Just what makes her black as hell, I wonder? Is it her willingness to have him back? What makes her dark as night? Is sounds like more than her complexion. Where is this going?

148

O me! what eyes hath love put in my head,
Which have no correspondence with true sight,
Or if they have, where is my judgment fled,
That censures falsely what they see aright?
If that be fair whereon my false eyes dote,
What means the world to say it is not so?
If it be not, then love doth well denote,
Love's eye is not as true as all men's: no,
How can it? O how can love's eye be true,
That is so vex'd with watching and with tears?
No marvel then though I mistake my view,
The sun it self sees not, till heaven clears.
    O cunning love, with tears thou keep'st me blind,
    Lest eyes well seeing thy foul faults should find.

4 *censures* judges **10** *vex'd* plagued; *watching* lying awake **11** *mistake my view* misjudge what I see **14** *find* discover

W. continues to complain. He remains faultless, making excuses again. This time he says his eyes must be seeing false. No, maybe not—maybe they see correctly but his judgment is wrong. No, he was right the first time—his eyes see false because they couldn't possibly see with all the lying awake and crying all the time. It's all the Dark Lady's fault. She's doing it on purpose, making him blind with tears so he can't see her *foul faults.*

I'm disappointed in W. After Sonnet 146, I was hoping he might show some moral fiber. Instead, he's sinking lower and lower, unable to help himself. And he sounds perplexed throughout Sonnet 148. He flits from one thing to another. He can't make up his mind what's going on or what he wants to say. We follow with the verse his confused, bothered state, jumping around with each quatrain. Especially dramatic is line 9, which opens the third quatrain with its complaint, *"How can it? O how can love's eye be true?"*

What does the Dark Lady say? I imagine: "Are you crying? I thought you were happy I came back to you. Feeling guilty again? Get a hold of yourself. You have to decide what it is you want. I know you have a love/hate relationship with me, but that's not my fault. You have to make up your mind. What are you going to do?"

149

Canst thou, O cruel, say I love thee not,
When I against my self with thee partake?
Do I not think on thee when I forgot
Am of my self, all tyrant for thy sake?
Who hateth thee that I do call my friend,
On whom frown'st thou that I do fawn upon?
Nay if thou lour'st on me do I not spend
Revenge upon my self with present moan?
What merit do I in my self respect,
That is so proud thy service to despise,
When all my best doth worship thy defect,
Commanded by the motion of thine eyes?
  But love hate on for now I know thy mind,
  Those that can see thou lov'st, and I am blind.

2 *partake* join forces, take part **3-4** *I forgot Am of my self* I am forgotten by myself **7** *lour'st* frown **8** *present moan* immediate sorrow **10** *thy service to despise* i.e., as to get in the way of serving you **11** *defect* insufficiency **12** *motion* bidding

Sonnet 149 is a reply to the Dark Lady. After all W.'s complaining, I hear her saying to him in frustration, "Since you don't love me, why don't you leave me." He replies, "How can you say that? You don't understand me. But now I understand you." Of course, he blames her. Sonnet 149 reads like a conventional sonnet except for the negative barbs thrown in. A conventional sonnet mistress would not be asked, *Who hateth thee?* And she would not be told that *all my best doth worship thy defect.* But she is cruel, he dotes on her, he is selfless for her sake, he excoriates himself, he is proud to serve her, he is commanded by the bidding of her eyes, he loves her, and his love is unrequited. Hatred is a bit strong to express the disdain of a sonnet mistress for her poet. But we know from the start that this is no conventional sonnet. When W. says, *O cruel*, we know he's addressing the Dark Lady and any similarity to convention is a deliberate way of contrasting this odd relationship to that odd conventional one.

The diction of this sonnet is as tortured as W.—the word order is as twisted in knots as his conscience. Some are simple, as in line 2, where "When I against my self with thee partake" stands for "When I partake with thee against my self." Others are more extreme, like lines 3-4, "when I forgot am of my self" for "when I am forgot(ten) of my self," (when I don't give a thought for myself). This distorted word order ends with the last four lines, which are stated directly, as if to make clear that W. understands what is going on. He is blinded by his tears and she loves only those who can see. Hate on, he says.

This doesn't sound like a real argument. W. doesn't expect us or the Dark Lady to believe that he thinks the reason she doesn't love him is because he can't see. He knows she has other reasons. *We* are not sure what they are.

If this were a conventional sonnet, we would understand that the poet would be asking for the impossible—his mistress would be beautiful *and* chaste. She *must* refuse his attentions (to remain chaste). The relationship with the Dark Lady is more confused. Does she really hate him? Or does he hate himself? Is he equating her complaisance with hatred because it makes him a sinner? Would the only way she could show him love be to remain chaste (both toward him and others)? Or does she hate him because he makes *her* a sinner? Does he make *her* feel guilty? Does *she* have a love/hate relationship with W.? Whatever the reason for W.'s perceptions, he is guilty of self-delusion. He refuses to comprehend the nature of the relationship and the complex feelings that underly it. Is the Dark Lady as frustrated with him as W. seemed to be with Y.M.?

150

Oh from what power hast thou this powerful might,
With insufficiency my heart to sway,
To make me give the lie to my true sight,

And swear that brightness doth not grace the day?
Whence hast thou this becoming of things ill,
That in the very refuse of thy deeds,
There is such strength and warrantise of skill,
That in my mind thy worst all best exceeds?
Who taught thee how to make me love thee more,
The more I hear and see just cause of hate?
Oh though I love what others do abhor,
With others thou shouldst not abhor my state.
    If thy unworthiness rais'd love in me,
    More worthy I to be belov'd of thee.

2 *sway* rule **5** *becoming of things ill* faculty of making bad things look good **7** *warrantise* guarantee **12** *state* condition

W. continues to whine. It's the same perversion of sonnet convention. The Dark Lady holds ultimate power over W., but when this mistress makes him swear that *brightness doth not grace the day* it's not because she's brighter and outshines it, but because she *makes* him lie. He accuses her of making *things ill* look *becoming*, he complains of the skill with which she makes the *worst* that she does seem to him to exceed the *best*. Who taught her, he asks, to *make* him love her more, the more he sees *just cause of hate*. Why should he love what others *abhor*? Finally, she shouldn't, as others do, *abhor* him.

These are strong words. What has the Dark Lady done to deserve them? What *just cause* does he have to hate her? Why do others *abhor* her? She may not be the model of Elizabethan beauty, but that's not the same as being abhorrent. Is she abhorred because she's adulterous? Is her relationship with W. the abhorrent deed? Is that his *just cause of hate*?

In the couplet, W. asks, as he did in Sonnet 142, for equal treatment. If you *rais'd love* in me (with a pun on sexual arousal) despite your unworthiness, I am all the more worthy of being loved by you, not hated. Has the Dark Lady accused W. of being unworthy on account of his being an adulterer? If so, he has responded by first complaining about her power over him (his usual denial of responsibility) and then he gets to the point—

she's as guilty as he is. If he can overlook her faults, she ought to do the same for him.

Despite the harsh words, there's a beauty of expression in this sonnet that adds an aching sweetness to its bitterness. The paradoxes that fill this sonnet are a reflection of the paradox of the relationship between W. and the Dark Lady. The *powerful might* that has *insufficiency my heart to sway*. The *brightness that doth not grace the day*. The *becoming of things ill*. The *unworthiness* that raises a *worthy* love. I find the most complicated expression the most interesting. In *the very refuse* of her deeds (that which is left over after the best parts of them have been drained away) there is still such *strength*, and *warrantise of skill* (guarantee of ability) that her *worst all best exceeds*. This whole phrase, especially the end, *thy worst all best exceeds*, in another context would be a compliment. If we read Sonnet 150 a certain way, it sounds almost like a conventional sonnet praising a conventional mistress—until *hate, abhor,* and *unworthiness* spoil the mood in the last six lines. What's the Dark Lady's mood, I wonder?

151

Love is too young to know what conscience is,
Yet who knows not conscience is born of love?
Then gentle cheater urge not my amiss,
Lest guilty of my faults thy sweet self prove.
For thou betraying me, I do betray
My nobler part to my gross body's treason,
My soul doth tell my body that he may
Triumph in love, flesh stays no farther reason,
But rising at thy name doth point out thee,
As his triumphant prize, proud of this pride,
He is contented thy poor drudge to be
To stand in thy affairs, fall by thy side.
    No want of conscience hold it that I call
    Her love, for whose dear love I rise and fall.

1 *conscience* sound judgment **3** *urge not my amiss* do not stress my sinfulness **8** *stays* waits for **10** *pride* sexual desire **13** *want* lack

This is a confusing sonnet. We learn from line 3 that W. has been accused of an *amiss*. We have to wait for the couplet to find out that the Dark Lady has suggested he lacks conscience for calling *Her love, for whose dear love I rise and fall.** (Remember the indignation over the pun on "prick" in Sonnet 20? You should read some of the commentary to this sonnet! Hysterical. Penises are one thing but erections, well polite people don't mention those.)† What's going on between these two? Is the Dark Lady complaining that she's just a sex object to W.? That she has sacrificed her honor for him and instead of getting love in return all she gets is love-making? And whining. (A common problem among sonneteers.)‡

This could explain W.'s indignant response. "What does love know of conscience," he asks? "How dare you accuse me of a lack of conscience! You have betrayed me by making me betray my soul. Yet I ask for no more than to call you 'love.' Can't I have even that much?"

That's the most generous interpretation. But if we look at what W. is saying, it sounds like that same male-centric view of the relationship. The sonnet is a disjointed argument. The connecting words, *Yet* (line 2), *Then* (line 3), *For* (line 5), and *But* (line 9) seem like they should make sense, but don't. If we ignore them, we have this series of statements:

> Love is too young to know what conscience is.
> Conscience stems from love.
> Do not criticize me lest you prove guilty yourself. (There's no consensus on the meaning of *gentle cheater*. I get the sense of an oxymoron. She is gentle—in the sense of noble,

---

* This is explained by Helen Vendler, who picks up on George Wyndham's analysis of this as a reply sonnet. See Vender, *The Art of Shakespeare's Sonnets*, 639-40 and Wyndham, *Poems*, 334.

† See Rollins, *New Variorum*, I, 387-88.

‡ After eliminating a number of sonnets from his revised 1619 edition of *Idea*, Michael Drayton wrote in a preface: "No far-fetched Sigh shall ever wound my breast, / Love from mine Eye a Tear shall never wring, / Nor in Ah-mes my whining sonnets dressed" [spelling modernized] (Evans, M., *Elizabethan Sonnets*, xxxii).

kind—but also a cheater, in some vague sense. I don't
think the exact meaning matters. We get the drift.)
You betray me, and I betray my soul.
My soul gives my body permission to love.
My passion requires no further reason to love you.
My passion is proud of naming you as his prize.
He is contented to be your drudge.
I do not consider it a lack of conscience to call you "love."

But these statements sound more like a man skirting around
his struggle to keep his pants on than one struggling with his
soul. We can hear W. saying, "yet . . . then . . . for . . . but" and
meaning it, but he keeps harping on his *gross body's treason*, his
flesh, *rising* at her name, pointing out his *triumphant prize*, standing
and falling by her side. All he can talk about is his penis! And
worse than that, he seems to think the Dark Lady must be
fighting the same battle he's fighting. "Be careful," he says, "or
you'll be guilty of the same faults I am." All this because she
chided him for calling her "love." It certainly *sounds* like he's
treating her like a sex object. W. seems to have a problem understanding the difference between sex and love. The Dark Lady
understands.

152

In loving thee thou know'st I am forsworn,
But thou art twice forsworn to me love swearing,
In act thy bed-vow broke and new faith torn,
In vowing new hate after new love bearing.
But why of two oaths' breach do I accuse thee,
When I break twenty: I am perjur'd most,
For all my vows are oaths but to misuse thee,
And all my honest faith in thee is lost.
For I have sworn deep oaths of thy deep kindness,
Oaths of thy love, thy truth, thy constancy,
And to enlighten thee gave eyes to blindness,
Or made them swear against the thing they see.
　　For I have sworn thee fair: more perjur'd eye,
　　To swear against the truth so foul a lie.

1 *I am forsworn* I break an oath **3** *bed-vow* marriage vows; *new faith torn* i.e., a new contract of fidelity torn up **7** *but to misuse* i.e., merely to deceive **8** *in thee is lost* is lost because of you **10** *truth* fidelity **11** *enlighten* brighten; *gave eyes to blindness* surrendered sight to blindness **13** *eye* eyes (with pun on *I*)

This is a big deal. Something's happened, but the details remain vague. W. tells us he has broken an oath by loving the Dark Lady—this strongly implies that he is married. And he then says the Dark Lady broke a *bed-vow*, implying that she is married, too. He also says that she has broken yet another vow—turning a new love into hate. He has complained about her hating him before, but this sounds different. He has never said anything before about vows or breaking them. It sounds like she's breaking up with him. We were able to explain how W. could call Y.M. "fair, kind and true" and even "constant" after the liaison sonnets, but to whom could he have sworn about the Dark Lady *Oaths of thy love, thy truth, thy constancy* if he is making love to her and she is married? This sounds like more finger pointing.

There's a larger question to consider. We've heard this story twice now, both times from W.'s point of view. How much do we really know, other than that W. is prone to exaggeration? We know a few things. W. has had a loving relationship with Y.M. He has had a love/hate relationship with the Dark Lady. He feels guilty about his relationship with her (Sonnet 146). He and the Dark Lady are both married (Sonnet 152). The Dark Lady and Y.M. had some sort of liaison (Sonnet 134). Y.M. complained a lot to W. and W. complained a lot to the Dark Lady. Do we know what happened between the Dark Lady and Y.M.? She tempted him. They went off together, or so says W.

What did *W.* actually know about the Dark Lady and Y.M.? He never really says. Did he hear rumors about them? Did he see them together? Did he see them kiss? Did one of them admit to having affair? Is the whole thing a jealous rage? Is she no more guilty than Desdemona?[*] I raise these questions to point

---

[*] The blameless wife of Othello whom he murdered in a jealous rage based on circumstantial evidence manufactured by the evil Iago.

out how vague the story is, how little we know, how plausible so many scenarios might be.

Sonnet 152 does tell us something about the relationship between W. and the Dark Lady. W. starts out by saying he is perjured but the Dark Lady is perjured twice, once by breaking her bed-vow, and once by breaking her vow with him. He then changes course and says he is perjured more because he has falsely vowed twenty times of her kindness, truth, love and constancy. He has given his eyes over to blindness and made them swear they've seen what isn't there. And he ends with his familiar curse: his eyes have sworn her fair and in doing so they have sworn *against the truth so foul a lie.* The question remains for us, having read this sonnet from W.'s point of view, are we reading truth, or lies?

153

Cupid laid by his brand and fell asleep,
A maid of *Dian's* this advantage found,
And his love-kindling fire did quickly steep
In a cold valley-fountain of that ground,
Which borrow'd from this holy fire of love,
A dateless lively heat still to endure,
And grew a seething bath which yet men prove,
Against strange maladies a sovereign cure.
But at my mistress' eye love's brand new fired,
The boy for trial needs would touch my breast,
I sick withal the help of bath desired,
And thither hied a sad distemper'd guest,
    But found no cure, the bath for my help lies,
    Where *Cupid* got new fire: my mistress' eyes.

1 *brand* torch 2 *Dian's* Diana's, goddess of chastity; *advantage* opportunity 4 *of that ground* i.e., nearby 6 *dateless* eternal; *still* always 7 *grew* became; *yet* to this day 8 *a sovereign cure* the best cure 9 *new fired* newly lit 10 *for trial needs would* as an experiment had to 11 *withal* with it 12 *distemper'd* diseased

Sonnet 153 is based on an ancient Greek epigram about an

unsuccessful attempt to quench Love's fire.* This and the next sonnet serve as an epilogue explaining the power the Dark Lady holds over W.

The first quatrain sets up the scene: Cupid falls asleep, one of Diana's maidens takes advantage of the moment to try to quench his torch in a *cold valley-fountain*. The second quatrain describes the creation of a bath that cures *strange maladies* as a result. Cupid wakes up and uses the Dark Lady's eyes to relight his torch. After Cupid checks his newly lit torch by touching W's breast with it, W., now *distemper'd* (sick) tries out the bath. The couplet tells us that the bath offers him no cure—he must find that in his mistress's eyes, the source of his distemper.

Sonnet 153 is in keeping with the themes of the Dark Lady series. The Dark Lady is mysterious and powerful. Her allure lights Cupid's torch. W. is enthralled and powerless. He is without any restraint or moral responsibility. He tries to escape to the bath for cure but finds it worthless against her power. She is his only remedy. Even Cupid is less culpable than the Dark Lady—she is the ultimate culprit. It's all her fault. W. is all victim. Sonnet 153 gives the Dark Lady immense power and stature. But it's the power of Faust. Did she ask for it, or was it foisted on her?

---

* Attributed to Marcianus Scholasticus (5th C. AD): "Beneath these plane trees, detained by gentle slumber, Love slept, having put his torch in the care of the Nymphs; but the Nymphs said one to another: 'Why wait? Would that together with this we could quench the fire in the hearts of men.' But the torch set fire even to the water, and with hot water thenceforth the Love-Nymphs fill the bath." Hutton, "Analogues," 385-403.

154

The little Love-God lying once asleep,
Laid by his side his heart inflaming brand,
Whilst many Nymphs that vow'd chaste life to keep,
Came tripping by, but in her maiden hand
The fairest votary took up that fire,
Which many Legions of true hearts had warm'd,
And so the General of hot desire,
Was sleeping by a Virgin hand disarm'd.
This brand she quenchèd in a cool Well by,
Which from love's fire took heat perpetual,
Growing a bath and healthful remedy,
For men diseas'd. But I, my Mistress' thrall,
    Came there for cure and this by that I prove:
    Love's fire heats water, water cools not love.

5 *votary* nymph of Diana **7** *General* commander (Cupid) **9** *by* nearby **12** *thrall* slave

Sonnet 154 is a variation of Sonnet 153. It's based on the same epigram but has a different emphasis, explaining that the reason for the quenching of Cupid's torch was to disarm his weapon of *hot desire* and enhance the cause of chastity. This explanation leaves only three lines for W. to tell us that he went to the bath for cure and had no success. The ending is different this time. Instead of saying his cure lies with the Dark Lady, he says he is incurable, resorting to proverb: *Love's fire heats water, water cools not love.* There's an echo in this line of the Songs of Solomon (8:7): "Many waters cannot quench love."*

In this version, the Dark Lady is less mysterious and powerful. Cupid has more power than she does. W. is still without responsibility, but at least the blame seems more directed at Love than at the Dark Lady.

What do these two sonnets, 153 and 154, have in common? They both express the inescapable power of erotic love. Even

---

* King James Bible. The echo was first noted by Thomas Carter, *Holy Scripture*, 224.

the goddess of chastity cannot quench its flame. Woman is the vehicle of erotic love and man, poor sap, is helpless before it.

The two sonnets show confusion about the role of women. Are they helpless like men, under Cupid's power, or are they extensions of Cupid, like Diana's maidens are extensions of her? Throughout the Dark Lady series, we have had no sense that W. has had any thought about the Dark Lady other than as a sex object. She is fair—or not. He wants to love her—or not. But he doesn't want to write poems about her that will last forever. He doesn't want her to have children so that her beauty will be perpetuated. He doesn't have sleepless nights thinking about her. The love of the Dark Lady series—Cupid's love—is not the same as the love of Y.M. series. These two sonnets put that difference in concrete terms.

But love in any form is powerful. I can't help but be reminded by these two sonnets, especially Sonnet 154, of the helplessness W. claimed in his attempt to cure himself of Y.M.'s love in Sonnet 118: *Drugs poison him who fell so sick of you.*

Conclusion

As you go through these 154 sonnets, they don't sound like someone telling a coherent story. Yet, out of them, we've been able to read of a relationship between two men, one younger than the other, complicated by the younger one stealing the affections of the other's mistress—a woman not described in the most flattering terms, but whose story remains vague. We don't know whether she has done very bad things or whether the writer of *The Sonnets* is blaming her for his own misbehavior. (I've talked a lot about misogyny in the Dark Lady series. I don't mean to imply that Shakespeare was a misogynist—that would be confusing the poet with his characters. Shakespeare always shows us who *we* are and leaves us to judge ourselves, not him.) We've also read about the apparently callous behavior of the youth who loves being fawned upon, and who teases his friend with comparisons to a Rival Poet.

These people are familiar. The handsome, talented young man who is just a bit too aware of his own charms, able to get away with more than most people. The poet who is eager to please his patron, convinced of his ability to immortalize with his verse. He is just that good. (This one really is that good, but I can't shake the sense that he was above all that, making fun of poets who take themselves *too* seriously. Which may explain the sonnets that seem overly bombastic.) The woman who is desirable but too easy to get. She is nothing but trouble. Although the men are guilty of the same deceit she is accused of, and they never tire of making excuses for themselves, she has no defenders. The story is familiar, too. Love that will last forever—but doesn't. Cheating that will never be repeated—but is. Shame that is tearfully expressed—and then banished under a pile of flimsy excuses. The story goes back as far as Ovid's Rome, two thousand years ago. We see it around us wherever we look.

I've asked a lot of questions and made a lot of guesses throughout this book. As I said in the Introduction, there are many ways to read *The Sonnets*. I have presented one way that tells a particular story. I like to think there are as many variations on that story as there are different answers to the questions I raised, but each variation teaches us the same thing. *The Sonnets* show us love in different guises—ecstatic, youthful, tender, mature, asexual, erotic. Most of all, they show us that love and relationships interact powerfully with one another. In this particular story, despite the protestations of undying love, all the relationships end poorly with only Cupid's fire left burning in the end, ready to continue with the next set of characters.

Appendix

The following is A. H. Bullen's modernized text of Christopher Marlowe's ca. 1590 translation of Book 1 of Ovid's *Amores* (A. H. Bullen, ed. *The Works of Christopher Marlowe*, 3 vols. London: John C. Nimmo, 1885, 3:103-140). The complete text, including Books 2 and 3, with the editor's footnotes may be found at Project Gutenberg: https://www.gutenberg.org/ebooks/21262.

Elegy 1

> Quemadmodum a Cupidine, pro bellis amoris scribere coactus sit.

We which were Ovid's five books, now are three,
For these before the rest preferreth he:
If reading five thou plain'st of tediousness,
Two ta'en away, thy labour will be less;
With Muse prepared, I meant to sing of arms,
Choosing a subject fit for fierce alarms:
Both verses were alike till Love (men say)
Bgan to smile and took one foot away.
Rash boy, who gave thee power to change a line?
We are the Muses' prophets, none of thine.
What, if thy mother take Diana's bow,
Shall Dian fan when love begins to glow?
In woody groves is't meet that Ceres reign,
And quiver-bearing Dian till the plain?
Who'll set the fair-tressed Sun in battle-ray
While Mars doth take the Aonian harp to play?
Great are thy kingdoms, over-strong and large,
Ambitious imp, why seek'st thou further charge?
Are all things thine? the Muses' Tempe thine?
Then scarce can Phœbus say, "This harp is mine."
When in this work's first verse I trod aloft,
Love slaked my muse, and made my numbers soft:
I have no mistress nor no favourite,
Being fittest matter for a wanton wit.

Thus I complained, but Love unlocked his quiver,
Took out the shaft, ordained my heart to shiver,
And bent his sinewy bow upon his knee,
Saying, "Poet, here's a work beseeming thee."
O, woe is me! he never shoots but hits,
I burn, love in my idle bosom sits:
Let my first verse be six, my last five feet:
Farewell stern war, for blunter poets meet!
Elegian muse, that warblest amorous lays,
Girt my shine brow with seabank myrtle sprays.

Elegy 2

> Quod primo amore correptus, in triumphum duci se a Cu-
> pidine patiatur.

What makes my bed seem hard seeing it is soft?
Or why slips down the coverlet so oft?
Although the nights be long I sleep not tho
My sides are sore with tumbling to and fro.
Were love the cause it's like I should descry him,
Or lies he close and shoots where none can spy him?
'Twas so; he strook me with a slender dart;
'Tis cruel Love turmoils my captive heart.
Yielding or striving do we give him might,
Let's yield, a burden easily borne is light.
I saw a brandished fire increase in strength,
Which being not shak'd, I saw it die at length.
Young oxen newly yoked are beaten more,
Than oxen which have drawn the plough before:
And rough jades' mouths with stubborn bits are torn,
But managed horses' heads are lightly borne.
Unwilling lovers, love doth more torment,
Than such as in their bondage feel content.
Lo! I confess, I am thy captive I,
And hold my conquered hands for thee to tie.
What need'st thou war? I sue to thee for grace:
With arms to conquer armless men is base.
Yoke Venus' Doves, put myrtle on thy hair,

Vulcan will give thee chariots rich and fair:
The people thee applauding, thou shalt stand,
Guiding the harmless pigeons with thy hand.
Young men and women shalt thou lead as thrall,
So will thy triumph seem magnifical;
I, lately caught, will have a new-made wound,
And captive-like be manacled and bound:
Good meaning, Shame, and such as seek Love's wrack
Shall follow thee, their hands tied at their back.
Thee all shall fear, and worship as a king
Iö triumphing shall thy people sing.
Smooth speeches, Fear and Rage shall by thee ride,
Which troops have always been on Cupid's side;
Thou with these soldiers conquer'st gods and men,
Take these away, where is thine honour then?
Thy mother shall from heaven applaud this show,
And on their faces heaps of roses strow,
With beauty of thy wings, thy fair hair gilded,
Ride golden Love in chariots richly builded!
Unless I err, full many shalt thou burn,
And give wounds infinite at every turn.
In spite of thee, forth will thine arrows fly,
A scorching flame burns all the standers by.
So, having conquered Inde, was Bacchus' hue;
Thee pompous birds and him two tigers drew;
Then seeing I grace thy show in following thee,
Forbear to hurt thyself in spoiling me.
Behold thy kinsman Cæsar's prosperous bands,
Who guards the conquered with his conquering hands.

Elegy 3

   Ad amicam.

I ask but right, let her that caught me late,
Either love, or cause that I may never hate;
I crave too much—would she but let me love her;
Jove knows with such-like prayers I daily move her.
Accept him that shall serve thee all his youth,

Accept him that shall love with spotless truth.
If lofty titles cannot make me thine,
That am descended but of knightly line,
(Soon may you plough the little land I have;
I gladly grant my parents given to save;)
Apollo, Bacchus, and the Muses may;
And Cupid who hath marked me for thy prey;
My spotless life, which but to gods gives place,
Naked simplicity, and modest grace.
I love but one, and her I love change never,
If men have faith, I'll live with thee for ever.
The years that fatal Destiny shall give
I'll live with thee, and die ere thou shalt grieve.
Be thou the happy subject of my books
That I may write things worthy thy fair looks.
By verses, horned Iö got her name;
And she to whom in shape of swan Jove came;
And she that on a feigned Bull swam to land,
Griping his false horns with her virgin hand,
So likewise we will through the world be rung
And with my name shall thine be always sung.

Elegy 4

> Amicam, qua arte quibusque nutibus in cæna, presente viro,
> uti debeat, admonet.

Thy husband to a banquet goes with me,
Pray God it may his latest supper be.
Shall I sit gazing as a bashful guest,
While others touch the damsel I love best?
Wilt lying under him, his bosom clip?
About thy neck shall he at pleasure skip?
Marvel not, though the fair bride did incite
The drunken Centaurs to a sudden fight.
I am no half horse, nor in woods I dwell,
Yet scarce my hands from thee contain I well.
But how thou should'st behave thyself now know,
Nor let the winds away my warnings blow.

Before thy husband come, though I not see
What may be done, yet there before him be.
Lie with him gently, when his limbs he spread
Upon the bed; but on my foot first tread.
View me, my becks, and speaking countenance;
Take, and return each secret amorous glance.
Words without voice shall on my eyebrows sit,
Lines thou shalt read in wine by my hand writ.
When our lascivious toys come to thy mind,
Thy rosy cheeks be to thy thumb inclined.
If aught of me thou speak'st in inward thought,
Let thy soft finger to thy ear be brought.
When I, my light, do or say aught that please thee,
Turn round thy gold ring, as it were to ease thee.
Strike on the board like them that pray for evil,
When thou dost wish thy husband at the devil.
What wine he fills thee, wisely will him drink;
Ask thou the boy, what thou enough dost think.
When thou hast tasted, I will take the cup,
And where thou drink'st, on that part I will sup.
If he gives thee what first himself did taste,
Even in his face his offered gobbets cast.
Let not thy neck by his vile arms be prest,
Nor lean thy soft head on his boisterous breast.
Thy bosom's roseate buds let him not finger,
Chiefly on thy lips let not his lips linger
If thou givest kisses, I shall all disclose,
Say they are mine, and hands on thee impose.
Yet this I'll see, but if thy gown aught cover,
Suspicious fear in all my veins will hover.
Mingle not thighs, nor to his leg join thine,
Nor thy soft foot with his hard foot combine.
I have been wanton, therefore am perplexed,
And with mistrust of the like measure vexed.
I and my wench oft under clothes did lurk,
When pleasure moved us to our sweetest work.
Do not thou so; but throw thy mantle hence,

Lest I should think thee guilty of offence.
Entreat thy husband drink, but do not kiss,
And while he drinks, to add more do not miss;
If he lies down with wine and sleep opprest,
The thing and place shall counsel us the rest.
When to go homewards we rise all along
Have care to walk in middle of the throng.
There will I find thee or be found by thee,
There touch whatever thou canst touch of me.
Ay me! I warn what profits some few hours!
But we must part, when heaven with black night lours.
At night thy husband clips thee: I will weep
And to the doors sight of thyself [will] keep:
Then will he kiss thee, and not only kiss,
But force thee give him my stolen honey-bliss.
Constrained against thy will give it the peasant,
Forbear sweet words, and be your sport unpleasant.
To him I pray it no delight may bring,
Or if it do, to thee no joy thence spring.
But, though this night thy fortune be to try it,
To me to-morrow constantly deny it.

Elegy 5

 Corinnæ concubitus.

In summer's heat, and mid-time of the day,
To rest my limbs upon a bed I lay;
One window shut, the other open stood,
Which gave such light as twinkles in a wood,
Like twilight glimpse at setting of the sun,
Or night being past, and yet not day begun;
Such light to shamefaced maidens must be shown
Where they may sport, and seem to be unknown:
Then came Corinna in a long loose gown,
Her white neck hid with tresses hanging down,
Resembling fair Semiramis going to bed,
Or Lais of a thousand wooers sped.
I snatched her gown: being thin, the harm was small,

Yet strived she to be covered therewithal;
And striving thus, as one that would be cast,
Betrayed herself, and yielded at the last.
Stark naked as she stood before mine eye,
Not one wen in her body could I spy.
What arms and shoulders did I touch and see!
How apt her breasts were to be pressed by me!
How smooth a belly under her waist saw I,
How large a leg, and what a lusty thigh!
To leave the rest, all liked me passing well;
I clinged her naked body, down she fell:
Judge you the rest; being tired she bade me kiss;
Jove send me more such afternoons as this!

Elegy 6

Ad Janitorem, ut fores sibi aperiat.

Unworthy porter, bound in chains full sore,
On movèd hooks set ope the churlish door.
Little I ask, a little entrance make,
The gate half-ope my bent side in will take.
Long love my body to such use make[s] slender,
And to get out doth like apt members render.
He shows me how unheard to pass the watch,
And guides my feet lest, stumbling, falls they catch:
But in times past I feared vain shades, and night,
Wondering if any walkèd without light.
Love, hearing it, laughed with his tender mother,
And smiling said, "Be thou as bold as other."
Forthwith love came; no dark night-flying sprite,
Nor hands prepared to slaughter, me affright.
Thee fear I too much: only thee I flatter:
Thy lightning can my life in pieces batter.
Why enviest me? this hostile den unbar;
See how the gates with my tears watered are!
When thou stood'st naked ready to be beat,
For thee I did thy mistress fair entreat.
But what entreats for thee sometimes took place,

(O mischief!) now for me obtain small grace.
Gratis thou mayest be free; give like for like;
Night goes away: the door's bar backward strike.
Strike; so again hard chains shall bind thee never,
Nor servile water shalt thou drink for ever.
Hard-hearted Porter, dost and wilt not hear?
With stiff oak propped the gate doth still appear.
Such rampired gates besiegèd cities aid;
In midst of peace why art of arms afraid?
Exclud'st a lover, how would'st use a foe?
Strike back the bar, night fast away doth go.
With arms or armèd men I come not guarded;
I am alone, were furious love discarded.
Although I would, I cannot him cashier,
Before I be divided from my gear.
See Love with me, wine moderate in my brain,
And on my hairs a crown of flowers remain.
Who fears these arms? who will not go to meet them?
Night runs away; with open entrance greet them.
Art careless? or is't sleep forbids thee hear,
Giving the winds my words running in thine ear?
Well I remember, when I first did hire thee,
Watching till after midnight did not tire thee.
But now perchance thy wench with thee doth rest,
Ah, how thy lot is above my lot blest:
Though it be so, shut me not out therefore;
Night goes away: I pray thee ope the door.
Err we? or do the turnèd hinges sound,
And opening doors with creaking noise abound?
We err: a strong blast seemed the gates to ope:
Ay me, how high that gale did lift my hope!
If Boreas bears Orithyia's rape in mind,
Come break these deaf doors with thy boisterous wind.
Silent the city is: night's dewy host
March fast away: the bar strike from the post.
Or I more stern than fire or sword will turn,
And with my brand these gorgeous houses burn.

Night, love, and wine to all extremes persuade:
Night, shameless wine, and love are fearless made.
All have I spent: no threats or prayers move thee;
O harder than the doors thou guard'st I prove thee,
No pretty wench's keeper may'st thou be,
The careful prison is more meet for thee.
Now frosty night her flight begins to take,
And crowing cocks poor souls to work awake.
But thou, my crown, from sad hairs ta'en away,
On this hard threshold till the morning lay.
That when my mistress there beholds thee cast,
She may perceive how we the time did waste.
Whate'er thou art, farewell, be like me pained!
Careless farewell, with my fault not distained!
And farewell cruel posts, rough threshold's block,
And doors conjoined with an hard iron lock!

Elegy 7

   Ad pacandam amicam, quam verberaverat.

Bind fast my hands, they have deservèd chains,
While rage is absent, take some friend the pains.
For rage against my wench moved my rash arm,
My mistress weeps whom my mad hand did harm.
I might have then my parents dear misused,
Or holy gods with cruel strokes abused.
Why, Ajax, master of the seven-fold shield,
Butchered the flocks he found in spacious field.
And he who on his mother venged his ire,
Against the Destinies durst sharp darts require.
Could I therefore her comely tresses tear?
Yet was she gracèd with her ruffled hair.
So fair she was, Atalanta she resembled,
Before whose bow th' Arcadian wild beasts trembled.
Such Ariadne was, when she bewails,
Her perjured Theseus' flying vows and sails.
So, chaste Minerva, did Cassandra fall
Deflowered except within thy temple wall.

That I was mad, and barbarous all men cried:
She nothing said; pale fear her tongue had tied.
But secretly her looks with checks did trounce me,
Her tears, she silent, guilty did pronounce me.
Would of mine arms my shoulders had been scanted:
Better I could part of myself have wanted.
To mine own self have I had strength so furious,
And to myself could I be so injurious?
Slaughter and mischiefs instruments, no better,
Deservèd chains these cursed hands shall fetter.
Punished I am, if I a Roman beat:
Over my mistress is my right more great?
Tydides left worst signs of villainy;
He first a goddess struck: another I.
Yet he harmed less; whom I professed to love
I harmed: a foe did Diomede's anger move.
Go now, thou conqueror, glorious triumphs raise,
Pay vows to Jove; engirt thy hairs with bays.
And let the troops which shall thy chariot follow,
"Iö, a strong man conquered this wench," hollow.
Let the sad captive foremost, with locks spread
On her white neck, but for hurt cheeks, be led.
Meeter it were her lips were blue with kissing,
And on her neck a wanton's mark not missing.
But, though I like a swelling flood was driven,
And as a prey unto blind anger given,
Was't not enough the fearful wench to chide?
Nor thunder, in rough threatenings, haughty pride?
Nor shamefully her coat pull o'er her crown,
Which to her waist her girdle still kept down?
But cruelly her tresses having rent,
My nails to scratch her lovely cheeks I bent.
Sighing she stood, her bloodless white looks shewed,
Like marble from the Parian mountains hewed.
Her half-dead joints, and trembling limbs I saw,
Like poplar leaves blown with a stormy flaw.
Or slender ears, with gentle zephyr shaken,

Or waters' tops with the warm south-wind taken.
And down her cheeks, the trickling tears did flow,
Like water gushing from consuming snow.
Then first I did perceive I had offended;
My blood the tears were that from her descended.
Before her feet thrice prostrate down I fell,
My fearèd hands thrice back she did repel.
But doubt thou not (revenge doth grief appease),
With thy sharp nails upon my face to seize;
Bescratch mine eyes, spare not my locks to break
(Anger will help thy hands though ne'er so weak);
And lest the sad signs of my crime remain,
Put in their place thy kembèd hairs again.

Elegy 8

> Execratur lenam quæ puellam suam meretricis arte instit-
> uebat.

There is—whoe'er will know a bawd aright,
Give ear—there is an old trot Dipsas hight.
Her name comes from the thing: she being wise,
Sees not the morn on rosy horses rise,
She magic arts and Thessal charms doth know,
And makes large streams back to their fountains flow;
She knows with grass, with threads on wrung wheels spun,
And what with mares' rank humour may be done.
When she will, cloudes the darkened heaven obscure,
When she will, day shines everywhere most pure.
If I have faith, I saw the stars drop blood,
The purple moon with sanguine visage stood;
Her I suspect among night's spirits to fly,
And her old body in birds' plumes to lie.
Fame saith as I suspect; and in her eyes,
Two eyeballs shine, and double light thence flies.
Great grandsires from their ancient graves she chides,
And with long charms the solid earth divides.
She draws chaste women to incontinence,
Nor doth her tongue want harmful eloquence.

By chance I heard her talk; these words she said,
While closely hid betwixt two doors I laid.
"Mistress, thou knowest thou hast a blest youth pleased,
He stayed and on thy looks his gazes seized.
And why should'st not please; none thy face exceeds;
Ay me, thy body hath no worthy weeds!
As thou art fair, would thou wert fortunate!
Wert thou rich, poor should not be my state.
Th' opposèd star of Mars hath done thee harm;
Now Mars is gone, Venus thy side doth warm,
And brings good fortune; a rich lover plants
His love on thee, and can supply thy wants.
Such is his form as may with thine compare,
Would he not buy thee, thou for him should'st care."
She blushed: "Red shame becomes white cheeks; but this
If feigned, doth well; if true, it doth amiss.
When on thy lap thine eyes thou dost deject,
Each one according to his gifts respect.
Perhaps the Sabines rude, when Tatius reigned
To yield their love to more than one disdained.
Now Mars doth rage abroad without all pity,
And Venus rules in her Æneas' city.
Fair women play; she's chaste whom none will have
Or, but for bashfulness, herself would crave.
Shake off these wrinkles that thy front assault;
Wrinkles in beauty is a grievous fault.
Penelope in bows her youths' strength tried,
Of horn the bow was that approved their side.
Time flying slides hence closely, and deceives us,
And with swift horses the swift year soon leaves us.
Brass shines with use; good garments would be worn;
Houses not dwelt in, are with filth forlorn.
Beauty, not exercised, with age is spent,
Nor one or two men are sufficient.
Many to rob is more sure, and less hateful,
From dog-kept flocks come preys to wolves most grateful.
Behold, what gives the poet but new verses?

And therefore many thousand he rehearses.
The poet's god arrayed in robes of gold,
Of his gilt harp the well-tuned strings doth hold.
Let Homer yield to such as presents bring,
(Trust me) to give, it is a witty thing.
Nor, so thou may'st obtain a wealthy prize,
The vain name of inferior slaves despise.
Nor let the arms of ancient lines beguile thee;
Poor lover, with thy grandsires I exile thee.
Who seeks, for being fair, a night to have,
What he will give, with greater instance crave.
Make a small price, while thou thy nets dost lay;
Lest they should fly; being ta'en, the tyrant play.
Dissemble so, as loved he may be thought,
And take heed lest he gets that love for naught.
Deny him oft; feign now thy head doth ache:
And Isis now will show what 'scuse to make.
Receive him soon, lest patient use he gain,
Or lest his love oft beaten back should wane.
To beggars shut, to bringers ope thy gate;
Let him within hear barred-out lovers prate.
And, as first wronged, the wrongèd sometimes banish;
Thy fault with his fault so repulsed will vanish.
But never give a spacious time to ire;
Anger delayed doth oft to hate retire.
And let thine eyes constrainèd learn to weep,
That this or that man may thy cheeks moist keep.
Nor, if thou cozenest one, dread to forswear,
Venus to mocked men lends a senseless ear.
Servants fit for thy purpose thou must hire,
To teach thy lover what thy thoughts desire.
Let them ask somewhat; many asking little,
Within a while great heaps grow of a tittle.
And sister, nurse, and mother spare him not;
By many hands great wealth is quickly got.
When causes fail thee to require a gift
By keeping of thy birth, make but a shift.

Beware lest he, unrivalled, loves secure;
Take strife away, love doth not well endure.
On all the bed men's tumbling let him view,
And thy neck with lascivious marks made blue.
Chiefly show him the gifts, which others send:
If he gives nothing, let him from thee wend.
When thou hast so much as he gives no more,
Pray him to lend what thou may'st ne'er restore.
Let thy tongue flatter, while thy mind harm works;
Under sweet honey deadly poison lurks.
If this thou dost, to me by long use known,
(Nor let my words be with the winds hence blown)
Oft thou wilt say, 'live well;' thou wilt pray oft,
That my dead bones may in their grave lie soft."
As thus she spake, my shadow me betrayed;
With much ado my hands I scarcely stayed;
But her blear eyes, bald scalp's thin hoary fleeces,
And rivelled cheeks I would have pulled a-pieces.
The gods send thee no house, a poor old age,
Perpetual thirst, and winter's lasting rage.

Elegy 9

> Ad Atticum, amantem non oportere desidiosum esse, sicuti nec militem.

All lovers war, and Cupid hath his tent;
Attic, all lovers are to war far sent,
What age fits Mars, with Venus doth agree;
'Tis shame for eld in war or love to be.
What years in soldiers captains do require,
Those in their lovers pretty maids desire.
Both of them watch: each on the hard earth sleeps:
His mistress' door this, that his captain's keeps.
Soldiers must travel far: the wench forth send,
Her valiant lover follows without end.
Mounts, and rain-doubled floods he passeth over,
And treads the desert snowy heaps do cover.
Going to sea, east winds he doth not chide,

Nor to hoist sail attends fit time and tide.
Who but a soldier or a lover's bold
To suffer storm-mixed snows with night's sharp cold?
One as a spy doth to his enemies go,
The other eyes his rival as his foe.
He cities great, this thresholds lies before:
This breaks town gates, but he his mistress' door.
Oft to invade the sleeping foe 'tis good,
And armed to shed unarmèd people's blood.
So the fierce troops of Thracian Rhesus fell,
And captive horses bade their lord farewell.
Sooth, lovers watch till sleep the husband charms,
Who slumbering, they rise up in swelling arms.
The keepers' hands and corps-du-gard to pass,
The soldier's, and poor lover's work e'er was.
Doubtful is war and love; the vanquished rise,
And who thou never think'st should fall, down lies.
Therefore whoe'er love slothfulness doth call,
Let him surcease: love tries wit best of all.
Achilles burned, Briseis being ta'en away;
Trojans destroy the Greek wealth, while you may.
Hector to arms went from his wife's embraces,
And on Andromache his helmet laces.
Great Agamemnon was, men say, amazed,
On Priam's loose-trest daughter when he gazed.
Mars in the deed the blacksmith's net did stable;
In heaven was never more notorious fable.
Myself was dull and faint, to sloth inclined;
Pleasure and ease had mollified my mind.
A fair maid's care expelled this sluggishness,
And to her tents willed me myself address.
Since may'st thou see me watch and night-wars move:
He that will not grow slothful, let him love.

Elegy 10

　　Ad puellam, ne pro amore præmia poscat.

Such as the cause was of two husbands' war,

Whom Trojan ships fetch'd from Europa far,
Such as was Leda, whom the god deluded
In snow-white plumes of a false swan included.
Such as Amymone through the dry fields strayed,
When on her head a water pitcher laid.
Such wert thou, and I feared the bull and eagle,
And whate'er Love made Jove, should thee inveigle.
Now all fear with my mind's hot love abates:
No more this beauty mine eyes captivates.
Ask'st why I change? because thou crav'st reward;
This cause hath thee from pleasing me debarred.
While thou wert plain I loved thy mind and face:
Now inward faults thy outward form disgrace.
Love is a naked boy, his years saunce stain,
And hath no clothes, but open doth remain.
Will you for gain have Cupid sell himself?
He hath no bosom where to hide base pelf.
Love and Love's son are with fierce arms at odds;
To serve for pay beseems not wanton gods.
The whore stands to be bought for each man's money,
And seeks vild wealth by selling of her coney.
Yet greedy bawd's command she curseth still,
And doth, constrained, what you do of goodwill.
Take from irrational beasts a precedent;
'Tis shame their wits should be more excellent.
The mare asks not the horse, the cow the bull,
Nor the mild ewe gifts from the ram doth pull.
Only a woman gets spoils from a man,
Farms out herself on nights for what she can;
And lets what both delight, what both desire,
Making her joy according to her hire.
The sport being such, as both alike sweet try it,
Why should one sell it and the other buy it?
Why should I lose, and thou gain by the pleasure,
Which man and woman reap in equal measure?
Knights of the post of perjuries make sale,
The unjust judge for bribes becomes a stale.

'Tis shame sold tongues the guilty should defend,
Or great wealth from a judgment-seat ascend.
'Tis shame to grow rich by bed-merchandise,
Or prostitute thy beauty for bad price.
Thanks worthily are due for things unbought;
For beds ill-hired we are indebted nought.
The hirer payeth all; his rent discharged,
From further duty he rests then enlarged.
Fair dames forbear rewards for nights to crave:
Ill-gotten goods good end will never have.
The Sabine gauntlets were too dearly won,
That unto death did press the holy nun.
The son slew her, that forth to meet him went,
And a rich necklace caused that punishment.
Yet think no scorn to ask a wealthy churl;
He wants no gifts into thy lap to hurl.
Take clustered grapes from an o'er-laden vine,
May bounteous love Alcinous' fruit resign.
Let poor men show their service, faith and care;
All for their mistress, what they have, prepare.
In verse to praise kind wenches 'tis my part,
And whom I like eternise by mine art.
Garments do wear, jewels and gold do waste,
The fame that verse gives doth for ever last.
To give I love, but to be asked disdain;
Leave asking, and I'll give what I refrain.

Elegy 11

    Napen alloquitur, ut paratas tabellas ad Corinnam perferat.

In skilful gathering ruffled hairs in order,
Napè, free-born, whose cunning hath no border,
Thy service for night's scapes is known commodious,
And to give signs dull wit to thee is odious.
Corinna clips me oft by thy persuasion:
Never to harm me made thy faith evasion.
Receive these lines; them to my mistress carry;
Be sedulous; let no stay cause thee tarry,

Nor flint nor iron are in thy soft breast,
But pure simplicity in thee doth rest.
And 'tis supposed Love's bow hath wounded thee;
Defend the ensigns of thy war in me.
If what I do, she asks, say "hope for night;"
The rest my hand doth in my letters write.
Time passeth while I speak; give her my writ,
But see that forthwith she peruseth it.
I charge thee mark her eyes and front in reading:
By speechless looks we guess at things succeeding.
Straight being read, will her to write much back,
I hate fair paper should writ matter lack.
Let her make verses and some blotted letter
On the last edge to stay mine eyes the better.
What needs she tire her hand to hold the quill?
Let this word "Come," alone the tables fill.
Then with triumphant laurel will I grace them
And in the midst of Venus' temple place them,
Subscribing, that to her I consecrate
My faithful tables, being vile maple late.

Elegy 12

Tabellas quas miserat execratur quod amica noctem negabat.

Bewail my chance: the sad book is returned,
This day denial hath my sport adjourned.
Presages are not vain; when she departed,
Napè by stumbling on the threshold, started.
Going out again, pass forth the door more wisely,
And somewhat higher bear thy foot precisely.
Hence luckless tables! funeral wood, be flying!
And thou, the wax, stuffed full with notes denying!
Which I think gathered from cold hemlock's flower,
Wherein bad honey Corsic bees did pour:
Yet as if mixed with red lead thou wert ruddy,
That colour rightly did appear so bloody.
As evil wood, thrown in the highways, lie,
Be broke with wheels of chariots passing by!

And him that hewed you out for needful uses,
I'll prove had hands impure with all abuses.
Poor wretches on the tree themselves did strangle:
There sat the hangman for men's necks to angle.
To hoarse scrich-owls foul shadows it allows;
Vultures and Furies nestled in the boughs.
To these my love I foolishly committed,
And then with sweet words to my mistress fitted.
More fitly had they wrangling bonds contained
From barbarous lips of some attorney strained.
Among day-books and bills they had lain better,
In which the merchant wails his bankrupt debtor.
Your name approves you made for such like things,
The number two no good divining brings.
Angry, I pray that rotten age you racks,
And sluttish white-mould overgrow the wax.

Elegy 13

    Ad Auroram ne properet.

Now o'er the sea from her old love comes she
That draws the day from heaven's cold axletree.
Aurora, whither slid'st thou? down again!
And birds for Memnon yearly shall be slain.
Now in her tender arms I sweetly bide,
If ever, now well lies she by my side.
The air is cold, and sleep is sweetest now,
And birds send forth shrill notes from every bough.
Whither runn'st thou, that men and women love not?
Hold in thy rosy horses that they move not.
Ere thou rise, stars teach seamen where to sail,
But when thou com'st, they of their courses fail.
Poor travellers though tired, rise at thy sight,
And soldiers make them ready to the fight.
The painful hind by thee to field is sent;
Slow oxen early in the yoke are pent.
Thou coz'nest boys of sleep, and dost betray them
To pedants that with cruel lashes pay them.

Thou mak'st the surety to the lawyer run,
That with one word hath nigh himself undone.
The lawyer and the client hate thy view,
Both whom thou raisest up to toil anew.
By thy means women of their rest are barred,
Thou settst their labouring hands to spin and card.
All could I bear; but that the wench should rise,
Who can endure, save him with whom none lies?
How oft wished I night would not give thee place,
Nor morning stars shun thy uprising face.
How oft that either wind would break thy coach,
Or steeds might fall, forced with thick clouds' approach.
Whither go'st thou, hateful nymph? Memnon the elf
Received his coal-black colour from thyself.
Say that thy love with Cephalus were not known,
Then thinkest thou thy loose life is not shown?
Would Tithon might but talk of thee awhile!
Not one in heaven should be more base and vile.
Thou leav'st his bed, because he's faint through age,
And early mount'st thy hateful carriage:
But held'st thou in thy arms some Cephalus,
Then would'st thou cry, "Stay night, and run not thus."
Dost punish me because years make him wane?
I did not bid thee wed an agèd swain.
The moon sleeps with Endymion every day;
Thou art as fair as she, then kiss and play.
Jove, that thou should'st not haste but wait his leisure,
Made two nights one to finish up his pleasure.
I chid no more; she blushed, and therefore heard me,
Yet lingered not the day, but morning scared me.

Elegy 14

    Puellam consolatur cui præ nimia cura comæ deciderant.

Leave colouring thy tresses, I did cry;
Now hast thou left no hairs at all to dye.
But what had been more fair had they been kept?
Beyond thy robes thy dangling locks had swept.

Fear'dst thou to dress them being fine and thin,
Like to the silk the curious Seres spin.
Or threads which spider's slender foot draws out,
Fastening her light web some old beam about?
Not black nor golden were they to our view,
Yet although [n]either, mixed of either's hue;
Such as in hilly Ida's watery plains,
The cedar tall, spoiled of his bark, retains.
Add they were apt to curl a hundred ways,
And did to thee no cause of dolour raise.
Nor hath the needle, or the comb's teeth reft them,
The maid that kembed them ever safely left them.
Oft was she dressed before mine eyes, yet never,
Snatching the comb to beat the wench, outdrive her.
Oft in the morn, her hairs not yet digested,
Half-sleeping on a purple bed she rested;
Yet seemly like a Thracian Bacchanal,
That tired doth rashly on the green grass fall.
When they were slender and like downy moss,
Thy troubled hairs, alas, endured great loss.
How patiently hot irons they did take,
In crookèd trannels crispy curls to make.
I cried, "'Tis sin, 'tis sin, these hairs to burn,
They well become thee, then to spare them turn.
Far off be force, no fire to them may reach,
Thy very hairs will the hot bodkin teach."
Lost are the goodly locks, which from their crown,
Phœbus and Bacchus wished were hanging down.
Such were they as Diana painted stands,
All naked holding in her wave-moist hands.
Why dost thy ill-kembed tresses' loss lament?
Why in thy glass dost look, being discontent?
Be not to see with wonted eyes inclined;
To please thyself, thyself put out of mind.
No charmèd herbs of any harlot scathed thee,
No faithless witch in Thessal waters bathed thee.
No sickness harmed thee (far be that away!),

No envious tongue wrought thy thick locks' decay.
By thine own hand and fault thy hurt doth grow,
Thou mad'st thy head with compound poison flow.
Now Germany shall captive hair-tires send thee,
And vanquished people curious dressings lend thee.
Which some admiring, O thou oft wilt blush!
And say, "He likes me for my borrowed bush.
Praising for me some unknown Guelder dame,
But I remember when it was my fame."
Alas she almost weeps, and her white cheeks,
Dyed red with shame to hide from shame she seeks.
She holds, and views her old locks in her lap;
Ay me! rare gifts unworthy such a hap!
Cheer up thyself, thy loss thou may'st repair,
And be hereafter seen with native hair.

Elegy 15

   Ad invidos, quod fama poetarum sit perennis.

Envy, why carp'st thou my time's spent so ill?
And term'st my works fruits of an idle quill?
Or that unlike the line from whence I sprung
War's dusty honours are refused being young?
Nor that I study not the brawling laws,
Nor set my voice to sail in every cause?
Thy scope is mortal; mine, eternal fame.
That all the world may ever chant my name.
Homer shall live while Tenedos stands and Ide,
Or to the sea swift Simois shall slide.
Ascræus lives while grapes with new wine swell,
Or men with crookèd sickles corn down fell.
The world shall of Callimachus ever speak;
His art excelled, although his wit was weak.
For ever lasts high Sophocles' proud vein,
With sun and moon Aratus shall remain.
While bondmen cheat, fathers [be] hard, bawds whorish,
And strumpets flatter, shall Menander flourish.
Rude Ennius, and Plautus full of wit,

Are both in Fame's eternal legend writ.
What age of Varro's name shall not be told,
And Jason's Argo, and the fleece of gold?
Lofty Lucretius shall live that hour,
That nature shall dissolve this earthly bower.
Æneas' war and Tityrus shall be read,
While Rome of all the conquered world is head.
Till Cupid's bow, and fiery shafts be broken,
Thy verses, sweet Tibullus, shall be spoken.
And Gallus shall be known from East to West,
So shall Lycoris whom he lovèd best.
Therefore when flint and iron wear away,
Verse is immortal and shall ne'er decay.
To verse let kings give place and kingly shows,
And banks o'er which gold-bearing Tagus flows.
Let base-conceited wits admire vild things;
Fair Phœbus lead me to the Muses' springs.
About my head be quivering myrtle wound,
And in sad lovers' heads let me be found.
The living, not the dead, can envy bite,
For after death all men receive their right.
Then though death racks my bones in funeral fire,
I'll live, and as he pulls me down mount higher

Bibliography

Citations to Shakespeare's plays reference the Globe Edition.

Abbott, E. A. 1870. *A Shakespearian Grammar: An Attempt to Illustrate Some of the Differences between Elizabethan and Modern English.* 3d ed. London: Macmillan. Reprint, New York: Dover Publications, 1966.

Alden, Raymond MacDonald. ed. 1916. *The Sonnets of Shakespeare.* Boston: Harcourt Brace.

Atkins, Carl D., ed. 2007. *Shakespeare's Sonnets: With Three Hundred Years of Commentary.* Madison: Farleigh Dickinson University Press.

_____. 2003. "The Application of Bibliographic Principles to the Editing of Punctuation in Shakespeare's *Sonnets.*" *Studies in Philology* 100:493-513.

_____. 2007. "The Importance of Compositorial Error and Variation to the Emendation of Shakespeare's Texts: A Bibliographic Analysis of Benson's 1640 Text of Shakespeare's *Sonnets.*" *Studies in Philology* 104:306-339.

Auden, W. H. 2000. *Lectures on Shakespeare.* Ed. Arthur Kirsch. Princeton: Princeton University Press.

Bartlett, John. 1894. *A Complete Concordance or Verbal Index to Words, Phrases and Passages in the Dramatic Works of Shakespeare with a Supplementary Concordance to the Poems.* London: Macmillan.

Beeching, H. C., ed. 1904. *The Sonnets of Shakespeare.* Athenaeum Press Series. Boston: Ginn.

Booth, Stephen, ed. 1977. *Shakespeare's Sonnets.* New Haven: Yale University Press.

Boswell, James, ed. 1821. *The Plays and Poems of William Shakespeare* ... [The third variorum.] 21 vols. London: Rivington.

Brooke, Tucker, ed. 1936. *Shakespeare's Sonnets.* London: Oxford University Press.

Carter, Thomas. 1905. *Shakespeare and Holy Scripture, with the Version He Used.* New York: E. P. Dutton. Reprint, New

York: AMS Press, 1970.

Cercignani, Fausto. 1981. *Shakespeare's Works and Elizabethan Pronunciation*. Oxford: Oxford University Press.

Clark, William George and Wright, William Aldis, eds. 1864. *The Complete Works of William Shakespeare. The Globe Edition*. New York: Frederick A. Stokes.

Duncan-Jones, Katherine, rev. ed. 2010. Shakespeare's Sonnets. Arden Shakespeare: Third series. Walton-on-Thames: Nelson

Durling, Robert M., ed. and transl. 1976. Petrarch's Lyric Poems: The Rime sparse and Other Lyrics. Cambridge: Harvard University Press.

Edmondson, Paul and Stanley Wells, eds. 2020. All the Sonnets of Shakespeare. Cambridge: Cambridge University Press.

Empson, William. 1947. Seven Types of Ambiguity. Rev. ed. New York: New Directions.

Evans, G. Blakemore, ed. 1996. Shakespeare's Sonnets. New Cambridge Shakespeare. Cambridge: Cambridge University Press.

Evans, Maurice, ed. 1994. Elizabethan Sonnets. Rev. Roy J. Booth. London: J. M. Dent.

Friedman, Martin B. 1971. "Shakespeare's 'Master Mistris': Image and Tone in Sonnet 20." Shakespeare Quarterly 22:189-91.

Gregory, Horace, ed. 1964. Love Poems of Ovid: Amores, The Art of Love, The Cures for Love. New York: New American Library.

Hutton, James. 1940-41. "Analogues of Shakespeare's Sonnets 153-54: Contributions to the History of a Theme." Modern Philology 38:385-403.

Ingram, W. G., and Theodore Redpath, eds. 1964. Shakespeare's Sonnets. London: London University Press.

Johnson, Samuel. 1756. Proposals for Printing by Subscription the Dramatic Works of William Shakespeare . . . In W. K. Wimsatt, Jr., ed., Samuel Johnson on Shakespeare. New York: Hill and Wang, 1960.

Kerrigan, John, ed. 1986. "The Sonnets" and "A Lover's Complaint." New York: Penguin.

Lee, Sidney. 1909. "Ovid and Shakespeare's Sonnets." Quarterly Review 210:455-76.

Lever, J. W. 1956. The Elizabethan Love Sonnet. London: Methuen.

Massey, Gerald, ed. 1866. Shakespeare's Sonnets Never Before Interpreted . . . London: Longmans, Green.

Moxon, Joseph. 1683-84. Mechanick Exercises on the Whole Art of Printing. London: J. Moxon. Reprint, ed. Herbert Davis and Harry Carter. 2d ed. Oxford: Oxford University Press, 1962. Reprint, New York: Dover Publications, 1978.

Montaigne, Michel de. 1958. The Complete Essays of Montaigne. Translated by Donald M. Frame, Stanford: Stanford University Press.

Ramsey, Paul. 1979. The Fickle Glass. New York: AMS Press.

Reed, Edward Bliss, ed. 1923. Shakespeare's Sonnets. Yale Shakespeare. New Haven: Yale University Press.

Roessner, Jane. 1979. "Double Exposure: Shakespeare's Sonnets 100-114." ELH 46:357-78.

Rollins, Hyder Edward, ed. 1944. A New Variorum Edition of Shakespeare: The Sonnets. 2 vols. Philadelphia: Lippincott.

_____, 1940. The Passionate Pilgrim, by William Shakespeare.Third Edition, 1612. New York: Scribner.

Schwarz, Kathryn. 2008. "Will in Overplus: Recasting Misogyny in Shakespeare's 'Sonnets.'" ELH 75:737-66.

Seymour-Smith, Martin, ed. 1963. Shakespeare's Sonnets. London: Heinemann.

Shindler, R. 1892. "The Stolen Key." Gentleman's Magazine 272:70-84.

Simpson, Richard. 1868. An Introduction to the Philosophy of Shakespeare's Sonnets. London: N. Trübner.

Stapleton, M. L. 1996. Harmful Eloquence. Ovid's Amores from Antiquity to Shakespeare. Ann Arbor: University of Michigan Press.

Tilley, Morris P. 1950. A Dictionary of the Proverbs in England in the

Sixteenth and Seventeenth Centuries. Ann Arbor: University of Michigan Press.

Tucker, T. G., ed. 1924. *The Sonnets of Shakespeare.* Cambridge: Cambridge University Press.

Vendler, Helen. 1997. *The Art of Shakespeare's Sonnets.* Cambridge: Harvard University Press.

Wilde, Oscar. 1921. *"The Portrait of Mr. W. H."* New York: M. Kennerly. In *The Short Stories of Oscar Wilde.* Norwalk, CT: Easton Press, 1976, 3-78.

Wilson, J. Dover, ed. 1966. *Shakespeare's Sonnets.* Cambridge: Cambridge University Press.

Wright, George T. 1988. *Shakespeare's Metrical Art.* Berkeley: University of California Press.

Wyndham, George, ed. 1898. *The Poems of Shakespeare.* London: Methuen.

Index

CPSIA information can be obtained
at www.ICGtesting.com
Printed in the USA
BVHW050757220921
617191BV00017B/1621